Foreign Investment, Human Rights and Environmental Protection

This book examines the integration of human rights and environmental standards within international investment agreements (IIAs). It explores the intricate relationship between foreign direct investment and sustainable development, emphasizing the necessity for reform in investment treaties to ensure they support rather than hinder human rights and environmental protection.

The book begins with an overview of the current international investment law landscape, focusing on its primary goal of investment protection. It then delves into how human rights and environmental standards can shape IIAs, suggesting a new approach to these treaties. The authors explore the incorporation of sustainable development principles into IIAs, the difficulty of balancing investor protection with state regulatory autonomy, and the evolving norms and standards in this area. The book includes detailed case studies on topics such as the interplay between labour standards, investment, and human rights, bilateral investment agreements, sustainable forest management, and the liberalization of water services.

Aimed at policymakers, legal scholars, and international law practitioners, this book provides a thorough framework for understanding and reforming IIAs. It offers groundbreaking insights into aligning investment treaties with global sustainable development goals, making it a vital resource for anyone interested in the intersection of investment, human rights, and environmental sustainability.

Shawkat Alam is a professor of international and environmental law at Macquarie Law School, Macquarie University, Australia.

Abdullah Al Faruque is a professor of law at University of Chittagong, Bangladesh.

Routledge Research in International Economic Law

International Trade Regulation
Evolving Dynamics and Shifting Foundations
Zhiqiong June Wang and Jianfu Chen

India and Investor-State Dispute Settlement
Affronting Sovereignty or Indicting Capriciousness?
Prabhash Ranjan

Investor-State Dispute Settlement and International Investment Agreements
The Case of the Gulf Cooperation Council Member States
David Price and Amelia Hallam

Rules for Trade in Services 2.0
Adapting the GATS to a Changing Trade Landscape
Gabriel Gari

International Trade with the Middle East and North Africa
Legal, Commercial and Investment Perspectives
Edited by Hossein Esmaeili, Vivienne Brand and Susan Karamanian

Preferential Trade Agreements and Cultural Products
Gilbert Gagné

Foreign Investment, Human Rights and Environmental Protection
Striking a Balance for Sustainable Development
Shawkat Alam and Abdullah Al Faruque

For more information about this series, please visit https://www.routledge.com/Routledge-Research-in-International-Economic-Law/book-series/INTECONLAW

Foreign Investment, Human Rights and Environmental Protection

Striking a Balance for Sustainable Development

Shawkat Alam and Abdullah Al Faruque

Routledge
Taylor & Francis Group
LONDON AND NEW YORK

First published 2025
by Routledge
4 Park Square, Milton Park, Abingdon, Oxon OX14 4RN

and by Routledge
605 Third Avenue, New York, NY 10158

Routledge is an imprint of the Taylor & Francis Group, an informa business

British Library Cataloguing-in-Publication Data
A catalogue record for this book is available from the British Library

Library of Congress Cataloging-in-Publication Data
Names: Alam, Shawkat, author. | Faruque, Abdullah al, author.
Title: Foreign investment, human rights, and environmental protection : striking a balance for sustainable development / Shawkat Alam, Abdullah al Faruque.
Description: Abingdon, Oxon [UK] ; New York, NY : Routledge, 2024. | Includes bibliographical references and index.
Identifiers: LCCN 2024031558 | ISBN 9780367759759 (hardback) | ISBN 9780367759742 (paperback) | ISBN 9781003164951 (ebook)
Subjects: LCSH: Investments, Foreign (International law) | Investments, Foreign—Law and legislation. | Environmental law, International. | Sustainable development—Law and legislation. | Human rights. | Social responsibility of business—Law and legislation. | International commercial arbitration.
Classification: LCC K3830 .A94 2024 | DDC 346.07—dc23/eng/20240714
LC record available at https://lccn.loc.gov/2024031558

ISBN: 978-0-367-75975-9 (hbk)
ISBN: 978-0-367-75974-2 (pbk)
ISBN: 978-1-003-16495-1 (ebk)

DOI: 10.4324/9781003164951

Typeset in Galliard
by Apex CoVantage, LLC

Contents

About the Authors

Shawkat Alam of Macquarie University specializes in international and environmental law, focusing on trade, investment, sustainability, and developing economies. He authored *Sustainable Development and Free Trade* (Routledge, 2008) and co-edited several books, including *International Environmental Law and the Global South* (Cambridge, 2015) and *Implementation of Sustainable Development in the Global South* (Hart, 2024). His research delves into legal and institutional frameworks for trade and sustainable development. His global collaborations lead to impactful outreach, providing a vital Global South perspective on trade, investment, climate change and sustainable development.

Abdullah Al Faruque is a professor in the Department of Law at the University of Chittagong, Bangladesh. He holds an LLM from the University of Dhaka and a PhD from the University of Dundee, UK. His research interests include labour law, human rights, environmental law, petroleum contracts, and the law of the sea. He has authored several notable publications, including *Nuclear Energy Regulation, Risk and the Environment* (Routledge). His work often focuses on the legal challenges and frameworks related to sustainable development and human rights in developing countries.

Abbreviations

ADR	alternative dispute resolution
BIT	bilateral investment treaty
CAR	corrective action request
COMESA	Common Market for Eastern and Southern Africa
CPTPP	Comprehensive and Progressive Agreement for Trans-Pacific Partnership
CSR	corporate social responsibility
DUAT	Direito de Uso e Aproveitamento da Terra
ECT	Energy Charter Treaty
EITI	Extractive Industries Transparency Initiative
ESG	environmental, social and governance
FAO	Food and Agriculture Organization of the United Nations
FDI	foreign direct investment
FET	fair and equitable treatment
FLEG	Forest Law Enforcement and Governance
FLEGT	Forest Law Enforcement Governance and Trade
FSC	Forest Stewardship Council
FTA	free trade agreement
GATT	General Agreement on Tariffs and Trade
GC	Global Compact
GHGs	greenhouse gas emissions
GSP	Generalized System of Preferences
GSP+	Special Incentive Arrangement for Sustainable Development and Good Governance
ICCPR	International Covenant on Civil and Political Rights
ICSID	International Centre for Settlement of Investment Disputes
IFC	International Finance Corporation
IIA	international investment agreement
ILO	International Labour Organization
ISDS	investor-state dispute settlement
ISO	International Organization for Standardization
ITPC	International Tropical Peatlands Centre
LDCs	least developed countries

MDGs	Millennium Development Goals
MFN	most favoured nation
MNC	multinational corporation
MNE	multinational enterprise
NAALC	North American Agreement on Labor Cooperation
NAFTA	North American Free Trade Agreement
NGO	non-governmental organization
NPM	non-precluded measure
NRAP	National REDD+ Action Plan
NT	national treatment
ODA	overseas development assistance
OECD	Organisation for Economic Co-Operation and Development
PCB	polychlorinated biphenyl
PEFC	Programme for the Endorsement of Forest Certification
PES	payments for ecosystem services
PPMs	process and production methods
REDD+	reduce greenhouse gas emissions from deforestation and forest degradation
REDD++	enhance forest carbon stocks through conservation, sustainable management and restoration
SDGs	Sustainable Development Goals
SFM	sustainable forest management
TNC	transnational corporation
UDHR	Universal Declaration of Human Rights
UNCTAD	United Nations Conference on Trade and Development
USO	universal services obligation
WTO	World Trade Organization

Cases

Aguas de Tunari, S.A. v. Republic of Bolivia, ICSID Case No. ARB/02/3, Letter from Arbitral Tribunal to NGO (29 January 2003)

Asian Agricultural Products Ltd. v. Republic of Sri Lanka, ICSID Case No. ARB/87/3, Award (27 June 1990)

Bayindir v. Pakistan, ICSID case No. ARB/02/3, Decision on Jurisdiction (14 November 2005)

Biloune and Marine Drive Complex Ltd v. Ghana Investments Centre and the Government of Ghana, UNCITRAL ad hoc Tribunal, Award on Jurisdiction and Liability (27 October 1989)

Case Concerning Oil Platforms (Iran v. United States of America), Judgment (6 November 2003), ICJ Reports 2003

Case Concerning the Barcelona Traction, Light and Power Company Limited (New Application: 1962) (*Belgium v. Spain*), Second Phase (1970) I.C.J. Rep. 3

CME v. Czech Republic, UNCITRAL Case, Partial Award (13 September 2001)

CMS Gas Transmission Co. v. Argentine Republic, ICSID Case No. ARB/01/8, Award (12 May 2005)

Compania del Desarrollo de Santa Elena v. Costa Rica, ICSID Case No. ARB/96/1, Award (17 February 2000)

Continental Casualty Company v. Argentina, ICSID Case No. ARB/03/9, Award (5 September 2008)

Corn Products v. United Mexican States, ICSID Case No. ARB (AF)/04/1 (2008)

Energy Int'l v. Argentine Republic, ICSID Case No. Arb/02/16, Award (28 September 2007)

Enron Corporation and Ponderosa Assets, L.P. v. Argentina, ICSID Case No. ARB/01/3, Award (22 May 2007)

Fraport AG Frankfurt Airport Services Worldwide v. Republic of the Philippines (Fraport), ICSID Case No. ARB/03/25, Award (16 August 2007)

Genin v. Estonia, ICSID Case No. ARB/99/2, Award (25 June 2001)

Impregilo S.p.A. v. Argentine Republic, ICSID Case No. ARB/07/17, Award (21 June 2011)

Inceysa Vallisoletana S.L. v. Republic of El Salvador (Inceysa), ICSID Case No. ARB/03/26 Award (2 August 2006)

LG&E Energy Corp. v. Argentine Republic, ICSID Case No. ArbRB/02/1, Award (25 July 2007)

Loewen Group, Inc. and Ronald L. Loewen v. United States of America, ICSID Case No. ARB(AF)/98/3, Award (26 June 2003)

Metalclad Corp. v. United Mexican States, Award, ICSID (Additional Facility) Case No. ARB (AF)/97/1 (30 August 2000)

Methanex Corporation v. United States of America, UNCITRAL (Final award of the Tribunal on Jurisdiction and Merits of 3 August 2005) ICSID Case

MTD v. Chile, ICSID Case No. ARB/01/7, Award (25 May 2004)

Occidental v. Ecuador, LCIA Case No. UN 3467 (1 July 2004)

Philip Morris Brands Sàrl, Philip Morris Products S.A. & Abal Hermanos S.A. v. Oriental Republic of Uruguay, ICSID Case No. ARB/10/7, Award (8 July 2016)

Ronald S. Lauder v. Czech Republic, UNCITRAL Case, Final Award (September 2001)

Salini Costruttori S.p.A. and Italstrade S.p.A. v. Kingdom of Morocco, ICSID case no. ARB/00/4, Decision on Jurisdiction (23 July 2001)

Saluka Investment BV v. Czech Republic (Saluka case), PCA, UNCITRAL, Partial Award (17 March 2006)

Saluka Investments BV (The Netherlands) v. Czech Republic (Partial Award) (UNCITRAL, 2006)

Sedco, Inc. v. National Iranian Oil Co., Interlocutory Award, 9 Iran-US Claims Tribunal Report (1985)

Sempra Energy International v. Argentine Republic, ICSID Case No. ARB/02/16, Award (28 September 2007)

SGS v. Pakistan, ICSID Case No. ARB/01/13, Decision of Tribunal on Objection to Jurisdiction (6 August 2003)

SGS v. Philippines, ICSID Case No. ARB/02/6, Decision of Tribunal on Objection to Jurisdiction (29 January 2004)

Suez, Sociedad General de Aguas de Barcelona, S.A., & Vivendi Universal, S.A. v. Argentine Republic, ICSID Case No. ARB/03/19, Award (April 2015)

Tecnicas Medioambientales Tecmed S.A. v. United Mexican States, ICSID Case No. ARB(AF)/00/2, Award (29 May 2003)

Tokios Tokeles v. Ukraine, ICSID case No. ARB/02/18, Decision on Jurisdiction (29 April 2004)

United Parcel Service of America, Inc. v. Canada, Decision on Petitions for *Compania del Desarrollo de Santa Elena v. Costa Rica*, ICSID Case ARB/96/1, Award (17 February 2000)

Urbaser v. Argentina, ICSID Case No. ARB/07/26, Award (8 December 2016)

International Instruments

BIT between the Netherlands and Venezuela 1991

Cooperation and Facilitation Investment Agreement between the Federative Republic of Brazil and Mozambique (Brazilian Model BIT, 2015)

China-Japan BIT (1988)

Bilateral Investment Treaty between the Republic of Colombia and . . . (Colombian Model BIT, 2017)

Convention on the Elimination of All Forms of Discrimination Against Women, opened for signature on 18 December 1979, 1249 UNTS 13 (entered into force 3 September 1981)

Declaration on the Right to Development, GA Res 41/128, UN GAOR, 41st sess, 97th plen mtg, (UN Doc A/Res/41/128 1986)

Free Trade Agreement between the Government of New Zealand and the Government of the People's Republic of China, signed on 7 April 2008 (entry into force on 1 October 2008)

GSP Regulation (EU) No. 978/2012

IISD Model Agreement on Investment for Sustainable Development, International Institute for Sustainable Development

The 2016 Model Indian Bilateral Investment Treaty (Model BIT, 2016)

International Covenant on Economic, Social and Cultural Rights, opened for signature on 16 December 1966, 999 UNTS 3 (entered into force on 3 January 1976)

Marrakesh Agreement Establishing the World Trade Organization, opened for signature on 15 April 1994, 1867 UNTS 3 ('Marrakesh Agreement') (General Agreement on Trade in Services) 1869 UNTS 183 (entered into force on 1 January 1995)

South African Development Community Model Bilateral Investment Treaty (Model BIT of the Southern African Development Community, 2012)

Agreement on Reciprocal Promotion and Protection of Investments between . . . . and the Kingdom of the Netherlands (Netherlands Model BIT, 2019)

OECD, *OECD Guidelines for Multinational Enterprises* (Revision 2000)

Reciprocal Investment Promotion and Protection Agreement, Morocco-Nigeria (3 December 2016)

Singapore WTO Ministerial Declaration regarding labour standards, adopted on 13 December 1996, https://www.wto.org/english/thewto_e/minist_e/min96_e/wtodec_e.html accessed 13 March 2024

UK-Philippines Bilateral Investment Treaties (1981)

US Securities and Exchange Commission, 17 C.F.R. § 229.1011 (2017)

UN General Assembly, *Transforming Our World: the 2030 Agenda for Sustainable Development* A/RES/70/1 (2015)

UNCITRAL Rules on Transparency in Treaty-based Investor-State Arbitration (adopted 9 July 2013, entered into force on 1 April 2014) (UNCITRAL Transparency Rules)

United Nations General Assembly, *United Nations Declaration on the Rights of Indigenous Peoples* (Sixty-First Session, Agenda Item 68, Report of the Human Rights Council, A/61/L.67. 2007)

United Nations Economic and Social Council, Commission on Human Rights, Fifty-Fifth Session of the Sub-Commission on the Promotion and Protection of Human Rights, *Norms on the Responsibilities of Transnational Corporations and Other Business Enterprises*, E/CN.4/Sub.2/2003/12/Rev.2 (2003)

The New Zealand-Thailand Closer Economic Partnership Agreement (2005) Available at: www.mfat.govt.nz/Trade-and-Economic-Relations, accessed 14 July 2022

Code of Conduct on Transnational Corporations, UN. ESCOR, Organizational Session for 1988, Provisional Agenda Item 2, at 4, UN Doc. E/1988, 39(Add.1) (1988)

Comment of Human Rights Committee, General Comment no. 24 (1994): Issues relating to reservations made upon ratification or accession to the Covenant or the Optional Protocol thereto, or in relation to declarations under article 41 of the Covenant

Comprehensive and Progressive Agreement for Trans-Pacific Partnership (CPTPP), signed 30 December 2018, entry into force on 14 January 2019

Development and International Economic Cooperation: Transnational Corporations, U.N. ESCOR, 2d Sec, Agenda Item 7(d), para. 13, U.N. Doc E/1990/94(1990)

Draft United Nations Code of Conduct on Transnational Corporations, U.N. Center on Transnational Corporations, Special Sess. (7–18 March, 1983, and 9–20 May, 1983), U.N. Doc.E/C.10/1982/6(1986)

Human Rights Committee, General Comment No. 31, The Nature of the General Legal Obligation Imposed on States Parties to the Covenant (26 May 2004), CCPR/C/21/Rev.1/Add.13

Model Text for the Indian Bilateral Investment Treaty (Bilateral Investment Treaty Between the Government of the Republic of India and . . .) (2015)

Report of the High Commissioner for Human Rights, U.N. Economic and Social Council, Human Rights, Trade and Investment (E/CN.4/Sub.2/2003/9)

The Agreement Between the Government of the Hong Kong Special Administrative Region of the People's Republic of China and the Government of the United Arab Emirates for the Promotion and Reciprocal Protection of Investments, https://investmentpolicy.unctad.org/international-investment-agreements/treaty-files/5865/download, accessed 19 July 2022

Agreement between the Government of Australia and the Government of the Republic of Indonesia concerning the Promotion and Protection of Investments (Jakarta, 17 November 1992)

Generalized System of Preferences, European Union, Treaty between the United States of America and the Oriental Republic of Uruguay concerning the encouragement and Reciprocal Protection of Investment, signed on 4th November 2005(entered into force on 1 November 2006)

UN Global Compact for the New Century, at http://unglobalcompact.org/un/gc/unweb.nsf/content/thenine.htm

United Nations Declaration on the Rights of Indigenous Peoples, Sixty-First Session, Agenda Item 68, Report of the Human Rights Council, 7 September 2007, A/61/L.67, General Assembly

United Nations Economic and Social Council, Commission on Human Rights, Fifty-Fifth Session of the Sub-Commission on the Promotion and Protection of Human Rights, *Norms on the Responsibilities of Transnational Corporations and Other Business Enterprises*, E/CN.4/Sub.2/2003/12/Rev.2 (2003)

Agreement between the Belgium-Luxembourg Economic Union, on the one hand, and the Republic of Tajikistan, on the other hand, on the Reciprocal Promotion and Protection of Investment, signed on 12 February 2009

Agreement between Japan and the Republic of Colombia for the Liberalization, Promotion and Protection of Investment, signed 12 September 2011

Canadian Model Foreign Investment Protection and Promotion Agreement (FIPA)

John Ruggie, Report of the Special Representative of the Secretary-General on the Issue of Human Rights and Transnational Corporations and Other Business Enterprises (9 February 2007) A/HRC/4/035

Human Rights, Trade and Investment Matters, Amnesty International UK (May 2006)

Human Rights, Trade and Investment, Report of the High Commissioner for Human Rights, U.N. Economic and Social Council, at 6, U.N. Doc. E/CN.4/Sub.2/2003/9(July 2, 2003).

OECD and International Energy Agency, Update on Recent Progress in Reform of Inefficient Fossil-Fuel Subsidies that Encourage Wasteful Consumption (2019)

Introduction

International investment law and investment agreements (IIAs) are primarily focused on investment protection and promotion, often at the expense of policy space for host states to address human rights and environmental issues. This narrow focus results in a lack of integration of Sustainable Development Goals (SDGs) within IIAs. Additionally, the democratic deficiencies in the IIA-making process and insufficient engagement with non-state stakeholders render these agreements exclusionary. Despite the undeniable potential of foreign direct investment (FDI) to contribute to sustainable development, IIAs with robust environmental and human rights provisions can significantly enhance the achievement of SDGs, particularly in developing countries.

In response to growing criticisms of IIAs, states are updating their old bilateral investment treaties (BITs) and concluding a new generation of IIAs aimed at improving both substantive and procedural rules of international investment law. Some IIAs now include provisions on environmental protection, sustainable development, and human rights commitments. However, these provisions are often merely declaratory and lack enforceability. The relevance of human rights and environmental protection remains marginal in most IIAs, typically confined to sporadic provisions or drafted in soft law language that lacks binding force.

Reconciling the dual goals of promoting FDI and integrating non-economic values, such as human rights and environmental concerns, into investment agreements is a formidable challenge for many developing countries. As these countries strengthen their national policies and regulatory frameworks to attract foreign investment, they must also balance these efforts with the integration of human rights and environmental protections. Reforming IIAs to be more oriented towards sustainable development is crucial. The current framework of international investment law fails to adequately address pressing global issues such as climate change, despite the clear relationship between foreign investment and fossil fuel consumption, particularly in the oil, gas, and coal sectors.

The reform of IIAs should emphasize the inclusion of strong, enforceable provisions on environmental protection and human rights. This requires a comprehensive overhaul of the IIA-making process to ensure greater

DOI: 10.4324/9781003164951-1

stakeholder engagement and the alignment of investment with global sustainability objectives. Moreover, IIAs should explicitly incorporate SDGs, providing host states with the necessary policy space to regulate in the public interest without fear of litigation. This includes adopting exception clauses that allow States to prioritize environmental and human rights considerations.

In summary, the international investment regime must evolve to integrate environmental and human rights considerations more effectively, ensuring that IIAs contribute to sustainable development rather than undermine it. Comprehensive reform of IIAs, emphasizing robust environmental and human rights provisions and enhanced stakeholder engagement, is essential for aligning the international investment framework with global SDGs. This alignment is crucial for addressing the critical challenges of our time, including climate change and the equitable distribution of resources and opportunities.

Chapter 1, 'Bridging Investment and Sustainability: The Role of Human Rights and Environmental Standards in Shaping International Investment Agreements', serves as a comprehensive introduction to the book. It outlines the central themes and sets the stage for subsequent analysis. The chapter begins by exploring the dual role of FDI in the economic development of developing countries, highlighting how BITs attract necessary investment for national development goals such as poverty alleviation, job creation and economic growth. FDI is presented as a crucial element of an open and effective international economic system, acting as a catalyst for development.

The narrative emphasizes the critical role of investment treaties in facilitating the exploration of natural resources, which has significant environmental implications both locally and globally, particularly in terms of transboundary impacts. It critically examines how these treaties, while promoting economic growth, often limit the ability of states to regulate social and environmental issues, thereby hindering their duty to protect human rights and environmental interests. This tension within the investment regime is explored through its negative impacts on human rights and environmental protection efforts.

The chapter also discusses the need to balance investor protection against arbitrary or discriminatory measures by host states with the necessity for these states to meet their international human rights and environmental obligations. It raises critical questions about achieving a balance between protecting investors' rights and allowing host states to pursue sustainable development objectives without compromising their environmental and human rights commitments.

Chapter 2, 'Reimagining Investment Treaties: Converging Human Rights and Environmental Protection Through Relevant Actors', proposes a coherent approach to the intersection between investment law, human rights and sustainable development. It emphasizes the importance of interpreting and applying the investment treaty regime in ways that support, rather than undermine, human rights and environmental protection.

The chapter advocates for an integrated approach that examines key issues within the broader context of international law, considering the roles of relevant actors, including transnational corporations (TNCs). TNCs play a significant role in realizing human rights and sustainability through their investments, and their participation is crucial for achieving a balanced and equitable investment framework. This perspective enriches our understanding of the investment regime and guides the evolution of investment practices towards more sustainable and equitable outcomes. By recognizing the interconnectedness of various international legal regimes and exploring how they can coexist and reinforce each other, the chapter highlights the necessity of moving beyond the traditional narrow focus on investment protection. It proposes a holistic approach that integrates investment law with broader social and ecological responsibilities, ensuring that investment treaties contribute positively to human rights and environmental sustainability.

Chapter 3, 'Conceptual Framework for Integrating Human Rights and Sustainable Development Into International Investment Agreements', explores the theoretical and conceptual foundations of the relationship between international investment law, human rights and environmental protection. It begins by outlining traditional principles governing international investment law and highlights the historical neglect of environmental and human rights considerations, which has led to significant negative externalities. This neglect has often resulted in a race to the bottom, where host countries lower standards to attract foreign investment, exacerbating environmental degradation and human rights abuses.

The chapter argues that contemporary international investment law is increasingly aligning itself with sustainable development principles. This shift is illustrated through examples of IIAs integrating environmental and human rights considerations, driven by the need to mitigate the adverse impacts of unchecked economic growth and growing consumer demand for sustainable and ethically sound products and services. Companies are now incentivized to adopt more sustainable practices to meet these expectations.

Despite these positive developments, the chapter acknowledges ongoing tensions between providing robust investor protections and preserving the regulatory autonomy of states. It examines how contemporary IIAs, while integrating human rights and sustainable development objectives, may perpetuate existing inequalities between developed countries and the Global South by impeding host countries' regulatory freedom. Furthermore, the chapter explores the anthropocentric view of the natural environment in these agreements and the emerging ideas of extending personhood to natural bodies and recognizing the rights of nature, which challenge traditional economic exploitation perspectives.

Chapter 4, 'Investment Protection, Human Rights and Environmental Sustainability: Emerging Standards and Evolving Norms', examines the intersection of human rights, sustainable development and international investment law. It analyses how provisions in investment treaties, such as national treatment (NT), most favoured nation (MFN) treatment, and fair and equitable treatment (FET), influence host states' abilities to maintain human rights and environmental standards. The chapter highlights that these provisions often restrict states' regulatory freedoms, making it difficult to favour local industries or enforce stringent environmental regulations. Additionally, the FET standard allows investors to challenge state actions deemed unfair, even if these actions are intended to protect human rights or the environment.

The discussion then transitions to soft law norms related to investment, human rights and the environment, particularly the corporate duty to protect human rights as articulated in the John Ruggie's framework on business and human rights. While not legally binding, this framework establishes essential principles for corporate conduct, urging businesses to respect human rights and avoid complicity in abuses. The chapter argues that these soft law instruments, though voluntary, set significant global standards that multinational enterprises (MNEs) cannot easily ignore due to potential public criticism and reputational damage. The chapter concludes by advocating for reforms and comprehensive frameworks to address the challenges of the current international investment regime, aiming for a more sustainable and equitable global investment landscape.

Chapter 5, 'Human Rights and Environmental Protection: Addressing Substantive Challenges in Regional and Bilateral Investment Agreements', explores the obligations within bilateral and multilateral treaties and their impact on host states' environmental and human rights responsibilities. The chapter aims to understand how these treaties balance investment protection with the need to uphold environmental and human rights standards.

A key focus is the interpretation of treaties to balance and avoid conflicts. The chapter emphasizes the significance of exception clauses in BITs and applicable laws, which integrate environmental protection and human rights into the investment treaty regime. These clauses are essential in ensuring that investment protections do not hinder a host state's ability to meet its environmental and human rights obligations. Furthermore, the chapter examines how arbitral tribunals incorporate human rights and environmental norms when interpreting BIT provisions. It highlights how tribunals manage the complex interaction between investment protections and broader societal obligations, providing insights into evolving jurisprudence in this area.

The chapter also critically analyses the emerging trend of third-party participation in arbitration processes. Traditionally, arbitration has been confidential and secretive, but there is a growing trend towards greater transparency and third-party involvement. By examining current arbitral practices, the chapter assesses how third-party participation can enhance transparency and accountability in arbitration proceedings.

Chapter 6, 'Investor-State Dispute Settlement: Harmonizing Investment Protection With Human Rights and Sustainability', explores the contentious investor-state dispute settlement (ISDS) mechanism. A major criticism of ISDS is its bypassing of domestic remedies, unlike other international law fields such as human rights and environmental law, which is seen as undermining domestic legal sovereignty and legal subsidiarity. Additionally, the confidentiality of ISDS proceedings, which are often not public unless agreed upon by both parties, fosters perceptions of a lack of accountability and public oversight. Another point of criticism is the potentially high compensation awarded under ISDS, which may favour investors over host states, straining public finances and prioritizing private profit over public interest. Furthermore, the inconsistency in arbitral tribunal decisions leads to unpredictability and instability in international investment law. The ISDS framework also has limited mechanisms to challenge arbitral awards, primarily through annulment and enforcement proceedings, which are often inadequate to address errors or biases. Concerns about the independence and impartiality of arbitrators, due to potential conflicts of interest, further undermine the system.

ISDS is perceived to interfere with states' rights to regulate crucial issues such as human rights, environmental protection, and national security, prioritizing investor rights over these public interests. To address these criticisms, ISDS reform is essential, focusing on enhancing transparency, ensuring adherence to human rights and environmental norms, and integrating public interest considerations into decision-making processes. Reforming international investment law and arbitration to rectify procedural deficiencies and address substantive imbalances is crucial to resolving the legitimacy crisis facing ISDS and restoring confidence in its fairness and efficacy.

Chapter 7, 'Business and Human Rights: The Interplay Between Labour Standards, Investment and Human Rights', examines how labour rights are integrated into investment treaties and trade agreements and their impact on labour governance in developing countries. The chapter highlights the increasing visibility of international labour issues due to the inclusion of labour, human rights and environmental provisions in many agreements.

It discusses the labour-investment nexus within the context of globalization, noting that trade and investment are often seen as weakening domestic labour protections and union movements. This race-to-the-bottom scenario leads to worsening labour conditions, lower unionization rates, and more authoritarian labour relations as countries lower standards to remain competitive. Despite the presence of international labour standards in domestic laws, MNEs and foreign investors may ignore or violate core labour rights, such as minimum wages, freedom of association and collective bargaining, particularly in countries with poor human rights records.

The chapter also presents the opposing view that foreign investments, under investment treaties, can enhance labour standards and protect labour rights in host states, contributing positively to labour governance. These contrasting perspectives underscore the complex relationship between labour and investment, reflecting tensions between the Global North and Global South. The chapter argues against the assumption that lowering domestic standards attracts foreign investment, suggesting that empirical data do not support this view. It calls for a nuanced understanding of the relationship between labour standards and foreign investment, advocating for a balanced approach that protects labour rights while promoting sustainable foreign investment.

Chapter 8, 'Promoting Sustainable Forest Management Through International Trade and Investment', explores sustainable forest management (SFM) as a framework to balance social and ecological conservation goals in forestry. The chapter emphasizes SFM's holistic approach, recognizing the diverse benefits of forest ecosystems beyond economic gains.

The chapter begins by examining the relationship between forest trade, international investment and SFM, highlighting how global trade and investment patterns can both threaten and support SFM. This dual role underscores the complexity of aligning international investment with sustainable forestry practices. A critical aspect discussed is the broader context of the international timber trade, which historically has overlooked the social and ecological benefits of forests. Effective SFM requires addressing these historical oversights and understanding the larger trade framework. Promoting achievable SFM that aligns with the global export of timber products involves recognizing the interplay between international trade and SFM. Supportive investments are crucial for enhancing SFM practices among various forest stakeholders.

The chapter emphasizes that this issue is particularly relevant for developing countries, which possess some of the world's most valuable forest resources but are vulnerable to economic exploitation and face challenges in implementing and enforcing SFM. Addressing these challenges is vital for SFM and conservation.

Chapter 9, 'GATS and the Liberalization of Water Services: Implications for Human Rights and the Environment', addresses the critical issue of providing safe drinking water and sanitation to impoverished populations, a major developmental challenge of the 21st century. Ensuring access to clean water requires substantial investments in infrastructure such as supply systems, sewerage and irrigation. Although clean water provision is a fundamental public service, its management has increasingly shifted towards privatization and commercial frameworks.

The chapter examines the impact of the General Agreement on Trade in Services (GATS) on water services liberalization. It highlights the tension between viewing water as an economic commodity and recognizing it as a vital public good essential for human rights. While GATS can potentially improve the water sector by increasing efficiency and attracting foreign investment, it raises concerns that treating water services like goods undermines their social aspects and risks human rights violations. The shift towards privatization has transformed the state's role from a direct provider to a regulator, allowing private entities to control water resources. This change can lead to prioritizing profit over public welfare, resulting in higher water prices and uneven resource distribution. The chapter calls for rigorous regulation and oversight to balance globalization benefits with local community needs, emphasizing that water services require special consideration in the liberalization debate due to their critical role in human development and their status as a human right.

1 Bridging Investment and Sustainability

The Role of Human Rights and Environmental Standards in Shaping International Investment Agreements

Introduction

In the pursuit of national development, countries worldwide are continuously striving to attract increased levels of investment. The primary goal of these efforts is to achieve key socio-economic objectives such as poverty alleviation and the creation of sustainable employment opportunities. Among the various forms of investment, FDI holds particular significance due to its multifaceted benefits to host economies. FDI introduces a comprehensive package of assets, including essential capital infusion, advanced technology, managerial expertise, and specialized skills. These resources are not only crucial for maximizing profits for the investing TNCs but also play a vital role in strengthening the economic framework of the host countries. The integration of these assets into local markets often leads to the production of goods for both domestic consumption and export, thereby generating additional income and employment opportunities.

One of the transformative impacts of FDI is its capacity to induce structural change and promote industrial upgrading. As foreign enterprises establish operations in developing countries, they introduce new technologies and business practices that can lead to significant improvements in productivity and efficiency. This process is instrumental in modernizing the economic landscape, elevating labour and environmental standards and facilitating the economic integration of developing countries into the global economy.

FDI's infusion of advanced technologies and innovative practices often results in the adoption of more efficient production methods and management techniques. This not only boosts the overall productivity of local industries but also enhances their competitiveness in the global market. Consequently, local firms are often compelled to innovate and improve their operations to keep pace with foreign counterparts, leading to a broader industrial upgrading.

Furthermore, the presence of foreign enterprises can have a profound impact on labour standards. These enterprises often bring with them higher standards of labour practices, which can result in improved working conditions, better wages and enhanced skills development for the local workforce. This not only raises the quality of employment but also contributes to human capital development in the host country.

DOI: 10.4324/9781003164951-2

In terms of environmental standards, foreign companies are typically subject to stringent regulations in their home countries. As they expand operations abroad, they often implement similar environmental practices, thereby fostering sustainable development in the host country. This can lead to better environmental management practices and a reduction in the ecological footprint of industrial activities.

The economic integration facilitated by FDI also opens up new markets and creates opportunities for local businesses to participate in global value chains. This integration helps countries to diversify their economies and reduce their dependence on a narrow range of exports. By engaging in international trade and investment, these countries can achieve more robust and resilient economic growth.

To facilitate and protect foreign investments, countries frequently enter into bilateral or regional investment agreements. These agreements are vital as they establish a legal framework that safeguards the interests of both the investing and host countries, ensuring smoother operations for foreign businesses. Currently, according to the United Nations Conference on Trade and Development (UNCTAD), there are 3277 BITs in effect.[1]

Negative Impacts of International Investment Treaties

Investment treaties play a pivotal role in shaping the economic and social landscapes of countries, with significant effects on human rights and environmental management. These agreements primarily aim to protect investors, stimulate economic cooperation and enhance investment flows. However, they often restrict host states' ability to govern social and environmental issues effectively. This limitation impedes the states' responsibilities to uphold and advocate for human rights and environmental concerns. One major issue is that investment treaties can limit the regulatory autonomy of host states, particularly in enacting and enforcing laws that protect the environment and human rights. This can deter governments from implementing stringent environmental protections or labour standards, fearing potential litigation and financial penalties.

Furthermore, the treaties facilitate the exploitation of natural resources, influencing both local and global environmental impacts due to investment activities. The focus on economic benefits often leads to prioritizing resource extraction and industrial activities, which can result in deforestation, pollution and biodiversity loss. The current investment law framework primarily centres on the interests of investors and host states, often overlooking the broader implications on local communities and indigenous populations. This focus neglects the potential or actual effects that investment projects, disputes and

1 UNCTAD, available at https://investmentpolicy.unctad.org/, accessed 2 November 2023.

awards might have on these critical stakeholders, who are directly impacted by the outcomes of such agreements.[2]

Investment in large natural resource projects, such as logging in forest areas or the use of chemicals in mining operations, frequently leads to significant environmental degradation. These investments can result in water pollution, deforestation, soil degradation and a host of other environmental harms. Specifically, extensive land-based projects often contribute to severe consequences like land expropriations, contamination of water sources, air pollution and even shifts in local migration patterns, as communities are forced to move due to altered landscapes and depleted resources. Thus large-scale, land-based investment projects, which often necessitate significant changes in land use and can disrupt local ecosystems, inherently involve a complex network of relationships. These projects frequently intersect with the lives of local communities, whose social identity, traditional way of life and livelihood are deeply intertwined with the land. This intersection can lead to significant negative impacts on the enjoyment of human rights and environmental protection efforts. As land is transformed for investment purposes, communities may face loss of access to resources, displacement or disruptions to their socio-economic practices, which can undermine their ability to sustain their way of life and meet their basic needs.

The investment regime, while designed to foster economic growth through capital inflow and development, often does so at a considerable social and environmental cost. The protection of investors often prioritizes economic interests, potentially leading to conflicts with human rights and environmental conservation. For instance, investors are granted protections against arbitrary or discriminatory actions by host states, which are crucial for ensuring fair treatment and fostering a stable investment climate. However, these protections can sometimes conflict with necessary government measures aimed at preventing human rights abuses or environmental degradation. Enforcement of investor obligations often rests solely on the concept of corporate social responsibility (CSR). While CSR can play a role in encouraging ethical behaviour, its voluntary nature and lack of binding enforcement mechanisms render it insufficient for ensuring compliance with human rights and environmental standards. Consequently, these agreements frequently prioritize investors' interests, overshadowing critical concerns such as environmental degradation, community displacement, and violations of human rights.

Interplay Between International Investment Law and Human Rights

The interplay between investment treaties and human rights has become a significant topic within the discourse of international investment law. This

2 Ladan Mehranvar, Jessica Hennings, Robin Marie Kelly, Lena Raxter and Ana Toimil. 'How the International Investment Law Regime Undermines Access to Justice for Investment-Affected Stakeholders' New York: Columbia Center on Sustainable Investment (CCSI) (January 2024) 2.

growing interest stems from the increasingly evident overlap between human rights norms and investment protection standards during dispute resolution and the interpretations of treaty provisions. Luis Gonzalez Garcia highlights at least five distinct ways in which human rights norms influence and intersect with international investment law.[3] First, there is the potential for an investor to commit or be complicit in human rights violations. Second, an investor's human rights might be violated by the state. Third, a state may implement measures grounded in human rights norms that could interfere with an investor's property rights. Fourth, during legal proceedings, both the state and the investor might reference practices from international human rights courts concerning procedural issues. Finally, a state might draw upon international human rights norms when applying or interpreting obligations related to investment protection.[4]

This interaction underscores a crucial area of study as it shapes how treaties are applied and understood in scenarios where investment considerations might conflict with the protection of human rights. Concerns regarding the implications of FDI on human rights, coupled with the exploitation of natural resources in host countries, have heightened awareness of human rights issues within the context of international investment. BITs, the primary instruments regulating these investments, typically do not address the international human rights obligations of the contracting parties.[5] Furthermore, these treaties generally lack provisions that obligate investors to adhere to human rights standards, thereby creating a significant gap in accountability. Under the prevailing investment law framework, foreign investors are seldom held accountable for human rights violations. Investment tribunals, as they currently operate, do not have the jurisdiction to adjudicate claims related to human rights abuses unless explicitly stated within the treaty. This creates a scenario where the only recourse for addressing such violations by investors might be through instruments specifically dedicated to human rights, rather than investment or commercial dispute mechanisms.

Investment protection is the cornerstone of the investment treaty regime. Many terms of BITs and substantive obligations are formulated in a broad manner and with open-ended terms that favour the interests of investors over host states.[6] Critics argue that these open-ended provisions can significantly

3 Luis Gonzalez Garcia, 'The Role of Human Rights in International Investment Law' available at https://www.matrixlaw.co.uk/wp-content/uploads/2016/05/The-role-of-human-rights-in-international-investment-law.pdf, accessed 21 October 2023.

4 Ibid.

5 Luke Eric Peterson and R. Gray Kevin, 'International Human Rights in Bilateral Investment Treaties and in Investment Treaty Arbitration' *A paper Presented by the International Institute for Sustainable Development (IISD) for the Swiss Department of Foreign Affairs* (2003), 6–8. According to M. Sornarajah, "[h]uman rights are seldom, if at all, referred to in bilateral investment treaties. There are few treaties which address this issue . . ." (*The International Law on Foreign Investment*, 2nd edn, Cambridge University Press 2004), 261–262.

6 For example, according to Article 5(1) of 2012 Model US Bilateral Investment Treaty, 'Each Party shall accord to covered investments treatment in accordance with customary international

curtail the ability of host states to control and regulate investments within their territories, essentially limiting their sovereignty over economic matters. In the current international legal landscape, where a globally binding multilateral treaty dedicated to enforcing human rights protections is absent, BITs are likely to remain the primary legal framework for investment protection.

This situation perpetuates a scenario where the balance of power in investment relationships leans heavily towards investors, often at the detriment of host states' rights and obligations to enforce local laws and regulations, including those pertaining to human rights and environmental standards. There are also ongoing concerns regarding human rights violations in the context of investment contracts between host countries and TNCs. Often, these contracts lack specific provisions to adequately address human rights issues, leading to significant challenges in ensuring that investments do not adversely affect the rights and well-being of local populations.

Impact on Human Rights as Labour Rights

Large-scale investment projects, which are typically accompanied by significant financial and operational commitments, often face challenges related to labour rights. Ensuring that workers are protected and provided with fair conditions is a crucial issue. Many workers involved in these projects risk being excluded from rights guaranteed by both national laws and international labour standards. International labour standards, overseen by entities such as the International Labour Organization (ILO), aim to set minimum criteria for worker rights around the globe. The ILO conventions mandate member states to align their legislation with these agreed-upon international benchmarks. Despite these provisions, compliance varies significantly. Many host countries of large investment projects have not ratified the core ILO conventions. As a result, the implementation of these international standards into their national laws remains inconsistent.

On the other side of the spectrum, TNCs often seek investment opportunities in countries with lower labour standards. The allure of cheaper labour costs can often outweigh the potential ethical concerns related to workers' rights. This economic strategy not only affects the labour market in host countries but also poses a challenge to the enforcement of international labour standards.

To combat these challenges, investment and trade agreements often contain labour provisions,[7] which are the most widely used trade policy tool for promoting and enforcing compliance with labour rights. For instance,

law, including fair and equitable treatment and full protection and security.' Similarly, Article 3(2) of the BIT between Australia and Uruguay states: 'Each Party shall ensure fair and equitable treatment in its own territory to investments.'

7 According to the ILO LP Hub 2022, labour provisions refer to any principle or standard or rule (including references to international labour standards) that addresses labour relations, minimum working conditions, terms of employment and/or other labour issues; any framework to promote cooperation and/or compliance with standards, through activities, dialogue and/or monitoring of labour issues; and/or any mechanism to ensure compliance with national

unilateral measures such as preferential trade arrangements come with labour conditionality clauses. Additionally, import bans on goods produced with forced labour are increasingly common. Regional trade agreements also often leverage trade policy measures to uphold labour rights, further emphasizing the global move towards protecting workers through economic agreements. Moreover, the inclusion of labour provisions in BITs and trade agreements can create a framework that supports decent work conditions. However, it is noteworthy that the majority of trade agreements featuring labour provisions typically occur between developed and developing countries. For example, the preamble of the China-New Zealand Free Trade Agreement emphasizes 'the right of their governments to regulate in order to meet national policy objectives' and preserve 'their flexibility to safeguard the public welfare'.[8]

Trade agreements, on the other hand, tend to focus on fostering dialogue, monitoring and cooperative activities aimed at preventing and resolving conflicts. These procedures are less adversarial and more geared towards collaboration and understanding. The emphasis is on continuous engagement and negotiation, rather than on litigation or arbitration. This approach reflects a preventive strategy, seeking to address issues before they escalate into formal disputes. For instance, most of the Canadian, EU, and US trade agreements with labour provisions include institutional mechanisms to facilitate the engagement of workers' and employers' organizations, non-governmental organizations (NGOs) and the broader public in various ways in the negotiation and implementation of such provisions.[9] This participatory approach is critical in enhancing the transparency and legitimacy of trade agreements. It allows for a broader range of perspectives to be considered, particularly those of the workers who are directly impacted by labour standards and conditions. By involving civil society and labour organizations, trade agreements can better address the real-world impacts of economic policies on labour rights.

Environmental Impacts of International Investment Agreements

The environmental impacts of IIAs extend beyond physical and economic damage; they also infringe upon fundamental human rights, particularly the right to health. Environmental degradation can drastically diminish air and water quality, compromising the basic health of affected communities. Additionally, the destruction of ecosystems can disrupt local livelihoods that depend on natural resources, exacerbating the challenges faced by these communities.

---

labour law and standards set out in the trade agreement, such as through the settlement of labour-related disputes.

8 Free Trade Agreement between the Government of New Zealand and the Government of the Peoples Republic of China, signed on 7 April 2008 (entry into force on 1 October 2008).

9 Marva Corley-Coulibaly, Gaia Grasselli and Ira Postolachi, 'Promoting and Enforcing Compliance with Labour Provisions in Trade Agreements: Comparative Analysis of Canada, European Union and United States Approaches and Practices' *ILO* (2023) xii.

In light of these issues, there has been an increasing emphasis on incorporating environmental protection within the framework of international economic law. This shift reflects a growing recognition of the need to protect affected communities from the adverse impacts of large-scale natural resource investments. The concept of rights-based environmental protection is gaining traction as a critical element in shaping policies and agreements in international investment. Environmental rights have long been enshrined in key international declarations. The 1972 Stockholm Declaration asserts that humanity has 'the fundamental right' to 'an environment of a quality that permits a life of dignity and well-being',[10] and the 1992 Rio Declaration stipulates, rather more vaguely, that human beings are 'entitled to a healthy and productive life in harmony with nature'.[11]

As substantive rights, environmental rights establish the expectation that the environment should be preserved to a specific standard,[12] entitling individuals to clean water, protection from pollution or contamination, and the enjoyment of natural resources safeguarded from degradation. These rights often manifest as procedural rights, playing a crucial role in regulating developments that impact the environment. Procedural environmental rights typically include the right to access information about pollutants from development projects, the right to participate in hearings on development proposals and the right to challenge developments that may be harmful to the environment.[13] When recognized and exercised, these procedural rights pose significant challenges to states and investors who seek approvals for economically significant projects. They ensure that the interests of affected communities and the environment are considered, promoting transparency and accountability in the decision-making process.

Despite their importance, environmental rights have not received substantial attention in the scholarly literature on the legal investment regime. This oversight may stem from the perceived threat these rights pose to traditional investor protections. Consequently, environmental rights have been somewhat neglected in IIAs. This neglect persists despite growing concerns over the environmental impacts of investment and trade, highlighting a critical gap in addressing environmental issues within the framework of international economic law.

Several environmental treaties have recognized the necessity of incorporating environmental considerations into development projects. These treaties typically require states to conduct environmental impact assessments before authorizing activities likely to have significant environmental consequences. This book aims to address the deficiencies in current discourse and practices by advocating for the integration of environmental rights as a fundamental aspect

10 Principle 1 of the Declaration of the United Nations Conference on the Human Environment, 1972, cited in Ben Boer, 'Introduction' to Ben Boer (ed), *Environmental Law Dimensions of Human Rights* (Oxford University Press 2015) 2.

11 Principle 1 of the Rio Declaration on Environment and Development, 1992, cited in ibid.

12 Stephen Turner, *A Global Environmental Right* (Routledge 2013) 23.

13 Ibid.

of human rights and environmental approaches to international investment law. It seeks to elevate the profile of environmental rights, ensuring they are not only recognized but actively incorporated into the governance of international investments. By doing so, the book aims to safeguard both environmental integrity and public welfare in the face of expansive economic development.

Convergence of Investment Law, Human Rights Norms and Environmental Protection

The convergence of international investment law, human rights norms and environmental protection is becoming increasingly pronounced, influencing the evolution and application of investment law. An emerging consensus supports the integration of human rights, including environmental rights, within investment treaties to ensure comprehensive promotion and protection.[14] Such an objective can be achieved through three strategies: interaction among the various actors of the transnational legal process, adjudication of disputes that proactively takes into account human rights considerations, and the internalization of human rights norms in the investment treaty regime.[15]

Key issues such as human rights and transparency are shaping the evolution of international investment frameworks. Although the existing treaty language, arbitral practices and changes in arbitration rules have not yet achieved a fully coherent and comprehensive balance between investment law and human rights law, there is a noticeable positive trend in this direction.

Several recent developments within the field highlight this shift. Increasingly, investment treaties are incorporating references to human rights, environmental protection, sustainable development and public policy objectives. This change is also evident in the evolution of treaty interpretation practices and the movement towards greater transparency in investment treaty arbitration. One notable example is the relatively recent incorporation of general exceptions clauses in BITs. These clauses often address emerging concerns, particularly in environmental and labour policies, reflecting a growing recognition of the need to integrate public interest safeguards into investment agreements. For example, Article 21(2) of the 2011 Japan-Colombia BIT[16] provides:

14 Report of the High Commissioner for Human Rights, U.N. Economic and Social Council, Human Rights, Trade and Investment (E/CN.4/Sub.2/2003/9).

15 For example, in the context of a multilateral investment convention: S. Zia-Zarifi, 'Protection without Protectionism: Linking a Multilateral Investment Treaty and Human Rights' in E.C. Nieuwenhuys and M.M.T.A. Brus (eds), *Multilateral Regulation of Investment* (Kluwer Law International 2001) 121. See also, Julien Cantegreil, 'Implementing Human Rights in the NAFTA Regime—The Potential of a Pending Case: *Glamis Corp v USA*' in Pierre-Marie Dupuy, Francesco Francioni and Ernest-Ulrich Petersmann (eds), *Human Rights in International Investment Law and Arbitration* (Oxford University Press 2009) 389; and H. Koh, 'Transnational Public Law Litigation' (1991) 100 *Yale Law Journal* 2347.

16 Agreement between Japan and the Republic of Colombia for the Liberalization, Promotion and Protection of Investment, signed on 12 September 2011.

> Each contracting Party may adopt, maintain or enforce any measure that it considers appropriate to ensure that investment activities in its area are undertaken in a manner not incompatible with its environmental law, provided that such measures are consistent with this Agreement.

More stringent provisions on environmental protection are found in Article 5(1) of the 2009 BIT between the Belgium-Luxembourg Economic Union and Tajikistan:[17]

> Recognising the right of each contracting Party to establish its own level of domestic environmental protection and environmental development policies and priorities, and to adopt or modify accordingly its environmental legislation, each Contracting Party shall strive to ensure that its legislation provides for high levels of environmental protection and shall strive to continue to improve its legislation.

One exemplary model in this regard is the Morocco-Nigeria BIT, which explicitly incorporates human rights in its preamble and articles. This BIT mandates that all parties ensure their laws and actions are consistent with the international human rights agreements to which they are party. It also requires investors to uphold human rights in the host state and adhere to core labour standards as per the ILO Declaration on Fundamental Principles and Rights at Work. This innovative approach not only makes human rights obligations binding but also adds a new dimension to regulating investment activities, linking investment promotion and protection directly with the protection of human rights.

The preambles of many BITs explicitly acknowledge the government's role in pursuing policy goals that are crucial for public welfare, such as health, safety, the environment and adherence to internationally recognized labour standards. These introductory clauses highlight the dual objectives of fostering economic growth through investment while also safeguarding important social and environmental values. A prime example is the 2005 US-Uruguay BIT, whose preamble states that both parties aim to achieve economic objectives 'in a manner consistent with the protection of health, safety, and the environment, and the promotion of consumer protection and internationally recognized labour rights'.[18]

Moreover, some BITs go a step further by acknowledging that it is inappropriate to encourage investment at the expense of weakening or reducing the protections afforded in domestic environmental or labour laws. This perspective is critical as it directly addresses the potential negative impacts

17 Agreement between the Belgium-Luxembourg Economic Union, on the one hand, and the Republic of Tajikistan, on the other hand, on the Reciprocal Promotion and Protection of Investment, signed on 12 February 2009.

18 Treaty between the United States of America and the Oriental Republic of Uruguay concerning the encouragement and Reciprocal Protection of Investment, signed on 4 November 2005 (entered into force on 1 November 2006).

of investment on host country regulations and standards, ensuring that economic development does not undermine local protections. These preambles and exception clauses are vital for maintaining a delicate balance between promoting FDI and preserving the social and environmental dimensions of host countries. They set a framework within which investments should operate, aligning them with broader societal goals and ensuring that they contribute positively to the host communities.

The 2016 Morocco-Nigeria BIT contains two provisions dealing with environmental protection as part of the State's right to regulate.[19] Article 13(1) recognizes, in preambular language, the 'important role in protecting the environment' of national legislation and multilateral conventions to which the States are a party. It also requires each Party to adopt measures considered appropriate 'to ensure that [any] investment activity in its territory is undertaken in a manner sensitive to environmental and social concerns'.[20] All these developments in investment treaty practice indicate a shift from the previously predominant approach of the promotion and protection of foreign investment to a broader public interest goal.[21] Increasingly, there is a trend that contemporary BITs are considering issues relating to human rights and environmental sustainability in an integrated, holistic way that aligns with obligations governing state-investor relations.

Book Themes

The intricate nexus between investment, human rights and the environment has garnered increasing attention within the realm of investment arbitration, driven by a growing demand from civil society. Advocates argue that incorporating human rights and environmental considerations into investment treaties can better align investor-state arbitration with the broader objectives of sustainable development. This perspective recognizes that human rights and environmental concerns are frequently invoked by state parties and affected communities in investment arbitration playing a crucial role in shaping the legal landscape for state parties, foreign investors, and communities alike.

The book delves into the complex interplay between investment protections provided under IIAs, and their implications for a host state's responsibilities

19 Reciprocal Investment Promotion and Protection Agreement between the Government of the Kingdom of Morocco and the Government of the Federal Republic of Nigeria (Morocco-Nigeria BIT) (adopted on 3 December 2016). The treaty has been ratified by the Moroccan Parliament on 30 August 2017 and is not yet in force, pending the ratification by Nigeria.

20 Article 13(4) of the Reciprocal Investment Promotion and Protection Agreement Between the Government of the Kingdom of Morocco and the Government of the Federal Republic of Nigeria (2016).

21 See generally, Karsten Nowrot, 'How to Include Environmental Protection, Human Rights and Sustainability in International Investment Law?' (2014) 15 *The Journal of World Investment & Trade* 612–644.

concerning human and environmental rights. It presents a critical examination of the theoretical and conceptual frameworks underlying international investment law, with a particular focus on its integration with human rights and environmental protection. It highlights a paradigm shift from prioritizing FDI for economic growth to embedding sustainable development within the legislative fabric of international investments. It scrutinizes the traditional approach that often leads to a race to the bottom in environmental and human rights standards due to the isolated consideration of trade and investment disciplines. As international investment law evolves, it is increasingly intersecting with sustainable development principles, prompting a re-evaluation of investment agreements to mitigate negative externalities. This shift aligns with global consumer demand for sustainable and ethically produced goods and services, encouraging the adoption of more holistic and responsible investment practices.

This book emphasizes how treaty interpretation serves as a critical tool in achieving a balance and preventing conflicts between investors' rights and states' obligations to protect human and environmental interests. The book posits that environmental rights should be viewed as a legitimate extension of human rights, challenging conventional perspectives and urging for their inclusion in the discourse on international investment law. As this book examines the intricate relationship between human rights, environmental protection and international investment law, it delves into the specific challenges and opportunities presented by this intersection. Each chapter methodically addresses the pertinent issues, exploring potential reforms and forecasting future trends. This comprehensive exploration underscores the continuously evolving dynamics of this relationship.

This book explores the tension between investor protections and the regulatory freedoms of states, emphasizing the need for a balance that supports state sovereignty while promoting human rights and environmental stewardship. It raises critical questions about potential conflicts between economic development initiatives and the safeguarding of environmental and human rights, suggesting that investment treaties can sometimes hinder a nation's efforts to meet its international commitments.

Addressing the broader issue of sustainable development in relation to investment protection, the book advocates for a more integrated approach. It argues that economic growth, environmental sustainability and social inclusion should be viewed as interconnected pillars guiding the interpretation and application of investment treaties. Through this lens, the book calls for reforms that ensure investment agreements contribute to holistic and sustainable development outcomes.

A central theme of the book is the strategic use of exception clauses within BITs and the applicable legal frameworks. These clauses play a pivotal role in integrating human and environmental rights into the investment treaty regime. By providing legal pathways for exceptions, these clauses ensure that enforcing investment protections does not come at the expense of crucial social and environmental considerations.

The book also critically examines how arbitral tribunals currently apply human rights norms and environmental law when interpreting the substantive provisions of BITs. It argues that greater attention to environmental rights is needed in the adjudication of disputes, noting that tribunals often overlook these aspects due to the traditionally economic focus of investment treaties. The book suggests that incorporating these considerations can lead to a more balanced and equitable investment regime that better reflects the multifaceted nature of sustainable development.

Most BITs are equipped with robust mechanisms for ISDS, designed to protect and enforce the rights of investors. These mechanisms typically allow investors to initiate arbitration against host states if they believe their rights under the treaty have been violated. However, a significant gap in these treaties is the lack of reciprocal enforcement mechanisms that hold investors accountable for their obligations, particularly in areas concerning human rights and environmental standards.

The asymmetry in dispute settlement mechanisms under these investment agreements not only undermines the principles of justice and equity but also poses significant challenges to the realization of sustainable development. By prioritizing investor protection over other critical concerns, the current framework of international investment law can perpetuate a cycle where economic interests override fundamental human and environmental rights. This book addresses the challenges and potential reforms in ISDS processes, advocating for greater transparency and public participation to enhance the legitimacy and accountability of arbitration outcomes.

The analysis extends to labour rights clauses in investment treaties and trade agreements, evaluating how these provisions are integrated and enforced. The book critiques the current fragmented approach that separates human rights, environmental rights and investment protection into silos. It argues that this separation undermines effective and sustainable development and calls for an integrated approach that bridges these divides. By critically analysing these linkages, the book recommends a framework where sustainable development is at the core of investment treaties. It suggests that future treaties should be designed with clear, enforceable clauses that ensure the protection of human, labour and environmental rights. This approach not only aligns with global development goals but also ensures that investment contributes positively to the social and environmental objectives of host countries.

The international investment regime cannot be isolated from sustainable development, which has emerged as an overarching paradigm in recent times. Linking investment to sustainable development is essential because many sectors of the economy, such as energy, transportation, manufacturing, chemicals and mining, require a shift from unsustainable production methods to sustainable ones, necessitating new investments.[22] Thus foreign investment

22 Howard Mann, 'Reconceptualizing International Investment Law: Its Role in Sustainable Development' (2013) 17(2) *Lewis & Clark Law Review* 521, 534.

needs to be viewed from broader perspective of sustainable development. However, the current scope of the international investment regime is insufficient to reflect the fuller relationship between investment and sustainable development.[23] This inadequacy is particularly evident in the management and regulation of water services, as demonstrated in Chapter 9. The chapter highlights that the current international investment regime falls short in capturing the intricate relationship between investment and sustainable development.

Reflecting on water's critical role as a human right and a key component of environmental sustainability, this book calls for GATS and other international trade agreements to prioritize these elements within their frameworks. There are substantial potential conflicts between trade liberalization and human rights, notably the right to access clean and affordable water. This book advocates for establishing trade rules that support, rather than undermine, the fulfilment of these essential human rights. As such, this book argues for a balanced approach that integrates market dynamics with public service obligations.

A key takeaway from this book is the promotion of a holistic approach to addressing these issues, integrating human rights, environmental protection, labour rights and investment protection. This integrated perspective is crucial, given that global economic sectors require a shift from unsustainable practices to sustainable ones, necessitating new investments. Viewing foreign investment through the broader lens of sustainable development is essential. To bridge this gap, the book suggests inclusion of explicit human rights and environmental provisions in BITs and multilateral investment agreements. Such provisions would better facilitate states' ability to fulfil their obligations under international human rights and environmental laws while maintaining adequate domestic policy space. Both human rights and investment aim, to varying degrees, to improve the welfare of people.

The book makes a coherent linkage between investment and human rights, taking into account the legitimate concerns of both. Given the inadequate human rights provisions in current BITs and multilateral investment agreements, the book suggests the inclusion of human rights provisions in such agreements, including provisions for environmental rights, to enable states to meet their obligations under international human rights instruments and international environmental law. This inclusion will allow states to maintain adequate domestic policy space to meet their human rights obligations under human rights treaties.

Overall, the insights from this book aim to enhance the understanding among scholars and policymakers, particularly in developing countries, about the interplay between investment protection and human rights, advocating for an integrated approach that promotes sustainable development.

23 Ibid. 543.

2 Reimagining Investment Treaties

Converging Human Rights and Environmental Protection Through Relevant Actors

Introduction

The international investment regime has traditionally centred on protecting investments, with its original framework not specifically designed to address issues related to human rights, the environment or the public interest. This initial oversight has raised increasing concerns about the adverse impacts that transnational foreign investment activities, particularly in natural resource exploration, can have on host states. Such activities often trigger significant environmental, human rights, sustainable development and other public interest issues. Acknowledging these challenges, the international investment regime is progressively incorporating considerations of human rights and environmental protection. This shift reflects an understanding of the intricate relationship between investment law and broader social and ecological responsibilities. It moves beyond the traditional perspective of international investment law as an isolated regime, necessitating a more comprehensive analysis. This analysis must explore the structural issues and normative frameworks underpinning both investment and environmental laws, as well as their intersections with human rights.

The international investment regime is structured around a variety of international agreements and treaties, serving as a fundamental framework for the protection of foreign investments. Key components of this regime include BITs, investment chapters within free trade agreements (FTAs), and broader regional or international treaties such as the Energy Charter Treaty (ECT) and the Convention on the Settlement of Investment Disputes between States and Nationals of Other States (ICSID Convention). Additionally, this framework encompasses investment contracts that are directly concluded between foreign investors and host states or their state entities.

Historically, the disciplines of investment law, human rights and environmental law were seen as distinct, with each operating in its own sphere without much overlap. The prevailing view was that investment law functioned as a self-contained regime, isolated from other branches of international law and

DOI: 10.4324/9781003164951-3

immune to the influence of external legal considerations.[1] This perspective maintained that the different areas were not amenable to balancing or integration, as they were fundamentally separate in their goals and applications. However, this traditional compartmentalization has been increasingly challenged. Investment treaties play a critical role in economic and social development in developing countries, often facilitating the exploitation of natural resources by foreign investors. These treaties, typically designed to protect foreign investments and encourage international economic relationships, can influence domestic policies and priorities. While they can attract FDI and boost economic growth, they sometimes restrict the ability of governments to implement policies that protect public welfare, including labour rights, environmental standards, and public health measures. Often, these agreements limit the ability of host states to regulate social and environmental issues effectively. Provisions commonly found in these treaties, such as clauses on expropriation, FET and umbrella clauses, may restrict states' abilities to fulfil their duties in protecting and promoting environmental interests and human rights.

This heightened attention to the interplay between international investment law, human rights and sustainable development is due to the increasing interplay between human rights norms and investment protection norms within the processes of dispute settlement and treaty interpretation. Recent cases have shown that the norms guiding human rights and those ensuring investment protection often converge, influencing the outcomes of disputes and the reading of treaty provisions. These cases have started to recognize non-investment obligations, such as human rights and environmental concerns, as pertinent factors in the resolution of investment disputes.[2] This evolving approach reflects the growing recognition of the interconnected nature of these fields within international law. Consequently, issues of human rights and environmental considerations have gained more prominence in the negotiation of recent investment treaties.

This shift is largely driven by ongoing debates and an increased awareness of the necessity to align business practices with human rights and environmental sustainability. This marks a transformative period in the understanding and application of international investment law. Growing concerns about the impacts of FDI and natural resource exploitation have brought the human rights dimensions within investment frameworks to the forefront. Despite this emerging overlap, BITs typically do not explicitly reference the international human rights obligations of the contracting states, nor do they impose direct obligations on investors to respect human rights. This omission underscores a

1 See, J.I. Charney, 'Is International Law Threatened by Multiple International Tribunals?' (1998) *Recueil des Course* 219, 271.

2 *Urbaser v. Argentina*, ICSID Case No. ARB/07/26, *Biloune and Marine Drive Complex Ltd v. Ghana Investments Centre and the Government of Ghana*, UNCITRAL ad hoc Tribunal, Award on Jurisdiction and Liability, 27 October 1989.

significant gap in integrating human rights considerations into the core framework of investment treaties. The absence of an explicit connection between human rights obligations and investment protections presents challenges in ensuring that investment activities do not undermine human rights standards in host countries.

Understanding the State's Role in Upholding Human Rights Obligations

State obligations to adhere to human rights treaties originate from two primary sources: human rights treaties that states have ratified or acceded to, and customary international law. These obligations encompass a wide array of human rights instruments that deal with diverse categories, including universal norms of civil, political and economic rights, as well as social and cultural rights. Additionally, there are group-specific rights that protect women, children, persons with disabilities and indigenous peoples.

Some human rights have also evolved into the character of customary international law and are considered norms of jus cogens. These are peremptory norms from which no derogation is permitted, representing the most fundamental principles of international law. Even if states have not ratified specific treaties, they are still obligated to comply with these core human rights principles that flow from customary international law or jus cogens norms.

The concept of human rights itself embodies broader standards of fairness, justice, equality and human dignity. In terms of their normative status within international law, human rights are given a high priority. Consequently, any international treaty that conflicts with a state's obligations to comply with human rights is considered either void or inconsistent to the extent of such a conflict.[3] The contention that the human rights occupy a hierarchically superior position among the norms of international law can be justified by the provisions of the UN Charter and the Vienna Convention on the Law of Treaties, 1969.[4] On the other hand, under current international law, general international human rights law affects the obligations of private actors such as foreign investors 'indirectly' through domestic laws.[5]

3 Olivier De Schutter, 'A Human Rights Approach to Trade and Investment Policies' *A Paper Presented to the Conference on Confronting the Global Food Challenge: Finding New Approaches to Trade and Investment That Support the Right to Food*, held on 24–26 November 2008, Geneva, Switzerland.

4 See generally, Ian Seiderman, *Hierarchy in International Law: The Human Rights Dimension* (Intersentia-Hart 2001); Louis Henkin, *The Age of Rights* (Columbia University Press 1990); Bruno Simma and Philip Alston, 'The Sources of Human Rights Law: Custom, Jus Cogens, and General Principles' (1988–89) 12 *Australian Yearbook of International Law* 82.

5 Human Rights Committee, General Comment No. 31, The Nature of the General Legal Obligation Imposed on States Parties to the Covenant (26 May 2004) CCPR/C/21/Rev.1/Add.13, para. 8; John Ruggie, Report of the Special Representative of the Secretary-General

A distinction exists between investment treaties and human rights treaties. Investment treaties primarily establish obligations between States, whereas human rights treaties impose obligations on a State towards its own population. Consequently, human rights treaties possess an 'objective character in that they are not reducible to bilateral exchanges of advantages between the contracting States'.[6] This difference between two types of treaty obligations has been also identified by the Human Rights Committee, which observes: 'Such treaties and the Covenant specifically, are not a web of inter-State exchanges of mutual obligations. They concern the endowment of individuals with rights'.[7]

Human rights treaties generally impose three types of obligations on states: the obligation to respect, protect and fulfil the rights of individuals. To respect rights means that states must refrain from interfering with civil and political rights. To protect rights requires states to prevent infringements by private parties. To fulfil rights involves taking positive measures to ensure economic, social and cultural rights are met. These obligations necessitate states to implement various legislative, policy and administrative measures.

Both types of obligations—positive and negative—can be impacted by foreign investment projects. For instance, the implementation of a controversial investment project might lead to government actions that suppress civil and political rights such as freedom of assembly and expression, thus violating human rights obligations. Additionally, many states are signatories to ILO Conventions and Standards, which encompass a range of labour rights including the right to freedom of association and the right to organize trade unions.

Soft law on the rights of indigenous peoples can also be relevant in numerous situations, further illustrating how investment law interacts with the expanding scope of international human rights law. The evolving development of soft law concerning marginalized groups, such as indigenous peoples, introduces new dimensions to the ongoing debate on how best to integrate human rights considerations into the realm of investment law.[8]

The discussion underscores several critical points about the relationship between state obligations under IIAs and human rights treaties. First, it is increasingly acknowledged that when conflicts arise between different norms or obligations, states should be able to prioritize their human rights obligations as outlined in multilateral human rights treaties. This ability is essential for defending regulatory measures that are implemented to protect human rights.

on the Issue of Human Rights and Transnational Corporations and Other Business Enterprises (9 February 2007) A/HRC/4/035, para. 44.

6 De Schutter (n 4) 84.

7 Comment of Human Rights Committee, General comment no. 24 (1994): Issues relating to reservations made upon ratification or accession to the Covenant or the Optional Protocol thereto, or in relation to declaration under Article 41 of the Covenant, at para. 17.

8 United Nations Declaration on the Rights of Indigenous Peoples, Sixty-First session, Agenda Item 68, Report of the Human Rights Council, 7 September 2007, A/61/L.67, General Assembly.

Accordingly, IIAs must be interpreted in a manner that aligns with human rights, recognizing that human rights norms occupy a superior position in the hierarchy of international law. This is premised on the fact that states have a fundamental obligation to protect human rights, which is mandated by both customary international law and the human rights treaties to which they are parties.

Moreover, it has long been established that a state's obligation to protect investments is not absolute. In the famous *Barcelona Traction case*, the ICJ observed:

> When a State admits into its territory foreign investments or foreign nationals, whether natural or juristic persons, it is bound to extend to them the protection of the law and assumes obligations concerning the treatment to be afforded them. These obligations, however, are neither absolute nor unqualified. In particular, an essential distinction should be drawn between the obligations of a State towards the international community as a whole, and those arising vis-à-vis another State in the field of diplomatic protection. By their very nature the former are the concern of all states. In view of the importance of the rights involved, all States can be held to have a legal interest in the protection; they are obligations *erga omnes*.
>
> Such obligations derive, for example, in customary international law, from the outlawing of acts of aggression, and of genocide, as also from the principles and rules concerning the basic rights of the human person, including protection from slavery and racial discrimination.[9]

In modern times, many states have adopted affirmative action policies within their constitutions to address historical injustices. These policies enable states to differentiate legally between foreign investors and nationals, ensuring that certain groups receive benefits aimed at rectifying past disparities.

Additionally, over the duration of investment treaty obligations, host states often ratify new human rights treaties that mandate the protection of newly recognized rights. As a result, these states are required to enact new laws and implement administrative measures to fulfil the obligations set forth in such human rights treaties.[10] Sornarajah writes: 'The burgeoning law on human rights and environmental protection . . . also creates instability in an area that has been designed particularly in the context of the single objective of the protection of the foreign investment.'[11]

Third, the property rights of foreign investors are not absolute and are subject to limitations in virtually every legal system. It is universally acknowledged

9 *Case Concerning the Barcelona Traction, Light and Power Company Limited* (New Application: 1962) (*Belgium v. Spain*) Second Phase (1970) I.C.J. Rep. 3, paras 33–34.

10 Surya P. Subedi, *International Investment Law: Reconciling Policy and Principle* (Oxford University Press 2008) 168.

11 Sornarajah (n 5) 86.

that these rights must be balanced with other public interests, such as the right to health and public order, among other essential public services. The property rights stipulated in major human rights instruments are qualified to allow for state interference in the public interest, demonstrating a global consensus on the necessity of such balance.

Finally, the privatization of essential public services as a condition of foreign investment can significantly impact the rights of marginalized groups. While privatization offers numerous benefits, such as increased efficiency of public resources and improved service delivery, it also requires careful regulation to ensure that it does not adversely affect the most vulnerable populations. This involves ensuring that privatization does not compromise access to essential services for these groups, thereby aligning investment practices with broader human rights and public interest goals.[12]

However, the process of privatization can often result in increased costs for essential services, potentially placing these services beyond the reach of impoverished populations. This issue is particularly prevalent in developing countries and economies in transition, where there is a rush to privatize in the effort to establish a free-market economy, often without implementing adequate regulatory and administrative safeguards to protect marginalized groups. While privatization in itself is not a violation of human rights, the act of privatizing can reduce the level of human rights accountability within the sector concerned. The impact of privatization on human rights manifests in two primary contexts. First, there is the risk that the privatized service delivery may not meet established human rights standards, leading to an erosion of quality and accessibility. Second, privatization can lead to human rights violations as a result of the activities of privatized service providers. Examples include environmental pollution following a breakdown in sewage systems or waste management facilities, which can have dire health and environmental consequences for the surrounding communities.[13]

Sustainable Development and International Investment Law

In the increasingly interconnected world of international trade and investment, the intersection of environmental rights and investment regimes has become a crucial area of concern. Environmental and sustainable development rights refer to, in part, the entitlements related to the environment, recognized under international law and national constitutions, which protect the

12 See, Robert Pritchard, 'Privatisation and Private Provision of Infrastructure' in Robert Pritchard (ed), *Economic Development, Foreign Investment and the Law* (Kluwer Law International and International Bar Association 1996) 67–92.

13 Ursula Kriebaum, 'Privatising Human Rights: The Interface between International Investment Protection and Human Rights' in A. Reinisch and U. Kriebum (eds), *The Law of International Relations: Liber Amicorum Huas Neuhold* (Eleven International Publishing 2007) 165, 167.

right to a healthy environment. Investment regimes, typically framed by BITs and multilateral agreements, regulate the conditions under which investments by foreign entities are made, protected and governed. Environmental rights have long been enshrined in the principles of key international environmental treaties. For example, the 1972 Stockholm Declaration provides that human beings have 'the fundamental right' to 'an environment of a quality that permits a life of dignity and well-being',[14] and similarly, in the 1992 Rio Declaration, which stipulates rather more vaguely, human beings are 'entitled to a healthy and productive life in harmony with nature'.[15]

Sustainable development rights[16] are available in both substantive and procedural forms. As a substantive right, environmental rights manifest in the expectation the environment should be preserved to a specific standard.[17] The holder of the right is entitled to, for example, clean water, protection of health from pollution or contamination, and protecting their enjoyment of natural resources from degradation. As procedural rights, environmental rights may be expressed through the right to information about pollutants resulting from particular development, the right to participate in hearings related to development proposals or the right to challenge a particular development.[18] The exercise of these procedural rights, when recognized or permitted, would present obvious challenges to states and investors intent on securing approval for projects of economic significance.

Sustainable development rights have not yet received substantial treatment in the scholarly literature on the legal investment regime. Investment agreements often prioritize economic growth and investor protection, sometimes at the expense of environmental considerations. Environmental regulations can be perceived as barriers to investment, leading to conflicts where economic interests clash with environmental sustainability. Cases like *Vattenfall v. Germany* highlight the tension between investors' rights under investment treaties and state obligations to uphold environmental standards. Such disputes often arise when governments implement new environmental policies that affect the profitability of foreign investments. The scholarly literature on the legal investment regime has largely neglected environmental rights, perhaps due to the perceived threat they pose to traditional investor protections. This oversight becomes increasingly concerning as environmental impacts associated with

14 Principle 1 of the Declaration of the United Nations Conference on the Human Environment, 1972, cited in Ben Boer, 'Introduction' to Ben Boer (ed), *Environmental Law Dimensions of Human Rights* (Oxford University Press 2015) 2.

15 Principle 1 of the Rio Declaration on Environment and Development, 1992.

16 According to the United Nations Environment Programme, environmental rights mean 'any proclamation of a human right to environmental conditions of a specified quality'. 'What are environmental rights?' available at https://www.unep.org/explore-topics/environmental-rights-and-governance/what-we-do/advancing-environmental-rights/what.

17 Stephen Turner, *A Global Environmental Right* (Routledge 2013) 23.

18 Ibid.

international investment and trade grows more pronounced. The integration of environmental standards is crucial in the context of existing IIAs, where the range of environmental concerns explicitly addressed is both limited and outdated. The language used in these agreements tends to be generic and reflects the era of the 1948 General Agreement on Tariffs and Trade (GATT), failing to incorporate modern environmental challenges like climate change and biodiversity.[19] Although these issues are acknowledged in the ECT, a multilateral agreement, such recognition is the exception rather than the rule.

The main objective of the IIAs is to promote and protect foreign investment. Despite the strong linkage between sustainable development and investment, most IIAs do not adequately facilitate the sustainable development issue of the host State. Only some recent IIAs contain commitments to sustainable development. For example, the Trans-Pacific Partnership Agreement 2016, the Comprehensive Economic and Trade Agreement 2016 and the EU-Singapore Free Trade Agreement 2014 EU-Vietnam Free Trade Agreement 2015 include commitments to sustainable development in their preambles. Most of the provisions relating to sustainable development are 'balancing' in nature aiming at preserving state regulatory powers, rather than imposing sustainable development obligations on the host states or foreign investors.[20]

The insufficiency of sustainable development provisions in many IIAs is due to their primary focus on investment protection and promoting the economic development of host states. Consequently, the needs and rights of non-state stakeholders are often overlooked in the drafting of these agreements.[21] However, as global commitment to the SDGs grows, there is increasing demand for IIAs that are compatible with SDGs. This includes taking regulatory measures for public interest purposes and integrating specific SDG targets that are relevant to foreign investment. For instance, SDG Target 17.5 calls for the adoption and implementation of investment promotion regimes for least developed countries (LDCs). Other targets concern the use of foreign investment as a means to end poverty and hunger; achieve food security and improved nutrition; promote sustainable agriculture; ensure access to affordable, reliable, sustainable and modern energy; and reduce inequality within and among countries. This agreement on SDG Target 17 indicates international consensus towards developing a mutually reinforcing role of foreign investment and SDGs.

To harness the full potential of FDI in supporting sustainable development, it is imperative that both host and home countries design laws, policies and practices with sustainability at the core. Investment treaties, in particular, need a reformation

19 K. Gordon and J. Pohl, 'Environmental Concerns in International Investment Agreements: A Survey' *OECD Working Papers on International Investment*, 2011/01, OECD Publishing. http://doi.org/10.1787/5kg9mq7scrjh-en 6.

20 Manjiao Chi, *Integrating Sustainable Development in International Investment Law, Normative Incompatibility, System Integration and Governance Implications* (Routledge 2018) 162.

21 Ibid. 2.

to ensure they support investments that advance, rather than undermine, sustainable development objectives. This involves a paradigm shift from viewing FDI merely as an economic tool to recognizing its powerful role in achieving broader environmental and social goals. By aligning IIAs with the SDGs, international consensus and actions can create a mutually reinforcing relationship between foreign investment and global sustainable development initiatives.

Human Rights and International Investment Law

Many scholars have sought to analyse the relationship between the relationship between foreign investment and human rights by presenting two opposite theories: the neoclassical theory and the dependency theory. According to the neoclassical theory, FDI contributes positively to the economic development and human rights. The neoclassical theory is based on liberalization of trade, investment, and cross-border mobility of capital and labour. On the other hand, dependency theory views global capitalism promoted by FDI as a threat to the economic and social well-being of developing countries.[22] Many experts believe that foreign investment has positive spillovers on development of a country. According to this view, 'the foreign investment tends to improve the condition of human rights in developing countries either as a direct result of a firm's activity or as the indirect result of improved conditions created by those investments'.[23] FDI provides access to capital, creates employment opportunities and can play an important role in bringing new technologies to developing countries while contributing to their economic wealth and social welfare.[24] According to this view, foreign investment is not naturally inimical to human rights. As such, international investment law and human rights can effectively complement each other.[25]

But there is no automatic relationship between the foreign investment and human rights. In fact, FDI has a mixed impact on human rights and labour practices in developing countries.[26] The relationship between foreign investment

22 See, Sherif H. Seid, *Global Regulation of Foreign Direct Investment* (Ashgate 2002), David L. Richards, Ronald D. Gelleny and David H. Sacko, 'Myth with a Mean Streak? Foreign Economic Penetration and Government Respect for Human Rights in Developing Countries' (2001) 45 *International Studies Quarterly* 219–239.

23 See, Debora Spar, 'Foreign Investment and Human Rights' (1999) 42(1) *Challenge* 55–80.

24 See UNCTAD, 'Economic Development in Africa, Rethinking the Role of Foreign Direct Investment (2006) available at https://unctad.org/system/files/official-document/gdsafrica20051_en.pdf, accessed 15 March 2024; T. Moran, Edward Graham and Magnus Blomström (eds), *Does Foreign Investment Promote Development?* (Peterson Institute for International Economics 2005).

25 James D. Fry, 'International Human Rights Law in Investment Arbitration: Evidence of International Law's Unity' (2007–2008) 18 *Duke Journal of Comparative and International Law* 77, 106.

26 Layna Mosely and Saika Uno, 'Racing to the Bottom or Climbing to the Top? Foreign Direct Investment and Human Rights' *A Paper Presented at the Annual Meetings of the American Political Science Association*, August 29–September 1, 2002, Boston.

and human rights in domestic settings depends on a number of factors including presence of a regulatory, legal and voluntary framework to provide guidance to business as well as adequate protection to individual rights. De Schutter suggests that the legal framework of FDI should be investigated from a human rights perspective, and a structural dimension of the issue requires macro-analysis to measure the impact of FDI on the human rights–driven development of the country.[27] Seid suggested that FDI can contribute to economic development of a country only when it is capable of determining entry and conditions of operation of such FDI.[28] There is currently no concrete evidence to suggest that FDI itself really impedes the progress of human rights in the developing world. Empirical evidence is needed to establish any positive or negative correlation between foreign investment and human rights.[29] The positive impact of FDI on economic development is not self-evident. According to the UNCTAD Trade and Development Report 2007, the expansion of the world economy and trade had not changed the persistent imbalances and the net capital flow from developing to developed states. Thus the relationship between foreign investment and human rights is far more complex than the simplistic assumption.

Closely related to the above, another issue is whether BITs promote FDI. It has been revealed by several studies that the impact of BITs on FDI is rather small and the results are mixed.[30] Most of the developing countries enter into BITs to seek foreign investment in order to pursue their national development objectives, such as poverty alleviation and creation of employment opportunities. But the importance of concluding BITs for attracting foreign investment is difficult to assess because any causal connection between the conclusion of BITs and increased foreign investment flows can hardly be established using statistical correlations.[31] The value of a BIT lies more in reducing risk for investors by stabilizing the legal framework within which the investment will operate rather than in directly attracting investment.[32] Some recent studies argued that BITs have a positive impact on attracting FDI through granting

27 See Olivier De Schutter, 'Transnational Corporations as Instrument of Human Development' in Philip Alston and Mary Robinson (eds), *Human Rights and Development: Towards Mutual Reinforcement* (Oxford University Press 2005) 403–444.

28 See, Sherif H. Seid, *Global Regulation of Foreign Direct Investment* (Ashgate 2002) 182.

29 See, Brian Potter, 'Vertical and Horizontal Races: The Impact of Multinational Corporations on Host Country Human Rights Regimes' *International Studies Association, 2009 Annual Convention*, New York, 15 February 2009 (it distinguishes between vertical and horizontal foreign direct investment and concludes that host rights violations are more likely with vertical than horizontal FDI).

30 UNCTAD World Investment Report, 2003, Mary Hallward-Driemeier, 'Do Bilateral Investment Treaties attract FDI? Only Bit . . . They Could Bit' *Policy Research Working Paper 3121*, available at http://econ.worldbank.org/files/29143_wps3121.pdf, accessed 12 January 2024.

31 Kenneth J. Vandevelde, 'Investment Liberalisation and Economic Development: The Role of Bilateral Investment Treaties' (1998) 36 *Columbia Journal of Transnational Law* 522, 525.

32 Ibid.

investment protection, although BITs are only one variable in creating a favourable investment climate.[33] By concluding BITs, developing countries stand to benefit in terms of increasing their attractiveness for FDI.[34]

Strategies Towards Convergence in IIAs

As the intersection between international human rights law and international investment law continues to expand, a growing consensus has emerged on the need to take into account human rights, including environmental rights, in investment treaties. This integration aims to address various human rights and transparency issues that are increasingly influencing international investment law. However, the current state of treaty language, arbitral practices and changes in investment arbitration rules reveal a lack of a coherent and comprehensive framework that balances investment law with human rights considerations. Despite these challenges, there has been positive development towards building such a relationship, as reflected in recent developments in BITs and arbitral decisions.[35] This trend is supported by the increased inclusion of environmental issues in treaty negotiations and the growing number of investment disputes that involve environmental concerns.[36] It reflects a broader understanding within the international community that sustainable development and environmental protection are integral to the governance of international investments.

The interaction between investment and non-investment obligations in investment treaties is a critical area of development.[37] Scholars have noted an increasing demand for improved transparency in arbitration processes and greater participation from civil society in arbitral proceedings. These changes are indicative of a broader trend where the lines between human rights, environmental

33 E. Neumayer and L. Spess, 'Do Bilateral Investment Treaties Increase Foreign Direct Investment to Developing Countries' (2005), available at https://eprints.lse.ac.uk/627/01/World_Dev_(BITs).pdf, accessed 19 August 2023; J. Tobin and S. Rose-Ackerman, 'Bilateral Investment Treaties: Do They Stimulate Foreign Direct Investment' available at www.upf.es/dret/civil/clef/sra.pdf, accessed 23 August 2021. However, some studies conclude that there is only limited evidence that FDI can be attracted by BITs. See, Aaron Cosbey, 'International Investment Agreements and Sustainable Development: Achieving the Millennium Development Goals' *International Institute for Sustainable Development*, September 2005, http://www.iisd.org, accessed 14 April 2022.

34 'The Role of International Investment Agreements in Attracting Foreign Direct Investment to Developing Countries' UNCTAD, United Nations, Geneva and New York, 2009.

35 Model BIT of the Southern African Development Community (SADC Model BIT, 2012, Brazilian Model BIT (2015), Colombian Model BIT (2017).

36 Ibid.

37 M. Hirsch, 'Interactions between Investment and Non-Investment Obligations in International Investment Law' in P. Muchlinski, F. Ortino and Ch. Schreuer (eds), *The Oxford Handbook of International Investment Law* (Oxford University Press 2008) 154–181; A. Reinisch, '"Investment and . . . .": The Broader Picture of Investment Law' in A. Reinisch and Ch. Knahr (eds), *International Investment Law in Context* (Eleven International Publishing 2008) 201–207.

protection and investment law are converging. This convergence is partly driven by growing recognition of the private sector's role in environmental protection and the changing perception of foreign investment in environmental treaties.[38]

Three key strategies have been identified to achieve the integration of human rights into the investment treaty regime. First, enhancing the interaction between the various actors involved in the transnational legal process is crucial. This includes governments, TNCs, civil society and international organizations. By fostering dialogue and collaboration among these actors, there can be a more coordinated effort to incorporate human rights considerations into investment treaties. Second, arbitration bodies are encouraged to proactively consider human rights issues in their adjudication of disputes. This approach requires arbitrators to interpret investment treaties in ways that do not undermine human rights norms, thereby promoting a balance between investor protection and human rights obligations. This approach is considered in more detail in Chapter 6. Third, integrating human rights norms directly into the frameworks of investment treaties can institutionalize these considerations.[39] This involves explicitly referencing human rights, sustainable development and public policy objectives in the treaties to ensure they are a fundamental part of investment arbitration.[40] This strategy is examined in more detail in Chapter 4.

The integration of human rights into international investment law is an ongoing process that requires concerted efforts across various legal and regulatory frameworks. By adopting the strategies outlined above and continuing to foster dialogue among all stakeholders, there is potential to create an investment treaty regime that respects and promotes human rights while also safeguarding investor interests. This balanced approach is essential for the sustainable development of global investments in the modern world.

IIAs and Human Rights: Practical Considerations and Strengthening the Engagement of Relevant Actors

BITs do not always offer benefits to developing countries. The operation of foreign investment can affect human rights negatively in a number of contexts. First, a developing country can relax its domestic regulatory standards

38 Jorge E. Viñuales, *Foreign Investment and the Environment in International Law* (Cambridge University Press 2012) 8.

39 S. Zia-Zarifi, 'Protection without Protectionism: Linking a Multilateral Investment Treaty and Human Rights' in E.C. Nieuwenhuys and M.M.T.A. Brus (eds), *Multilateral Regulation of Investment* (Kluwer Law International 2001) 121. See also, Julien Cantegreil, 'Implementing Human Rights in the NAFTA Regime—The Potential of a Pending Case: Glamis Corp v USA' in Pierre-Marie Dupuy, Francesco Francioni and Ernest-Ulrich Petersmann (eds), *Human Rights in International Investment Law and Arbitration* (Oxford University Press 2009) 389; and H. Koh, 'Transnational Public Law Litigation' (1991) 100 *Yale Law Journal* 2347.

40 Model BIT of the Southern African Development Community (SADC Model BIT, 2012, Brazilian Model BIT (2015), Colombian Model BIT (2017).

including environmental and human rights in order to attract foreign investment of what is known as 'race to the bottom'. It is argued that competition to attract foreign investment results in the competitive reduction of social welfare, labour standards and respects for human rights.[41] It is often alleged that TNCs, who are the primary sources of FDI, with their huge economic leverage and global reach can exercise profound influence in social and economic and political spheres of developing countries and their activities can directly or indirectly affect the enjoyment of human rights of the people of these countries.[42]

Second, in some cases, TNCs have been held directly responsible for violations of human rights, such as abusive labour practices or forced evictions.[43] The TNCs' security arrangements with the host state through the employment of public or private security forces for the safety of investment facilities can lead to the violation of civil and political rights of the host community if such security forces suppress a local community's opposition to a particular project.[44] The negative impact on human rights by the activities of TNCs, which exacerbates social tension, has the potential to produce a popular backlash within that state against all FDI.[45]

Third, TNCs can indirectly violate human rights through their complicity in the abuse of human rights by the host government through the support of or acquiescence to activities of such governments.[46] TNCs operating in countries with authoritarian regimes may be complicit with human rights violations by maintaining silence and inactivity in the context of oppression by such governments.[47] TNCs can also be implicated in human rights violations when they invest in countries with poor human rights records and widespread corruption.[48] Some TNCs may deliberately invest in developing countries to circumvent the liability and costs associated with stringent environmental regulations in their home countries. The involvement of TNCs through contractual arrangements can be perceived as an endorsement of the host government's human rights record or as providing financial support that enables the government to repress

41 Dani Rodrcik, *Has Globalisation Gone Too Far?* (Institute for International Economics 1997).
42 For detailed discussion on how corporate activities can lead to each category of human rights, see Monash University Castan Centre for Human Rights Law, *Human Rights Translated: A Business Reference Guide*, Published by United Nations Human Rights, Office of the High Commissioner for Human Rights, 2008.
43 Abdulah Al Faruque, 'Mapping the Relationship between Investment Protection and Human Rights' (2010) 11(4) *The Journal of World Investment and Trade* 539, 552.
44 Ibid.
45 Glen Kelley, 'Multilateral Investment Treaties: A Balanced Approach to Multinational Corporations' (2000–2001) 39 *Columbian Journal of Transnational Law* 483–532.
46 Faruque (n 43).
47 Sir Geoffrey Chandler, 'The Responsibilities of Oil Companies' in Asbjorn Eide, Helge Ole Bergesen and Pia Rudolfson Goyer (eds), *Human Rights and the Oil Industry* (Intersentia 2000) 14.
48 Faruque (n 43).

its population.[49] Additionally, forming joint ventures with state-owned enterprises in countries with a history of human rights abuses can expose TNCs to accusations of complicity or of benefiting from these abuses.[50]

Transnational Corporations: A Key Player for Further Convergence

Today there is no denying the significant amount of power and influence that TNCs have around the globe. They exercise dominant control over global trade, investment and technology, and the annual revenue of some of these corporations exceeds that of the gross national product of many countries.[51] This makes some TNCs even more powerful than national governments themselves. Flowing from this power is the ability of TNCs to influence political, social and cultural values in the countries in which they operate. Not only can they influence living standards but TNCs can also have significant impact on cultural values and the environment. Thus as Kinley and Tadaki, two legal researchers in this area, state: 'by virtue, specifically of their economic and political muscle, TNCs are uniquely positioned to affect, positively and negatively, the level of enjoyment of human rights'.[52]

In terms of human rights, the great expansion of the global economy has brought advantages and disadvantages. The speed at which TNCs have grown around the world is unprecedented. It has been calculated, for example, that of the top 100 economies in the world today, 51 are corporations and only 49 states.[53] With such power at their hands, TNCs have the ability to do great good and great harm. On the one hand, through commercial activity driven by corporations, many human rights are positively affected. Examples of this include economic and social rights to work and wages, shelter, food and water, health care, education and raised standards of living generally.[54] Overall, corporations are contributing to the improvement of living standards and enjoyment of human rights for communities around the world.[55]

49 Peter Woicke, 'Putting Human Rights Principles into Development Practice through Finance: The Experience of the International Finance Corporation' in Philip Alston and Mary Robinson (eds), *Human Rights and Development: Towards Mutual Reinforcement* (Oxford University Press 2005) 340.
50 Ibid.
51 David Kinley and Junko Tadaki, 'From Talk to Walk: The Emergence of Human Rights Responsibilities for Corporations at International Law' (2004) 44(4) *Virginia Journal of International Law* 931, 933.
52 Ibid.
53 Sarah Anderson and John Cavanagh, *Top 200: The Rise of Global Corporate Power* (Institute of Policy Studies 2000).
54 David Kinley and Justine Nolan, 'Trading and Aiding Human Rights: Corporations in the Global Economy' (2007) 25(4) *Nordic Journal of Human Rights Law* 353, 356.
55 See, Deepa Narayan, Robert Chambers, Meera Kaul Shah and Patti Petesch, *Voices of the Poor: Crying Out for Change* (Oxford University Press 2000).

However, the influence of corporations on human rights is not all benign. TNCs have been and continue to be minor or major abusers of human rights. Some corporations are guilty of treating workers badly—in terms of pay, conditions and working environments; some pollute the environment in ways that have dramatic and serious effects far beyond their immediate surroundings; some discriminate against people with disabilities, women or indigenous people; and some work alongside governments that perpetrate gross human rights violations.[56] The ability of international law to deal with these violations has been limited.

Social Dimensions of Investment Projects

The negative social and environmental impact of investment operations can be partially the inevitable consequence of the exclusionary process and partially due to the unsustainable practices and negligence of TNCs towards the local community. Adverse social impacts may arise in various phases of natural resource development, albeit in varying degrees. However, the exploration and development stage can cause the greatest disruptions including displacement of indigenous peoples and their livelihoods, environmental pollution, loss of biological diversity, deforestation, destruction of cultural properties, severe health problems and other social problems. Alleged human rights violations by TNCs are among the most debated and controversial issues since their huge economic leverage and global reach can exercise profound influence in social and economic and political spheres of the developing countries and their activities can directly or indirectly affect enjoyment of human rights of the people of these countries. The government's overriding needs for foreign investment may exacerbate the situation.

The environmental and social problems caused by TNCs can give rise to resentment and conflict between them and the local or indigenous communities that can destabilize the relationship between the company and host community.[57] Such conflict can be fuelled by pressure groups, including local NGOs and local communities, whose coalition with other local and international activist groups can build vehement resistance to the

56 Beth Stephens, 'The Amorality of Profit: TNCs and Human Rights' (2002) 20 *Berkeley Journal of International Law* 45, 47.

57 See, for useful discussion on contexts of petroleum company-community conflict: Gary MacDonald and Timothy McLaughlin, 'Extracting Conflict' in Rory Sullivan (ed), *Business and Human Rights: Dilemmas and Solutions* (Greenleaf Publishing 2003) 232–242. See also, G. Manuel Eduardo Echeverra, 'Conflicts between Resource Development and Indigenous People' in *Mining and Oil & Gas Development in Latin America*, Mineral Law Series, Rocky Mountain Mineral Law Foundation, vol. 2001, Number 3 (discussing many incidents of community/petroleum company conflict in Ecuador); see also, George S. Akpan, 'Host Community Hostility to Mining Projects: A New Generation of Risk?' in Elizabeth Bastida, Thomas Walde and Janeth Warden-Fernandez (eds), *International and Comparative Mineral Law and Policy: Trends and Prospects* (Kluwer Law International 2005) 311–329.

development of a project through their concerted actions. Such actions can include dissemination of information, raising awareness-building activities in the host community about the negative impact of the operation of investment projects. The negative social impacts of operations and human rights abuse by TNCs can result in huge NGO campaigns, media coverage and public outrage against the concerned company. The disrepute brought to the TNCs by the negative publicity may cause depreciation of their shares in the stock market and may lead to denial of access to new deposits in a particular country. Shareholders' divestment of their share from a TNC accused of human rights violation or environmental pollution can keep it away from practices which harm biodiversity conservation, enjoyment of human rights and sustainable development. The TNCs accused of violations of human rights can be sued in both the host countries and their home countries for holding them accountable for the human rights abuse. The threat of litigation as a consequence of negative social and environmental impacts and human rights abuses is now considered to be one of the significant risk factors for TNCs.

Social impact assessment and its integration should be an integral part of the investment project design and implementation considering the fact that failure to understand community needs and aspiration at the initial stage of the project can sow the seeds of social tensions and potential conflict in the future. Carrying out social impact assessment to address social and human rights issues in the investment project is important for increasing the public acceptability and success of the project, obtaining a license to operate, and reducing risks of potential conflict and consequent uncertainties. Apart from social planning, a social impact assessment for the project is crucial to understanding the social and human rights risks the company may face. A social impact assessment is the main instrument for balancing the social concerns on the one hand and the economic gains in investment projects on the other. However, since the social impacts of the operation can be a significant risk factor for the companies, a separate and self- contained social impact assessment increasingly become essential. The necessity of a separate social impact assessment can be justified on the underlying difference between the nature of environmental and social impact of TNCs' operation. Similarly, a conflict risk assessment is specially required for the companies operating in a country with long history of ethnic or civil conflict to grasp the potential implications of such conflict on the operations of the project.

Effective participation of the community in the investment project can empower the communities and strengthen their role. Importantly, community engagement can reduce conflict among competing indigenous and local interests, ensure accountability of the decision makers and increase public acceptance of a given project. Public participation can play an instrumental role in making the project sustainable by ascribing a greater degree of legitimacy and acceptability to the project. The evolving norms relating to public participation of indigenous peoples in natural resource development in their lands is now clearly recognized by the international human rights law.[58]

TNCs' negotiation of a separate agreement with the local community can also be an important modality of their channelling concerns and interest and social pressure which can be an important step in reaching a durable solution of community-company conflicts. Negotiation of a separate agreement with the local community is increasingly becoming a viable alternative to articulate and accommodate public participation, social provision and the compensation issue. TNCs' proactive efforts to protect human rights within their own operations and to promote human rights where the corporation has the possibility of influencing the government with human rights records can be seen as key elements of their compliance with human rights obligations.[59] For this purpose, it is essential that companies operate in accordance with international human rights norms and respect the basic civil and political rights of local or indigenous community in the operating area. It should be mentioned here that currently many codes of CSR have been developed to regulate corporate behaviour in way that they are in compliance with human rights norms and practices.

Making TNCs Accountable for Human Rights and Sustainability

The root cause of the TNC and human rights predicament today lies in the governance gaps that have been created by globalization—between the ambit and effect of economic forces and actors, and the capacity of society to manage their adverse consequences.[60] TNCs have been able to operate in a legal vacuum regarding their human rights violations. The governance gaps caused by globalization have provided a permissive environment for wrongful acts by companies of all kinds without adequate sanctioning or reparation.[61] The lack of control over corporations at the international level has occurred because of

58 For instance, Article 15(2) of the ILO Convention No. 169 of 1989 requires the State to consult with indigenous peoples in case of exploration or exploitation of natural resources in their land with a view to ascertaining whether and to what degree their interests would be prejudiced by such activities. Article 17(2) states that the peoples concerned shall be consulted whenever consideration is being given to their capacity to alienate their lands or otherwise transmit their rights outside their own community.

59 See, Jens Scierbeck, 'Operational Measures for Identifying and Implementing Human Rights issues in Corporate Operations' in Asbjorn Eide, Helge Ole Bergesen and Pia Rudolfson Goyer (eds), *Human Rights and the Oil Industry* (Intersentia 2000) 168.

60 John Ruggie, 'Report of the Special Representative of the Secretary-General on the Issue of Human Rights and Transnational Corporations and Other Business Enterprises: Business and Human Rights: Mapping International Standards of Accountability for Corporate Acts' UN Doc. A/HRC/4/035, 9 February 2007, 82, available at http://www.business-humanrights.org/Documents/SRSG-report-Human-Rights-Council-19-Feb-2007.pdf, accessed 21 October 2008 (hereinafter *The Report*).

61 Ibid.

two main reasons. The first is because historically, international human rights law was introduced to protect individuals from the arbitrary power of states, not corporations.[62] Corporations have generally been considered as private enterprises and thus have not been held to hold human rights responsibilities. In general, the treatment of corporations in both domestic and international law is premised on the notion that they are private, not public entities—that is they are more like individuals than like states.[63] Under this view, like individual people, corporations with respect to human rights violations are treated as right holders rather than duty holders.[64] There has been difficulty therefore in the creation or adaptation of international law regimes that impose human rights responsibilities upon TNCs because as Sinden argues: 'it is seen as a radical departure from traditional international human rights law, which views non state actors as mere objects of international law rather than subjects of it'.[65]

The second factor that has contributed to the invisibility of TNCs' accountability at the international level is that traditionally regulation of corporations has been almost exclusively a domestic matter.[66] The human rights responsibilities of domestic law are not usually embedded in corporations or commercial law themselves but in separate anti-discrimination, workplace health and safety, and labour laws. Moreover, except in exceptional circumstances, these domestic human rights laws are designed to operate intra-territorially only. As a result, the extraterritorial operations of TNCs, the very feature that defines them, are substantially regulated neither by international nor domestic laws with respect to their impact on human rights.[67]

Current Scope of the Law Applying to TNCs and Its Effectiveness

The effectiveness of current laws governing TNCs is limited to say the least. Kinley and Tadaki argue that 'although wide, the current scope of what might loosely be called international human rights law duties of TNCs is spread thinly and unevenly'.[68] They assert that although legal or quasi-legal duties are imposed on corporations, these duties have only potential authority and remain largely ill-defined and ineffective. According to Kinley and Tadaki,

62 Kinley and Tadaki (n 51) 937.

63 Amy Sinden, 'The Power of Rights: Imposing Human Rights Duties on Transnational Corporations for Environmental Harms' (Legal Studies Research Paper, Temple University Beasley School of Law, 2006) 11.

64 Ibid. 39.

65 Ibid.

66 David Kinley and Adam McBeth, *Human Rights Trade and Multinational Corporations in Business and Human Rights* (Rory Sullivan Edition 2003) 52.

67 Ibid.

68 Kinley and Tadaki (n 51) 948.

although an international legal framework may be emerging, the substantive legal content is nearly absent.[69] This argument is indeed compelling.

To begin with, the Universal Declaration of Human Rights (UDHR), the principal legal instrument for addressing human rights violations, makes no specific mention of corporations.[70] Although the preamble contains the often-quoted provision that 'every individual and every organ of society . . . shall strive'[71] to promote respect for human rights and to secure their recognition and observance, which has been interpreted by Louis Henkin as including 'no one, no company, no market, no cyberspace',[72] it is difficult to avoid the conclusion that the provision expresses no more than an aspiration to 'strive' to promote respect for human rights, rather than impose a legally binding obligation.[73] Further, there is no denying that the emphasis of the UDHR is on states as the primary bears of human rights responsibilities not corporations. As Kinley states, 'the drafters of the UDHR could not have foreseen in 1948 that select states' powers might one day be dwarfed by corporate power'.[74]

Consequently, the UDHR and international human rights law in general place emphasis on states as the primary bearers of human rights responsibilities, rather than corporations. This limitation in the international legal framework, which fails to recognize corporations as having human rights responsibilities, has led to the development of various approaches aimed at imposing some level of responsibility on corporations.[75] However, the effectiveness of these approaches varies significantly.

The United Nations developed two specific mechanisms to regulate corporations and their impact on human rights: the Norms on the Responsibilities of Transnational Corporations and Other Business Enterprises with Regard to Human Rights (the Norms) and the Global Compact (the GC). The Norms have been described as the only non-voluntary CSR framework adopted at the international level.[76]

While the Norms affirm that states retain the primary responsibility for protecting human rights, they also establish standards for businesses to follow within their spheres of activity and influence, covering areas such as the

69 Ibid.

70 *The Report* (n 57) 38.

71 Universal Declaration of Human Rights, G.A. Res. 217A (III), U.N. GAOR, 3d Sess., U.N. Doc A/810 (1948) (hereinafter *UDHR*).

72 Louis Henkin, 'Keynote Address: The Universal Declaration at 50 and the Challenge of Global Markets' (1999) 25 *Brooklyn Journal of International Law* 17, 25.

73 *The Report* (n 57) 38.

74 Kinley and Nolan (n 54) 359.

75 Ibid. 361.

76 David Weissbrodt and Muria Kruger, 'Norms on the Responsibilities of Transnational Corporations and Other Business Enterprises with Regard to Human Rights' (2003) 97 *American Journal of International Law* 901, 903.

security of persons, the protection of workers' rights, and environmental preservation.[77] When the UN Sub-Commission on the Promotion and Protection of Human Rights approved the Norms, many leading international human rights NGOs expressed their support.[78] Fifteen human rights NGOs, including Amnesty International, Human Rights Watch, Christian Aid and Oxfam GB, issued a joint press release indicating their intention to use the Norms in their work to protect and promote human rights.[79] Despite this strong backing from NGOs, the Norms have faced significant criticism since their inception.

It is argued that although the Norms undoubtedly represent an improvement in terms of both formulation and implementation of human rights standards over previous attempts at the international level, they still fall short of establishing an effective international regulatory regime for corporate human rights responsibility.[80] While the Norms make a promising start by employing multiple monitoring techniques at both national and international levels, they neither introduce multiple sanctions to enforce obligations against TNCs nor establish a robust enforcement mechanism. Furthermore, despite these efforts, the Norms were not well received by business organizations.[81] The International Chamber of Commerce and the International Organization of Employers criticized the Norms in a statement to the member states of the UN Commission on Human Rights, describing them as vague and unclear. They argued that the Norms would lead to the 'privatization' of human rights by shifting the responsibility for human rights regulation from governments to businesses.[82] During the 60th Session of the UN Commission on Human Rights in 2004, the legal standing of the Norms was tested. The Commission, while acknowledging the importance of the Norms, concluded that they had no legal standing.[83] Consequently, the Norms do not impose any enforceable obligations on TNCs to uphold human rights responsibilities.

77 Daniel Braaten, 'Transnational Corporations, Human Rights, and the United Nations: The Global Compact as Soft Law' (Thesis University of Nebraska) 6.

78 Ibid.

79 Ibid.

80 Surya Deva, 'UN's Human Rights Norms for TNCs and Other Business Enterprises: An Imperfect Step in the Right Direction?' (2004) 10 *ILSA Journal International and Comparative Law* 493.

81 Joint views of the ICC and the IOE on the draft 'Norms on the Responsibilities of Transnational Corporations and Other Business Enterprises with Regard to Human Rights' (Letter submitted to the United Nations Commission on Human Rights, International Chamber of Commerce: Paris, 24 November 2003), available at http://www.business-humanrights.org/Links/Repository/179848/link_page_view, accessed 6 November 2008.

82 Ibid.

83 The 60th Commission on Human Rights, *Norms on the Responsibilities of Transnational Corporations and Other Business Enterprises with Regard to Human Rights* (Geneva, 15 March–24 April 2004), available at http://www.casin.ch/web/pdf/normstncshumanrights.pdf, accessed 16 November 2008.

Soft Law and the Way Forward

The alternative to the Norms has been the GC; whereas the Norms focused on regulating corporations directly, the GC has focused on engaging with corporations to facilitate problem-solving.[84] The GC is a voluntary set of principles that was designed to assist businesses in aligning their operations and strategies with ten universally accepted principles in the areas of human rights, labour, the environment and anti-corruption.[85] However, similarly to the Norms, critics of the GC point to a variety of issues that undermine the legitimacy and effectiveness of the initiative. Specifically, they point to the fact that member companies can pick and choose which of the ten GC principles they want to focus on instead of internationalizing all of the principles at once; they argue that the GC is more of a public relations tool for business than an effective regulator.[86]

The most common criticism of the GC is the fact that they are not able to be enforced on corporations. Voluntary and non-binding nature of the GC is argued to be 'irrevocably dooming the initiative to little more than window dressing'.[87] According to Braaten, 'it is the lack of hard law enforcement that particularly aggravates certain NGOs and activists'.[88] Ramesh Singh, chief executive of ActionAid, claims that the GC 'at the moment is so voluntary that it really is a happy-go-lucky club'.[89] However, whilst these arguments hold merit, there are also significant advantages to the soft law approach to human rights regulations. As Braaten argues:

> in order to effectively evaluate the effectiveness of the GC one has to look beyond its non-binding nature and critically evaluate the GC for what it purports to do. The GC is a soft law initiative and as such should be evaluated based on what soft law initiatives are supposed to do which are to fill in regulatory gaps and point to more binding measures.[90]

Responsibility in the GC is directly associated with the concept of CSR. The main objective of the GC is to raise awareness among the different actors on the grave effects caused by globalization and to help teach those actors, who share the same opinions, on ways to address these human rights issues. Ruggie argues that this concept is likely to succeed in the protection of human

84 Braaten (n 78) 7.
85 Ibid.
86 Ibid. 8.
87 Kinley and Tadaki (n 51) 951.
88 Braaten (n 78) 8.
89 Ramesh Singh, quoted in Gustavo Capdevila, 'UN Global Compact with Business "Lacks Teeth"—NGOs' *Inter Press News Services*, 6 July 2007, available at http://www.corpwatch.org/article.php?id=14549, accessed 3 November 2008.
90 Braaten (n 78) 8.

rights without any need for more enforceable obligations.[91] According to Ruggie, 'the more effective the CSR, the less the pressure will be to accomplish the same ends by other—and potentially far less friendly—means'.[92] This is a convincing argument. Corporations are fundamentally driven by profit, and historically, social change has not been a primary concern for them. However, with the growing public focus on CSR, businesses now recognize it as a valuable marketing tool that can generate business and profit. As noted in a leading business review, 'CSR opens a way for companies to use the discourse of social responsibility to expand their range of activities globally and make a profit.'[93] If the GC serves as a tool to help corporations achieve this, then it becomes an effective mechanism for promoting human rights responsibilities, even if the underlying motivation is profit driven.

While this approach appears to concede to the power and profit-driven motives of TNCs, it is a pragmatic step forward given the current limitations of international law in directly enforcing human rights obligations on TNCs. Soft law emerges as an effective strategy under these circumstances. Ideally, the future goal would be to formally recognize TNCs as holders of human rights obligations through the enforcement of hard law. However, this is not yet the case.

It is important to remember that corporations, especially powerful TNCs, are unlikely to participate in a regulatory environment perceived as threatening to their business interests unless it is legally enforced. This is precisely why many business organizations opposed the Norms. In the current context, attempting to enforce hard law or customary law on international corporations—especially when the UDHR makes no explicit reference to them—seems almost futile. Creating a safe environment, such as the GC, can at least encourage corporations to adhere to their human rights responsibilities, as it aligns with their financial interests. Therefore criticisms of the GC's non-binding nature overlook the rationale behind its creation. As far as filling regulatory gaps is concerned, the GC serves as an effective instrument.

Conclusion

This chapter has explored the convergence of human rights, sustainable development and international investment law through the perspective of relevant actors. States play a key role in creating, and being subject to, international human rights and sustainable development obligations that are then applied through domestic legislation. As this chapter has explored in detail, there are

91 John Ruggie, 'The Theory and Practice of Learning Networks: Corporate Social Responsibility and the Global Compact' (2002) 5(Spring) *Journal of Corporate Citizenship* 27–36.

92 Ibid. 35.

93 Michael Porter and Mark Kramer, 'The Competitive Advantage of Corporate Philanthropy' in *Harvard Business Review on Corporate Responsibility* (Harvard Business School Press 2003).

obligations under both the human rights and sustainable development regimes which have challenged states to consider holistically against IIA commitments, especially in terms of their relationship with regulating the most significant actor in bringing in FDI being TNCs.

This chapter has explored the challenges in regulating TNCs with the view of promoting a more synthesized approach towards human rights, environmental sustainability and IIA obligations. Specifically, this chapter has identified that further work in addressing governance gaps, regulating TNCs via a multi-scalar approach and using a combination of soft law instruments, is necessary to integrate human rights and environmental sustainability outcomes into FDI decision-making. Without addressing these key issues associated with TNCs, a key actor remains unaccountable for the human rights and environmental impacts associated with their investments.

3 Conceptual Framework for Integrating Human Rights and Sustainable Development Into International Investment Agreements

Introduction

With the world hurtling towards global warming and the rise of social media creating new threat horizons for hard-won human rights protections, the world is in a very different place and context compared to when international investment law started to become its own distinct discipline. The rubric of chasing FDI and the state giving unparalleled protections to foreign investors have fallen to the wayside, replaced with growing concern for the need to ensure that holistic development objectives can be met, and that foreign investment is not being utilized to create negative social costs on environmental preservation and human rights. The rise of sustainable development has provided a useful lens to reconceptualize and challenge the assumptions and theoretical framework that underpin international investment law, namely, the need to promote FDI with a narrow objective of achieving economic growth. With the calamities associated with climate change already here, and nations being tested to implement adaptation and mitigation strategies immediately, regulatory and policy freedom has never been more important as the state plays an ever-increasing role in protecting communities.

This chapter will examine the theoretical and conceptual framework for investment, human rights and environment protection. After a brief introduction to the key concepts that have traditionally driven international investment law, this chapter will highlight the consequences of treating trade and investment as distinct disciplines, separate from environmental and human rights considerations. This approach has often led to a race to the bottom, resulting in significant environmental damage and human rights abuses. More than ever, international investment law is becoming increasingly integrated with sustainable development, and this chapter will provide several illustrative examples of where this integration is occurring within IIAs. Several factors contribute to this increased alignment. First, there is a growing need to address the negative externalities associated with unchecked economic growth. Unrestrained investment practices can lead to significant environmental degradation and human rights violations. By incorporating sustainable development principles into IIAs, these adverse impacts can be mitigated, ensuring that economic

DOI: 10.4324/9781003164951-4

growth does not come at the expense of environmental sustainability and human rights. Second, there is a rising consumer demand for products and services with strong green and human rights credentials. In today's market, consumers are increasingly conscientious about the ethical and environmental implications of their purchases. Firms are incentivized to adopt sustainable practices and align with human rights standards to meet these consumer expectations and maintain their market competitiveness.

Whilst there has been a greater push for stronger integration between international investment law, human rights and sustainable development, however, key conceptual issues remain. This chapter will analyze these ongoing tensions, focusing on the balance between providing investor protections and maintaining the policy and regulatory freedom of states to legislate for human rights and environmental protections. One significant area of concern is the justice and fairness of the ISDS processes. These processes are often criticized for their lack of transparency, public scrutiny, and accountability. This chapter will explore how justice can be achieved within these frameworks, questioning whether the current mechanisms adequately address the needs and rights of all stakeholders involved, particularly when disputes involve critical public interests. This chapter will also consider normative issues associated with the intersection of sustainable development, human rights and IIAs. This includes a discussion on whether the current structure of IIAs perpetuates control over the Global South by developed countries and whether there has been any movement towards an ecocentric approach by considering how it can expand its remit of protection to include public goods. International investment law can no longer be considered in isolation from human rights and environmental protection. This raises several interesting questions in a discipline that has traditionally pushed for minimal state intervention and the prioritization of investor concerns.

The Remit of IIAs in Safeguarding Investor Interests and the Challenges Posed by an Evolving Global Landscape

The world today sits at an interesting junction. Historically, whilst minimum standards of behaviour towards foreign investment can be traced back to the colonial era through friendship, commerce and navigation treaties,[1] the late 1980s and 1990s saw a flurry of IIAs being negotiated and implemented. This era saw many host states establishing investor protections with the hope to provide greater investor certainty and attract FDI. Whilst each IIA establishes specific obligations that each state owes to its protected investors, this period

1 Kenneth J. Vandevelde, 'A Brief History of International Investment Agreements' in Karl P. Sauvant and Lisa Sachs (eds), *The Effect of Treaties on Foreign Direct Investment: Bilateral Investment Treaties, Double Taxation Treaties, and Investment Flows* (Oxford University Press 2009) 3.

proliferated many of the 'mainstream' obligations that we see are common in IIAs today, including protection against non-discrimination, FET, providing full protection and security of investments, a prohibition against illegal expropriation, observance of undertakings and enabling the free transfer of funds related to investments.[2] The obligation to protect investments against non-discrimination can be further unpacked to include the NT and MFN principles, namely, ensuring that investments are not treated no less favourably than the treatment that is accorded to national investors or investors from a third state, respectively. NT ensures that foreign investments are treated no less favourably than domestic investments, while MFN treatment guarantees that foreign investors receive treatment no less favourable than that accorded to investors from any third state. These principles are fundamental to creating a non-discriminatory and equitable investment environment.

In the context of globalization and the dominance of neoclassical economic theory, the drive to pursue foreign operations was rationalized by the goal of achieving lower marginal costs and competitive advantages in an increasingly interconnected global supply chain. Dunning's ownership-location-internalization (OLI) theory provides a framework for understanding the motivations behind FDI. According to this theory, the ability for firms to obtain monopoly advantages by accessing privileged markets, technological benefits, and increased innovation that are associated with FDI acted as a significant impetus for going global.[3] Coupled with locational, political and social advantages that a host country could offer, firms increasingly relocated their operations overseas under the mantra to achieve maximum profitability.[4] This paradigm reveals that FDI is therefore highly situation-dependent, with firms making investment decisions based on a complex interplay of factors that include economic advantages, strategic opportunities and the attractiveness of host country incentives. Consequently, states found themselves under pressure to create favourable conditions to attract and retain foreign investment. This dynamic often led to a competitive race among states to offer the most appealing investment climates, sometimes at the expense of environmental and social standards.

However, the 2000s saw a marked shift from this burgeoning era of BITs and foreshadowed a turning point for the policy rationale for justifying FDI. Investors were now testing the boundaries on the protections that were being offered

2 See, Jean d'Aspremont, 'International Customary Investment Law: Story of a Paradox' in Tarcisio Gazzini and Eric De Brabandere (eds), *International Investment Law: The Sources of Rights and Obligations* (Martinus Nijhoff 2012).

3 See J.H. Dunning, 'The Determinants of International Production' (1973) *Oxford Economic Papers* 25; J.H. Dunning, 'Toward an Eclectic Theory of International Production: Some Empirical Tests' (1980) 11 *Journal of International Business Studies*; J.H. Dunning, 'The Eclectic Paradigm of International Production: A Restatement and Some Possible Extensions' (1988) 19 *Journal of International Business Studies.*

4 Ibid.

by IIAs through ISDS mechanisms. The number of ISDS cases rose from zero in 1990 to 11 in 2000, and then grew rapidly to 35 in 2010 and 69 in 2020.[5] At its height, there were 85 cases initiated in 2015 and 2018, bringing a total of 1303 known treaty-based ISDS cases to date.[6] In turn, this explosion of ISDS cases created scepticism and pushback from states that were highly concerned that IIA protections that were being provided to foreign investors were too unilateral in favour of investors. This concern became material as the cost of defending these claims rose exponentially. For litigation costs alone, a respondent state would pay an average of US$5 million in legal and other professional services fees, and where awards were granted to claimant investors, the average size of an award was US$75 million. A series of high-profile cases such as *Occidental v. Ecuador* and the Yukon cases demonstrating the exorbitant costs paid by host states for ISDS, with payments being paid to private investors to the amounts of US$1.8 billion and US$50 billion, respectively.[7]

To date, ISDS arbitration continues to undermine policies and legislation aimed at improving human rights and environmental conservation.[8] For many developing countries in particular, IIAs have threatened their ability to build capacity in their local economies and institute ambitious legislation that would enable their communities to fulfil their sustainable development aspirations.

The impact that ISDS has had on environmental legislation has been significant for several states. In *Tecmed v. Mexico*[9] the revocation of a hazardous waste landfill permit due to concerns about public health and environmental protection was classified as indirect expropriation. Similarly, in *Suez and Interagua v. Argentina*[10] an action intended to protect the human right to water was judged not to meet the standard of FET. These disputes provide concrete illustrations on the impact that ISDS can have in curtailing regulatory freedom and the ability for host states to pursue economic, social, cultural and environmental rights. This has been such a live issue that for some states, the inclusion of ISDS has been banned from any future free trade and investment

5 UNCTAD, 'Investor-State Dispute Settlement Cases: Facts and Figures 2020' (IIA Issues Note, 2020), available at https://unctad.org/system/files/official-document/diaepcbinf2021d7_en.pdf, accessed 20 January 2024.

6 UNCTAD, 'Investment Dispute Settlement Navigator' (UNCTAD 2024), available at https://investmentpolicy.unctad.org/investment-dispute-settlement, accessed 20 January 2024.

7 Lise Johnson and Lisa E. Sachs, 'The Outsized Costs of Investor-State Dispute Settlement' (2016) 16(1) *Academy of International Business Insights* 12–13; see also M. Hodgson, 'Costs in Investment-Treaty Arbitration: The Case for Reform' (2014) 1 *Transnational Dispute Management*.

8 Gillian Moon, 'Protecting Human and Environmental Rights in International Investment Agreements' (*East Asia Forum*, 6 August 2021), available at https://www.eastasiaforum.org/2021/08/06/protecting-human-and-environmental-rights-in-international-investment-agreements/, accessed 20 January 2024.

9 *Tecnicas Medioambientales Tecmed S.A. v. Mexico*, Award of May 2003, 43 ILM 133 (2004).

10 Suez, Sociedad General de Aguas de Barcelona, S.A., & Vivendi Universal, S.A v. Arg. Republic, ICSID Case No. ARB/03/19.

agreement negotiations.[11] Notwithstanding the direct costs associated with ISDS litigation or repealing environmental legislation, there is also a hidden cost associated with the chilling effect that the threat of ISDS regulation has had in creating environmental or human rights regulations. This cost will remain unknown as regulators withdraw from implementing measures which can materially improve human rights expression and sustainable development.

Moreover, the continued environmental degradation and climate change highlight the urgency of addressing these issues. Developing countries, in particular, are disproportionately affected by the negative externalities of foreign investments that prioritize profit over sustainable practices. The integration of sustainable development and human rights into IIAs is not merely a theoretical exercise but a practical necessity to ensure that economic growth does not come at the expense of environmental integrity and social equity. FDI has played a crucial role in contributing to environmental destruction and shifting carbon emissions to developing countries,[12] and can inhibit the free expression of human rights, such as placing their investment in host states that are capable of crushing efforts for better wages or working conditions.[13] Instances such as the BHP copper and gold mine disaster at Ok Tedi in Papua New Guinea[14] and the Bhopal disaster also illustrate the real-world impact that foreign firms can have on the local environment and human rights. These changing facts on the ground, at a time when states need to implement ambitious policy and legislation, have driven states to push back on IIAs and the limits that have been placed on their regulatory freedom and sovereignty by these agreements. To date, states are increasingly moving towards mainstreaming sustainable development and human rights considerations into investment decision-making, as more measures are being implemented to achieve triple-bottom approaches towards social, environmental and economic objectives.

Towards an Integrated Approach: IIAs and Sustainable Development

Sustainable development is an organizing principle that, in its broadest sense, seeks to ensure that the human development needs of present generations

11 See Julia Calvert, 'Beyond "Once Bitten, Twice Shy": Defending the Legitimacy of Investor-State Dispute Settlement in Peru and Australia' (2023) 30(5) *Review of International Political Economy* 1799–1823, available at https://doi.org/10.1080/09692290.2022.2134172, accessed 20 January 2024.

12 Huang Yanyan, Chen Fuzhong, Wei Huini, Xiang Jian, Xu Zhexiao and Akram Rabia, 'The Impacts of FDI Inflows on Carbon Emissions: Economic Development and Regulatory Quality as Moderators' (2022) 9 *Frontiers in Energy Research*, available at: https://doi.org/10.3389/fenrg.2021.820596, accessed 20 January 2024.

13 David Law, 'Globalisation and the Future of Constitutional Rights' (2008)102 *Northwest University Law Review* 1313.

14 https://wwf.panda.org/discover/knowledge_hub/where_we_work/new_guinea_forests/problems_forests_new_guinea/mining_new_guinea/ok_tedi_forest_new_guinea/

are being met without jeopardizing the needs of future generations. Sustainable development seeks to balance economic, social and environmental considerations to provide a more holistic decision-making framework. Its precise contents are encapsulated through several sub-principles, including but not limited to principles of intergenerational equity, precautionary principle, common but differentiated responsibilities and the need to achieve distributive or procedural justice. Intergenerational equity emphasizes the responsibility to preserve resources and the environment for future generations. The precautionary principle advocates for proactive measures to prevent environmental harm when there is scientific uncertainty. Common but differentiated responsibilities acknowledge that developed and developing countries have different capabilities and obligations in addressing global environmental challenges. Distributive justice focuses on the fair allocation of resources and benefits, while procedural justice ensures that all stakeholders have a voice in decision-making processes.

In the context of international investment law, the United Nations SDGs highlight the importance of forming strategic partnerships to build the capacity of communities to achieve their development aspirations.[15] These partnerships often involve collaboration with the private sector, leveraging their capital and expertise to support sustainable development initiatives.

International investment plays a crucial role in capacity building. When appropriately regulated, international investment law can encourage FDI and stimulate economic growth. It provides resources and capabilities for communities to develop and build resilience to calamities such as climate change and serves as a conduit for knowledge transfers. In contrast to the pollution haven hypothesis,[16] which suggests that unchecked FDI can encourage a race to the bottom as states lower human rights and environmental standards for the pursuit of foreign capital, a sustainable development approach challenges decision makers to consider the broader social and environmental benefits associated with investment. This perspective argues that integrating sustainable development principles into FDI can enhance human development metrics by promoting investments that contribute to social welfare and environmental protection. This is particularly vital for states where access to capital is limited, and sustainable investment can catalyse significant developmental progress.[17]

15 See SDG 17: UN General Assembly, *Transforming Our World: The 2030 Agenda for Sustainable Development*, 21 October 2015, A/RES/70/1, available at https://www.refworld.org/docid/57b6e3e44.html, accessed 22 January 2024.

16 See Monica Singhania and Neha Saini, 'Demystifying Pollution Haven Hypothesis: Role of FDI' (2021) 123 *Journal of Business Research* 516–528, available at https://doi.org/10.1016/j.jbusres.2020.10.007, accessed 20 January 2024.

17 Javad Izadi and Bobur Madirimov, 'Effect of Foreign Direct Investment on Sustainable Development Goals? Evidence from Eurasian Countries' (2023) *Journal of Sustainable Finance and Investment*, available at http://doi.org/10.1080/20430795.2022.2163846, accessed 20 January 2024.

In direct contrast to the pollution haven and race-to-the-bottom hypothesis, some critics argue that FDI can in effect 'green' industries by facilitating the transfer of green technology and creating positive spillovers and knowledge transfers to domestic firms.[18] This viewpoint suggests that FDI can enhance local capacities for environmental protection and innovation, leading to more sustainable industrial practices. By incorporating advanced technologies and sustainable practices, foreign investors can help domestic industries improve their environmental performance and competitiveness.

However, this is by no means a fait accompli. FDI does not inherently stimulate sustainable development, and without sufficient checks and balances, it may crowd out domestic investment, worsen income inequality, reduce labour rights and working conditions, and the activities of foreign investors in host countries can have a significant impact on the promotion of human rights and the protection of the environment.[19] Whether FDI will benefit or cost an individual society is highly dependent on the facts and circumstances in each country, including the capacity to exercise good governance, the effectiveness of its regulatory regimes, the vulnerability to capture from rent-seeking behaviour and the level of human rights standards already existing within society. It is incumbent on governments and decision makers to ensure that foreign investment can achieve triple bottom line outcomes by carefully drafting IIAs to ensure that it is conducive to sustainable development and the protection of human rights.

Outside of good governance, the impact that FDI will have on sustainable development and positive human rights outcomes is highly dependent on additional macroeconomic and microeconomic factors. At a macroeconomic level, besides the enforcement of environmental regulations, the level of impact that FDI can have on the environment depends on which sector that FDI is directed to, and whether this sector is highly damaging to the environment or not.[20] Investment into pollution intensive industries is contrary to the objectives of sustainable development which aims to achieve more holistic gains, rather than economic gains at the expense of intergenerational equity. At a microeconomic level, managerial methods and the type of technology used by foreign firms can also have a significant impact on sustainable development outcomes.[21] Consideration of both these macro- and micro-economic factors

18 K. Gallagher and L. Zarsky, *The Enclave Economy* (MIT Press 2007).

19 J. Anthony VanDuzer, Penelope Simons and Graham Mayeda, *Integrating Sustainable Development into International Investment Agreements: A Guide for Developing Countries* (Commonwealth Secretariat, UK, 2012), 31, available at https://www.iisd.org/system/files/meterial/6th_annual_forum_commonwealth_guide.pdf, accessed 20 January 2024.

20 Michaela Kardos, 'The Relevance of Foreign Direct Investment for Sustainable Development: Empirical Evidence from European Union' (2014) 15 *Procedia Economics and Finance* 1349–1354, available at: http://doi.org/10.1016/S2212-5671(14)00598-X, accessed 20 January 2024.

21 J. Witkowska, 'Foreign Direct Investment and Sustainable Development in the New EU Member States: Environmental Aspects' (2011) 14(3) *Comparative Economic Research* 5–23.

is required as a starting point to determine whether FDI inflows will create unbalance between economic, social and environmental outcomes, or present a threat for communities' ability to express and enjoy their human rights.

Human Rights and Sustainable Development Provisions in IIAs

The integration of human rights and environmental considerations into IIAs is a crucial step in ensuring that international investment contributes positively towards sustainable development. By embedding these principles into investment agreements, states can foster a balanced approach that aligns economic growth with social and environmental objectives. This shift is particularly important for developing countries, which often face significant challenges in balancing the need for foreign investment with the protection of human rights and the environment. To further enhance the effectiveness of these provisions, IIAs should include enforceable obligations that hold investors accountable for their actions. This could involve mechanisms for monitoring and reporting on human rights and environmental impacts, as well as penalties for non-compliance. Additionally, there should be a concerted effort to harmonize international investment law with international human rights and environmental standards, ensuring a coherent and consistent approach across jurisdictions.

While the vast majority of IIAs do not contain human rights or sustainable development provisions, more contemporary IIAs are moving towards introducing measures that require foreign investors to comply with the host state's human rights or environmental legislation.[22] According to the Expert Mechanism on the Right to Development, these obligations are notable for reminding foreign firms of tangible consequences for an alleged breach of human rights obligations and can minimize jurisdictional objections to human rights counterclaims by states in ISDS arbitration.[23] Human rights obligations can also be extended to protected investors in IIAs by also extending human rights legislation of the home state. However, this has been criticized for lacking substantive changes in human rights enforceability given that these investors

22 Article 15.1 of 2012 Model BIT of the Southern African Development Community, Article 5.3 of the Netherlands Model BIT (March 2019 version), Article 13 of India Model BIT (2016) Article 14 of the Morocco-Nigeria BIT (2016), Draft Pan-African Investment Code, Article 13 of India Model BIT (2016). See Expert Mechanism on the Right to Development, 'Right to Development under International Investment Law' (Human Rights Council, 3–5 April 2023, A/HRC/EMRTD/7/CRP.2), 8, available at: https://www.ohchr.org/sites/default/files/documents/issues/development/emd/session7/A_HRC_EMRTD_7_CRP.2%20for%20the%20web.pdf, accessed 20 January 2024.

23 Expert Mechanism on the Right to Development, 'Right to Development Under International Investment Law' (Human Rights Council, 3–5 April 2023, A/HRC/EMRTD/7/CRP.2), 8, available at: https://www.ohchr.org/sites/default/files/documents/issues/development/emd/session7/A_HRC_EMRTD_7_CRP.2%20for%20the%20web.pdf, accessed 20 January 2024.

would be subject to these obligations in any instance, and they do not create an obligation on home states to improve their human rights legislation.[24] It is worth noting, however, that such provisions are an exception rather than a rule, and that even where human rights or sustainable development carve-outs are provided in an IIA, these only provide a defence for the host state against a counterclaim by a protected investor.[25]

The progress towards integrating human rights and sustainable development obligations into modern IIAs has been slow, but notable. In 2011, a survey conducted by the Organisation for Economic Co-Operation and Development (OECD) revealed that 8% of IIAs explicitly considered the environment.[26] Since then, this has now grown to 12.5% of IIAs which contain a substantive environmental clause.[27] Furthermore, since the finalization of the SDGs in 2015, 224 IIAs have been concluded and 31% of those IIAs contain provisions which directly address the SDGs.[28] A further 5.69% of all IIAs also contain the protection of the environment as an explicit objective in the preamble of an IIA.[29] The Expert Mechanism on the Right to Development points out several examples in which sustainable development has been incorporated into an IIA, which include the following:

1 References to sustainable development in their preambles (e.g., the Brazil-India BIT [2020] and the Islamic Republic of Iran–Slovakia BIT [2016]).
2 Using a definition of 'investment' that requires a contribution to the sustainable development of the host country in order to qualify (e.g., the Morocco-Nigeria BIT [2016]).
3 Providing for public policy exceptions which allow the host State to take measures to protect public policy objectives such as protecting public health and the environment (e.g., the Canada-Mongolia BIT [2016] and the Georgia-Japan BIT [2021]).
4 Imposing an obligation on States not to relax labour or environmental standards in order to attract foreign investment (e.g., the Colombia–United Arab Emirates BIT [2017] and the Japan-Morocco BIT [2020]).

24 Ibid.
25 Ibid.
26 Katheryn Gordon and Joachim Pohi, 'Environmental Concerns in International Investment Agreements' (OECD, Working Papers on International Investment, 2011), available at: https://www.oecd-ilibrary.org/finance-and-investment/environmental-concerns-in-international-investment-agreements_5kg9mq7scrjh-en, accessed 20 January 2024.
27 Kezhen Su and Wei Shen, 'Environmental Protection Provisions in International Investment Agreements: Global Trends and Chinese Practices' (2023) 15(11) *Sustainability* 8525, available at https://doi.org/10.3390/su15118525, accessed 19 January 2024.
28 Expert Mechanism on the Right to Development (n 22) 3.
29 Kezhen and Shen (n 27).

5 Obligations on investors relating to responsible business conduct (e.g., the Brazil-Ethiopia BIT [2018]).
6 Provisions precluding corrupt practices (e.g., the Georgia-Japan BIT [2021]).
7 Provisions promoting compliance with sustainable development in FDI (e.g., the European Union–Singapore Free Trade Agreement [2019]).
8 Provisions which explicitly deal with related activities, such as encouraging capability building through close cooperation with the local community (Brazil-Malawi BIT [2015]).[30]

The mechanism by which IIAs integrate sustainable development into the agreement varies. Su et al note that these provisions can be categorized into four main typologies.[31] First, environmental and human rights protections are commonly manifested in IIAs by safeguarding the host states' regulatory authority. This is the most common and oldest type of environmental clause. It protects the host state's control over foreign investments through an exemption or carve-out clause. Second, environmental and human rights are integrated into IIAs by identifying either environmental or human rights protection as an explicit treaty goal.[32] The introductions to agreements such as the North American Free Trade Agreement (NAFTA), the Canada-EU Comprehensive Economic and Trade Agreement, and the ECT include mentions of treaty goals, including environmental protection. Third, environmental or human rights obligations may be enforced by mandating a states' ongoing responsibility to ensure its protection.[33] This least common category obligates the host state to uphold environmental standards to prevent a regulatory race to the bottom. It ensures that the host state maintains a certain level of environmental standards and measures, allowing IIAs to fully address environmental protection issues.

Finally, IIAs are increasingly adopting a hybrid approach which takes a combination of any of the above forms.[34] To illustrate, the Netherlands Model BIT (2019) systematically tackles environmental concerns through a hybrid model. It highlights environmental protection as a shared goal and mandates high-level environmental protection standards. Its preamble states that the BIT's policy goals can be achieved without compromising the host state's enforcement power necessary for achieving targets such as environmental protection. In Article 6, 'Sustainable Development', the contracting parties ensure their investment do not infringe on environmental protection. They also pledge not to decrease the level of environmental protection prescribed by

30 Expert Mechanism on the Right to Development (n 20).
31 Kezhen and Shen (n 27).
32 Ibid.
33 Ibid.
34 Kezhen and Shen (n 27).

domestic legislation but reaffirm the host state's treaty obligations under international environmental protection agreements. Article 7, 'Corporate Social Responsibility', also outlines the responsibilities of investors and investments in environmental protection. The India Model BIT (2015) also addresses investor behaviour by requiring investors to adhere to environmental, social and governance (ESG) principles and rules in Article 12.

Despite the growing integration of sustainable development and human rights provisions into modern IIAs, most ISDS arbitration panels have only been receptive to human rights or sustainable development arguments as due process or procedural fairness issues.[35] Increasingly, more effective human rights counterclaims by states rely upon arguments based on jurisdictional clauses, applicable law clauses, definitions of 'investments', the customer rules of treaty interpretation, preambles to BITs, relevant protections standards and rules on awarding damage compensation.[36] It remains to be seen whether states will start to rely directly on substantive sustainable development or human rights provisions.

'Green' IIAs: A New Way Forward or Continuation of the Same?

Systemic issues remain which challenge the capability of IIAs in realizing positive human rights and sustainable development outcomes. The lack of an appeal process reduces the robustness of decisions, making arbitrators vulnerable to errors in fact or in law.[37] IIAs provide investors with many protections, however many IIAs lack any real obligations on investors to adhere to human rights and environmental standards. This makes IIAs one-sided and fails to achieve a sufficient balance between providing investor protections and promoting human rights and sustainable development. IIAs also enable investors to engage in forum shopping, which is made easier given how truly global the marketplace has become and the ability for companies to incorporate in jurisdictions that can be covered under an IIA. These issues undermine the capacity for states to institute human rights or environmental protection legislation without it being challenged by protected investors.

There are two key challenges that remain for effective integration of sustainable development and human rights outcomes into IIAs: the legitimacy crisis

35 Vivian Kube and EU Petersmann, 'Chapter 11: Human Rights Law in International Investment Arbitration' in Andrea Gattini, Attila Tanzi and Filippo Fontanelli (eds), *General Principles of Law and International Investment Arbitration* (Brill Publishing 2018).

36 Ibid.

37 David Boyd, 'Paying Polluters: The Catastrophic Consequences of Investor-State Dispute Settlement for Climate and Environment Action and Human Rights' (Special Rapporteur on the Issue of Human Rights Obligations Relating to the Enjoyment of a Safe, Clean, Healthy and Sustainable Environment, UN General Assembly, Doc Number A/78/168, 13 July 2023) 6, available at: https://documents-dds-ny.un.org/doc/UNDOC/GEN/N23/205/29/PDF/N2320529.pdf?OpenElement, accessed 20 January 2024.

associated with the restriction to state sovereignty and regulatory freedom and the lack of transparency and consistency in ISDS arbitration. These two issues impact the progression of sustainable development implementation specifically as they restrict the ability for host nations to institute measures which can foster sustainable economic growth and impede the ability to achieve procedural justice when investors are challenging such measures.

Sustainable Development and the Imperative of Maintaining Regulatory Freedom and State Sovereignty

The increasing integration of sustainable development, human rights, and environmental conservation values into international investment law marks a significant progression. However, this integration is far from complete and raises several pragmatic issues for IIAs. First, there remains an inherent tension between IIAs, ISDS processes and the sovereignty enjoyed by states to make policy and regulations. States often find themselves in a challenging position, having to balance the protections offered to investors under IIAs with their sovereign right to regulate in the public interest. This remains an unresolved tension that is intensifying over time, as states play an increasingly important role in implementing measures that promote human rights protection and sustainable development. By states willingly giving up their ability to ensure that measures do not infringe on investor protections contained in IIAs, it may restrict their ability to ensure that foreign investors adhere to minimum human rights and environmental standards, or in the alternative, create a regulatory chill which will prevent such regulations from being implemented in the first instance. The infringement on state sovereignty occurs when IIAs contain provisions that constrain a state's regulatory autonomy. These provisions often prioritize investor protections, making it difficult for states to enact and enforce regulations that may affect the profitability of foreign investments. As a result, states may find themselves unable to implement necessary measures to safeguard human rights and the environment without facing the risk of costly ISDS claims. The regulatory chill phenomenon further exacerbates this issue. The threat of ISDS litigation can deter states from adopting progressive human rights and environmental regulations. Policymakers might avoid implementing robust regulatory frameworks due to fear of potential disputes and financial liabilities arising from ISDS claims. This chilling effect undermines the state's ability to pursue policies aligned with SDGs and human rights protection.

Contemporary IIAs have aimed to address this tension by introducing carve outs or exemptions which enable states to still legislate for critically important social values such as human rights protection and sustainable development. Under Article 9.16 of the Comprehensive and Progressive Agreement for Trans-Pacific Partnership (CPTPP)

> Nothing in this chapter shall be construed to prevent a Party from adopting, maintaining or enforcing any measure otherwise consistent with this

> chapter that it considers appropriate to ensure that investment activity in its territory is undertaken in a manner sensitive to environmental health or other regulatory objectives.[38]

There is a clear intent for provisions such as Article 9.16 to ensure that states can still enjoy regulatory freedom and have sufficient policy space to introduce measures addressing sustainable development. Yet, such measures have been heavily criticized for introducing a circular logic and does not provide any significant additional protections for states. According to Kawharu,[39] these measures merely affirm the right to regulate in a manner consistent with other terms of the investment chapter. Gleeson and Labonte share this position, particularly in the context of regulatory freedom and public health.[40] For this reason, IIAs and the ISDS process have been labelled as 'incompatible' with human rights principles, especially when considering concerns about the independence, transparency, accountability, and predictability of ISDS processes.[41]

Public Participation and the Legitimacy Crisis Associated With ISDS Arbitration

ISDS arbitration continues to take divergent approaches when interpreting human rights or sustainable development provisions in IIAs, resulting in an inconsistent body of jurisprudence.[42] ISDS arbitration often occurs behind closed doors, with limited ability for third parties to make submissions to the arbitration panel as amicus curiae briefs. This presents a serious, systemic issue for encouraging public participation in the ISDS process and ensuring that procedural fairness is achieved for communities who are directly impacted by ISDS arbitration. Practically, host states are also prevented from fully representing their case to an arbitration panel, most critically, conveying the policy rationale as to why they have instituted measures to protect human rights interests or implement environmental protection. ISDS arbitrators are thus only privy to one side of the discussion, to the benefit of protected investors.

38 Comprehensive and Progressive Agreement for Trans-Pacific Partnership (CPTPP), signed 30 December 2018, entry into force 14 January 2019, Article 9.16.

39 Amokura Kawharu, 'The Admission of Foreign Investment Under the TPP and RCEP: Regulatory Implications for New Zealand' (2015) 16 *Journal of World Investment and Trade* 1050.

40 D. Gleeson and R. Labonte, *Trade Agreements and Public Health* (Palgrave Macmillan 2020) 28–29.

41 Alfred-Maurice de Zayas, 'Report of the Independent Expert on the Promotion of a Democratic and Equitable International Order' *United Nations Human Rights Council*, 14 July 2015, 13th session, UN Doc A/HRC/30/44. See also John Hendy, 'A Threat to the Sovereignty of Courts and Parliaments' (2015) 128 *Graya* 52–56.

42 UNCITRAL, 'Possible Reform of Investor-State Dispute Settlement (ISDS) Note by the Secretariat' *Vienna*, 27 November 2017, available at https://documents-ddsny.un.org/doc/UNDOC/LTD/V17/067/48/PDF/V1706748.pdf?OpenElement, accessed 20 January 2024.

These arguments are often critical in determining whether a measure is reasonably necessary and thus could legitimately rely upon an exemption or carve out from IIA protections.

The use of *amicus* briefs is a legitimate mechanism to enable submissions on critical legal issues of public concern and this was the driving rationale for its first use in *Methanex v. United States*.[43] Furthermore, the use of *amicus* briefs also enables arbitration panels to obtain highly probative evidence and opinion that can test the legitimacy of proposed measures aimed at protecting human rights and the environment. In evaluating a tobacco ban and counterclaims that the measure was protecting the health of the community, the tribunal in *Philip Morris v. Uruguay*[44] relied almost exclusively on amicus curiae submissions from the World Health Organization and the Pan American Health Organization to come to its decision in favour of Uruguay.[45]

Nevertheless, there have been plenty of instances where ISDS arbitration panels have rejected the use of *amicus* briefs and have effectively locked out the voices of communities that are directly impacted by a proposed measure and an investment. In the case of *Aguas de Tunari v. Bolivia*, a dispute under the International Centre for Settlement of Investment Disputes (ICSID) related to a water concession in Cochabamba, Bolivia, the arbitrators concluded that they did not have the authority to include amici in the proceedings. Despite receiving requests to submit *amicus* briefs from various entities and individuals, the Tribunal determined that there was no current necessity to summon witnesses or solicit additional submissions from non-parties during the jurisdictional phase of its work. More concerningly, the Tribunal also noted that the grant for an *amicus* brief, given the specific wording in the IIA, was a power held between the parties to the dispute and not the Tribunal.[46] Since this decision, states are moving to clarify that the use of *amicus* briefs can be a discretion held by the arbitration panel to enable more submissions from a non-disputing party where they can provide probative value.[47]

43 *Methanex v. United States*, Final Award of the Tribunal on Jurisdiction and Merits (3 August 2005) para. 1.

44 *Philip Morris Brands Sàrl, Philip Morris Products S.A. & Abal Hermanos S.A. v. Oriental Republic of Uruguay*, ICSID Case No. ARB/10/7, Award (July 8, 2016) (hereinafter *Philip Morris v. Uruguay*).

45 See Pei-Kan Yang, 'A Critique of ICSID's Amicus Curiae Decisions in Philip Morris v. Uruguay: Review of Amicus Submissions in a Fragmented World' (2021) 14(2) *Contemporary Asia Arbitration Journal* 245–274, available at SSRN: https://ssrn.com/abstract=3976975, accessed 20 January 2024, who criticized that the amicus curiae rules were not applied consistently by the arbitration panel.

46 *Aguas de Tunari v. Bolivia*, Letter from Arbitral Tribunal to NGO (29 January 2003) 2.

47 See Statement of the NAFTA Free Trade Commission on Non-Disputing Party Participation of 7 October 2003. See also UNCITRAL Rules on Transparency in Treaty-based Investor-State Arbitration (adopted 9 July 2013, entered into force 1 April 2014) (UNCITRAL Transparency Rules) art 4(3).

The shift to enable greater participation of amicus curiae submissions in ISDS arbitration will remain an important area of reform. These submissions not only enable better decision-making by allowing arbitration panels greater access to expert opinion that is of probative value, it promotes informed public dialogue and democratic accountability since a 'transparent arbitral process allows citizens to monitor actively the conscientiousness of the government's disbursement of public money'.[48] Yet as Baltag acknowledges,[49] as a consequence that the primary purpose of *amicus* briefs is to bring a different, impartial and informative perspective to proceedings, 'they may not have full access to the proceedings and to the file, nor in an availability of the proceedings to the outside world with the acceptance of *amici*'. Given these inherent restrictions, there is scope to introduce institutions such as a multilateral investment court[50] that will address these systemic issues that are contributing to a legitimacy crisis that is associated with ISDS arbitration.

Normative Challenges With Green IIAs: A Postcolonial Critique on the Intersection Between Sustainable Development, Human Rights and IIAs

Sustainable development is not a homogenous concept and there are many different approaches advanced in contemporary sustainable development literature.[51] Interestingly, a postcolonial critique provides a useful lens to assess the pre-existing power dynamics and relationships between states, especially between developed nations and the Global South. A postcolonial critique of green IIAs brings forth legitimate questions as to whether this presents a new form of control by developed countries against the Global South. This is a pertinent issue during IIA negotiations, where developed countries hold economic power and may impose provisions which may not be in the interest of a developing country party and could hamper their regulatory freedom. The lack of capacity to participate effectively in IIA negotiations, due to knowledge and information asymmetries stemming from a lack of experience, insufficient resources to implement

48 Epaminontas E. Triantafilou, 'Amicus Submissions in Investor-State Arbitration after Suez v. Argentina' (2008) 24(4) *Arbitration International* 571, 575.

49 Crina Baltag, 'The Role of *Amici Curiae* in Light of Recent Developments in Investment Treaty Arbitration: Legitimizing the System?' (2020) 35(1–2) *ICSID Review—Foreign Investment Law Journal* Winter/Spring, 279–310, available at https://doi.org/10.1093/icsidreview/siaa021, accessed 20 January 2024.

50 See, for instance, G. Van Harten, 'Key Flaws in the European Commission's Proposals for Foreign Investor Protection in TTIP' *Osgood Hall Law School Legal Studies Research Paper Series No. 16*, Volume 12 issue 4, York University, Toronto, available at http://papers.ssrn.com/sol3/papers.cfm?abstract_id=2692122.

51 See, A. Anghie, *Imperialism, Sovereignty and the Making of International Law* (Cambridge University Press 2005); A. Escobar, *Encountering Development: The Making and Unmaking of the Third World* (Princeton University Press 1995).

obligations and other institutional weaknesses, challenges the perspective that parties enter into an IIA negotiation on equal footing.

There is a second power asymmetry emerging from the steady growth in ISDS arbitration. Investors themselves are directly challenging the regulatory freedom enjoyed by developing countries that are effectively overriding legitimate state concerns.[52] According to Echandi and Newson, this can be traced back to the national post-colonial preoccupation with protecting investors during the resource extraction phase of investment history,[53] whereby developed countries exercised effective control over the Global South through the proxy of private corporations. During the 20th century decolonialization period, newly independent states sought to eliminate the political and economic influence of their former colonizers and assert the power of their own laws. This led to anxiety among foreign investors[54] and in this context, BITs were established to solidify rules governing expropriation, FET and the MFN and NT principles. Yet private firms have developed into powerful entities that exert control in their own right, and through their access to capital—and more nefarious actions such as rent-seeking behaviour and corruption—can have a more direct impact on the Global South and their development trajectory.

Breaking the entrenched power dynamics inherent in IIAs remains a significant struggle for the Global South. These agreements often perpetuate historical power imbalances, as evident in cases where private entities can inhibit or even overturn legislation drafted by developing countries. This dynamic allows private firms to continue practices reminiscent of extractivist colonialism, exacerbating inequality and undermining the sovereignty of host states.[55] However, sustainable development presents a framework for rethinking these relationships. Emphasizing capacity building and developing partnerships provides the Global South with avenues to break free from traditional dependencies on developed countries. By fostering South-South cooperation, sustainable development challenges the notion that IIAs must echo the colonial power dynamics of the past. This approach advocates for mutual support and shared growth among developing countries, reducing reliance on former colonial powers and

52 Frank Garcia, Lindita Ciko, Apuruv Gaurav and Kirrin Hough, 'Reforming the International Investment Regime: Lessons from International Trade Law' (2015) 18(4) *Journal of International Economic Law* 861–892.

53 Roberto Echandi and Maree Newson, 'Influence of International Investment Patterns in International Economic Law Rulemaking: A Preliminary Sketch' (2014) 17 *Journal of International Economic Law* 847.

54 See, M. Sornarajah, *The International Law on Foreign Investment* (3rd edn, Cambridge University Press 2010).

55 David Boyd, 'Paying Polluters: The Catastrophic Consequences of Investor-State Dispute Settlement for Climate and Environment Action and Human Rights' (Special Rapporteur on the Issue of Human Rights Obligations relating to the Enjoyment of a Safe, Clean, Healthy and Sustainable Environment, UN General Assembly, Doc Number A/78/168, 13 July 2023), available at: https://documents-dds-ny.un.org/doc/UNDOC/GEN/N23/205/29/PDF/N2320529.pdf?OpenElement, accessed 20 January 2024.

creating a more balanced global economic system. There is potential to allow IIAs to require investor home states to provide technical and capacity building assistance for host states,[56] which from a normative perspective, contests the view that contemporary IIAs are perpetuating colonialist power dynamics.

Challenging the Status Quo: Anthropocentric Perspectives

Integrating sustainable development principles into IIAs not only challenges the anthropocentric approach traditionally taken by these agreements but also promotes an ecocentric viewpoint that recognizes the intrinsic role the environment plays in sustaining human development. Traditionally, IIAs have been narrowly focused on protecting investor interests to encourage FDI. However, incorporating sustainable development into IIAs is a crucial first step towards acknowledging the limits that unbridled economic growth imposes on the natural environment. The conventional approach of IIAs has often prioritized economic growth and investor protection, sometimes at the expense of environmental and social considerations. This has led to criticisms that IIAs contribute to environmental degradation and social inequity. By integrating sustainable development principles, IIAs can begin to address these issues, promoting a more balanced approach that considers the long-term impacts of investment on both people and the planet.

To move beyond their anthropocentric foundations and fully embrace an ecocentric approach, IIAs must undergo significant reforms. One innovative proposal is to explicitly enable natural entities to become parties to investment treaties. Currently, IIAs typically recognize nationals and their investments as parties. By altering this framework to include natural bodies, such as rivers, forests, or ecosystems, states can ensure that the environment has a direct stake in investment decisions. Additionally, IIAs can include clauses that allow states to take measures to protect the rights of nature as exceptions to general obligations like indirect expropriation or FET. These clauses would provide legal grounds for states to implement environmental protections without fear of violating investment agreements. This approach aligns with the growing global recognition of the rights of nature, as seen in various legal systems around the world that have granted legal personhood to natural entities. For example, the Rights of Nature movement has gained traction in countries like Ecuador and New Zealand, where rivers and forests have been granted legal rights. Incorporating similar principles into IIAs would represent a significant shift towards an ecocentric legal framework, where the environment is valued not just for its utility to humans but for its intrinsic worth.

56 J. Anthony Van Duzer, Penelope Simons and Graham Mayeda, *Integrating Sustainable Development into International Investment Agreements: A Guide for Developing Countries* (Commonwealth Secretariat, UK, 2012), 258, available at: https://www.iisd.org/system/files/meterial/6th_annual_forum_commonwealth_guide.pdf, accessed 20 January 2024.

While the idea of granting rights to nature may seem radical, it is increasingly gaining recognition in international law. This concept is rooted in indigenous philosophies that perceive humans as integral parts of a broader ecosystem, rather than as separate entities that dominate nature. The rights of nature movement diverges from the anthropocentric view that regards nature solely as a resource for human use.[57] Instead, it seeks to confer legal rights upon natural entities, similar to those granted to humans and corporations. These rights include providing natural bodies with legal standing to challenge decisions in courts or granting them legal personhood to become parties to treaties or agreements. Increasingly, legal systems around the world are recognizing the inherent rights of nature, as seen in the constitutional recognition of the rights of nature in Ecuador's Constitution (2008),[58] the statutory recognition of the Whanganui River as a legal person in New Zealand,[59] and the Bangladeshi Supreme Court decision which recognized the legal personhood of rivers in Bangladesh which considered a proposal for land reclamation along the banks of the Turag River.[60] In this case, the Bangladesh Supreme Court High Court Division declared *in loco parentis* the protection of Bangladeshi river systems to the National River Conservation Commission, who is now responsible to prevent pollution and illegal encroachment.

One potential impact of introducing rights of nature into IIAs is that it may potentially sidestep long-standing issues faced by host states in ensuring that they have sufficient regulatory space to introduce measures to protect the environment. A law that is introduced to ensure that an entity does not cause environmental damage may, depending on the facts and circumstances of each matter and IIA, be considered a form of indirect expropriation by a host state, or a breach of the MFN or NT principles. However, a natural body having sufficient legal personhood to defend against irreparable environmental damage is not a measure or policy introduced by a host state; it is a completely separate entity that is asserting that another entity is breaching standards established under an IIA.

A radical reimagining of IIAs towards an ecocentric approach requires a fundamental reconsideration of what constitutes an 'investment' and how it should be protected. Traditionally, IIAs have defined investments as assets controlled or contributed by a foreign national, such as tangible and intangible property rights, shares and interests in a company, legal rights, or reinvested returns. These definitions, while varying slightly between agreements, generally adopt a narrow view that focuses primarily on private interests and

57 Craig M. Kauffman and Pamela L. Martin, 'Rights of Nature for 2030 and Beyond' in *The Politics of Rights of Nature* (MIT Press 2021) 4.

58 Constitution of the Republic of Ecuador, 2008, chapter 7.

59 Te Awa Tupua (Whanganui River Claims Settlement) Act 2017, section 14.

60 Judgement on Civil Petition for Leave to Appeal No 3039 of 2019 (Supreme Court of Bangladesh Appellate Division) (17 February 2020).

financial returns. However, this conventional definition often overlooks the broader public goods associated with investments, which can be significant motivators for foreign investors. For example, investments that contribute to positive environmental outcomes or advance human rights objectives may not fit neatly within the existing definitions of 'investment' in many IIAs. Yet, these aspects are increasingly important in today's global economy, where CSR objectives are gaining traction.[61]

To illustrate, a large foreign firm may wish to invest in preserving a high-value forested area within a developing country. The firm's goals include carbon sequestration, supporting local indigenous communities, and safeguarding the intrinsic ecological value of the forest. If the state introduces a law which enables logging in that area or directly transfers ownership of that site to the government to support a large-scale infrastructure project, the foreign firm may have recourse to seek the protection of an IIA. However, due to the traditionally narrow definition of investment, the arbitration process might not fully consider the non-monetary aspects of the investment, such as the value of carbon sequestration, the rights of indigenous communities, or the intrinsic ecological value of the forest. Current IIAs typically focus on tangible and intangible property rights, shares, and financial returns, which can limit the scope of compensation for indirect expropriation to purely economic terms. Expanding the definition of investment within IIAs to include non-monetary and public goods aspects could address this limitation. By recognizing investments in environmental and social values, IIAs could better protect projects aimed at sustainable development. This broader definition would challenge the anthropocentric focus of existing agreements and allow public goods to come under the protection of IIAs.

While IIAs have been criticized for creating a regulatory chill on states—deterring them from enacting policies that might affect foreign investments—this mechanism could be leveraged positively. It could foster a chilling effect on policies or legislation that threaten sustainable development, environmental values, or human rights.[62]

Conclusion

This chapter has explored the conceptual framework for integrating investment, human rights, and environmental protection within international investment law. After providing a brief introduction it provided an overview of the key concepts that have traditionally driven international investment law,

61 Archie B. Carroll, 'Corporate Social Responsibility: The Centrepiece of Competing and Complementary Frameworks' (2015) 44 *Organizational Dynamics* 95.

62 See K. Tienhaara, 'Regulatory Chill in a Warming World: The Threat to Climate Policy Posed by Investor-State Dispute Settlement' (2018) 7(2) *Transnational Environmental Law* 229–250, available at http://doi.org/10.1017/S2047102517000309, accessed 20 January 2024.

highlighting how treating investment as a separate discipline, without considering environmental and human rights impacts, has led to a race to the bottom resulting in environmental damage and human rights abuses.

One major challenge is the legitimacy crisis stemming from restrictions on the regulatory freedom of states and the lack of transparency and good governance in ISDS arbitration. These issues exacerbate the normative critiques of IIAs, particularly from postcolonial and anthropocentric perspectives. Developing countries face ongoing challenges in breaking free from existing power dynamics, which are often amplified by imbalances between private firms and the Global South.

The anthropocentric critique further questions whether green IIAs can truly prioritize the environment and whether investments should also encompass public goods that benefit local communities. The convergence of sustainable development with international investment law offers a critical opportunity for the Global South to fulfil development aspirations and utilize capital for productive uses that deliver public goods. For sustainable development to thrive under international investment law, it is imperative for states to leverage IIAs as tools to achieve broader developmental goals, rather than solely focusing on protecting private investor interests. Without substantial reform, there is a fundamental question of whether contemporary IIAs are genuinely aligning with sustainable development and the promotion of human rights. The global economy stands at a crucial juncture, with the potential to learn from past mistakes of unchecked economic growth, environmental degradation, and human rights suppression, and to ensure that future foreign investments contribute positively to both economic and ecological sustainability.

4 Investment Protection, Human Rights and Environmental Sustainability

Emerging Standards and Evolving Norms

The Changing Landscape of International Investment Regime

The framework governing international investment operates through various layers, including customary international law, bilateral and multilateral treaties, and national legislation specific to host countries. These sources collectively form the backbone of the global investment regime, ensuring the protection and promotion of investments across borders. However, the effectiveness of these measures often hinges on the political stability and legislative consistency of the host nations. Changes in government or shifts in political ideologies can lead to modifications in investment guarantees, suggesting potential instability in unilateral national protections. Therefore the reliance on international agreements becomes crucial as they provide binding obligations that transcend national changes, offering a more stable environment for investment protection, human rights and environmental sustainability.

Currently, there are over 3,000 IIAs or investment-related provisions, predominantly structured as BITs. These treaties can be categorized into three primary forms: BITs themselves, investment-related provisions within broader FTAs, and components of regional economic integration agreements like NAFTA, the Southern Common Market, and the ECT. In the absence of a comprehensive, globally binding multilateral treaty and the lack of definitive customary international law, BITs have risen as the principal mechanism for promoting and securing foreign investments.

BITs typically impose rigorous standards on host countries, particularly those whose domestic legal frameworks may not adequately safeguard foreign investments. They enforce principles of fairness and non-discrimination, ensuring that foreign investors enjoy NT (the same protections as local investors) and MFN treatment (the best treatment given to any foreign investor). Additional guarantees include FET, constant protection and security of investments aligned with international law, prohibition of arbitrary or discriminatory measures, and legal stability aimed at protecting investors against undue government interference. A key feature of BITs is their provision for dispute resolution through neutral arbitration, which mitigates risks associated with potential judicial biases in host countries. This aspect offers a reliable and

DOI: 10.4324/9781003164951-5

impartial venue for investors to address grievances, enhancing the attractiveness of BITs by providing a sense of security for investment protection.

The flexibility of BITs during negotiations allows for provisions to be tailor-made to fit the specific needs and circumstances of the contracting states. This adaptability contributes significantly to their popularity, enabling countries with varying economic profiles and strategic priorities to benefit from customized agreements. Despite the widespread adoption of BITs and their crucial role in the global investment regime, they are often regarded as *lex specialis*—special laws that apply to specific cases rather than creating broad, customary international law. This specialized nature can lead to inconsistencies and conflicts with other international norms, particularly in areas like human rights and environmental protection.

The negotiation and implementation of BITs often involve complex considerations that balance investment protection with the rights of the host country's population and the preservation of its environment. This intersection creates a challenging landscape for policymakers who must navigate the sometimes-conflicting demands of promoting economic development through foreign investment while also upholding international standards related to human rights and environmental protection. The need for a comprehensive approach that integrates these diverse but interconnected legal realms is becoming increasingly apparent, as the implications of investment decisions continue to reach far beyond the economic sphere into the broader social and environmental contexts.

Relationship Between Human Rights, Environmental Sustainability and International Investment Standards

The adoption of BITs across countries with varying levels of economic development and political systems signifies their importance as tools for enhancing investment flows. However, the influence of these treaties extends beyond mere economic transactions; they also have significant implications for human rights and environmental laws. As nations engage in these treaties, the protection standards set forth can have profound effects on local communities and natural environments, often intersecting significantly with human rights concerns and environmental sustainability.

National Treatment

The concept of national treatment has deep roots in international trade and investment law, originating with the GATT and extending to the realm of BITs and broader international economic regulations. This principle is foundational in ensuring that foreign products, services, and investors receive the same treatment as their domestic counterparts, which is crucial for maintaining a level playing field and preventing discrimination based on nationality.

Historically, the NT clause was advocated in the 19th century by Latin American nations under the Calvo Doctrine, aimed specifically at countering the imposition of an international minimum standard of treatment that could potentially favour foreign entities over domestic ones. This historical context highlights the principle's role in balancing the rights and obligations of foreign and domestic entities within a nation's borders. In modern international agreements, NT is codified in Article III of GATT and Article XVII of the General Agreement on Trade in Services (GATS). These legal provisions require that member countries of the World Trade Organization (WTO) must treat foreign firms no less favourably than domestic ones in similar circumstances. This requirement is pivotal in trade liberalization, ensuring that internal measures, whether they are laws, regulations, or administrative procedures, do not discriminate against foreign products or services, thus fostering fair competition.[1]

However, the application of the NT standard involves not only preventing overt discrimination but also addressing broader social and economic implications within the host state. These implications may include issues related to investment laws, privatization efforts, consumer protection, labour rights, competition policies, and the protection of intellectual property rights. The inclusion of these areas under the umbrella of NT shows its expansive impact on the regulatory environment of host states, necessitating a delicate balance between encouraging foreign investment and protecting domestic interests. Furthermore, the obligation of NT helps neutralize protectionist tendencies that might favour domestic producers and investors over their foreign counterparts. This neutrality is essential for countries that wish to integrate into the global economy while ensuring equitable treatment for all economic actors involved. Thus, while the principle of NT promotes economic fairness, it also requires states to carefully consider how their domestic policies might affect international relations and investor confidence.

In the realm of goods, GATT Article III specifically prohibits discrimination by ensuring that imported goods are not subject to internal taxes or regulations that are more burdensome than those applied to like domestic goods. This includes not only tax measures but also laws and regulations affecting the sale, purchase, transportation or use of goods. The objective is to prevent protective measures that could undermine the benefits of tariff reductions negotiated between countries. In the case of US Section 337, the Panel observed that the intent of Article III is to guarantee that internal measures are not implemented on both imported and domestic products in a way that provides protection to domestic industries (Article III:1).[2] The obligation of NT stringently restricts the implementation of protectionist measures. As highlighted in the *Japan—Alcoholic Beverages II* case (1996), the primary and overarching aim of Article III is to prevent protectionism through the use of internal tax and regulatory measures. Specifically, Article III is designed to ensure that

1 Andrea K. Bjorklund, 'National Treatment' in August Reinisch (ed), *Standards of Investment Protection* (Oxford University Press 2008) 29–58.
2 GATT Panel Report, US Section 337, para. 5.10.

internal measures are not applied to imported or domestic products in a manner that protects domestic industries. To this end, Article III requires WTO members to maintain equal competitive conditions for imported products compared to domestic products.[3]

For services, GATS Article XVII extends the NT obligation to sectors inscribed in a member's schedule, contingent on any conditions specified therein. This ensures that foreign service providers are treated no less favourably than domestic providers in regulated sectors, promoting fair competition and access to markets. The requirement of likeness in both goods and services trade is used to assess whether the products, services, and their respective suppliers are competitively comparable.

Focusing on trade in goods, NT extends to a broad spectrum of state actions. Under Article III:2 of GATT, there is a stipulation that imported goods must not face higher taxes than similar domestic products, nor should they be taxed differently compared to directly competitive or substitutable domestic products in a way that protects the local market. This specific Article targets taxation measures exclusively. However, Article III:4 of GATT widens this scope significantly. It mandates that imported goods should receive treatment that is no less favourable than that given to similar domestically produced products in relation to all applicable laws, regulations, and requirements.[4] This broader provision ensures a more comprehensive level of equity in treatment between imported and domestic goods, covering various non-tax regulatory measures.

The concept of NT in BITs plays a crucial role in shaping how host states engage with foreign investors while maintaining the capacity to enact policies aimed at protecting human rights and promoting social welfare. The extent of the potential impact of the NT standard on the protection and promotion of human rights may depend on the different Interpretations of the various elements of the NT obligations in the BITs.[5] Sometimes the NT provision contains exceptions in order to provide incentives to foreign investors as states are free to provide more favourable treatment to foreign investors. While the principle of NT is designed to ensure equality, many BITs include clauses that allow exceptions to this rule. These exceptions are often included to enable host states to provide incentives to foreign investors, potentially offering more favourable treatment to attract investment. For instance, states might implement tax breaks or regulatory advantages exclusive to foreign entities to boost economic development.

3 Appellate Body Report, Japan—Taxes on Alcoholic Beverages, WT/DS8/AB/R, WT/DS10/AB/R, WT/DS11/AB/R, adopted 1 November 1996, DSR 1996: I, p. 16.

4 See Holger Hestermeyer, 'Article III' in R. Wolfrüm, P.-T. Stoll and H. Hestermeyer (eds), *WTO—Trade in Goods* (Koninklijke Brill NV 2010), 121–165.

5 Federico Ortino, 'Non-Discriminatory Treatment in Investment Disputes' in Pierre-Marie Dupuy, Francesco Francioni and Ernest-Ulrich Petersmann (eds), *Human Rights in International Investment Law and Arbitration* (Oxford University Press 2009) 364.

Conversely, many investment treaties contain general exceptions from their NT obligations for measures taken for diverse reasons, such as protecting public health, public morality and national security.[6] Because the unqualified obligation of NT may restrict the host states to take positive social and welfare measures for the host population, in particular, the disadvantaged segments of the society. In order to pave the way for keeping regulatory space for the host states, recent BITs provide some specific exceptions to this obligation. For example, the South Africa–Tanzania BIT of 2005 exemplifies how exceptions to NT can be structured to safeguard human rights and promote social equity. Article 3(2) of the treaty affirms the principle of NT, but it is Article 4(c) that introduces a vital exception. This clause specifies that the treaty should not compel a party to extend benefits derived from laws aimed at achieving equality or designed to protect or advance disadvantaged groups. This type of exception is crucial for allowing host states to implement affirmative action and other measures targeting social disparities without fear of contravening the BIT.

Thus exceptions to NT that may allow a state to take measures which result in discriminatory or adverse effects on foreign investors may be justified on public policy grounds.[7] The 'exceptions' to the NT that result in less favourable treatment to the foreign investor are justified by the host states for promoting important policy objectives including human rights.

Most Favoured Nation Treatment

The MFN treatment obligation stands as a cornerstone principle in IIAs, especially within the framework of BITs. Its primary objective is to ensure equality of opportunity in investment, guaranteeing that investors from one state receive treatment no less favourable than that accorded to investors from any third state. This principle aims to create a level playing field for investors, thereby fostering a fair and non-discriminatory international investment environment.

Three critical questions determine compliance with the MFN obligation in the context of BITs:

1 *Investment advantage*: An investment advantage encompasses benefits such as preferential access to markets, favourable regulatory conditions or tax incentives. These advantages enhance the competitive position of investors and can significantly impact their investment decisions. For instance, if a state offers lower tax rates or streamlined regulatory procedures to investors from one country, it must extend these benefits to investors from all other countries that have BITs with the host state.
2 *Likeness of investments or investors*: The 'likeness' of investments or investors is assessed based on several factors, including the nature and characteristics

6 See also, UNCTAD, *National Treatment*, Vol. IV, UNCTAD/IIT/11 (1995).
7 Federico Ortino (n 5) 360.

of the investments, their economic activities and their regulatory treatment. This assessment ensures that only comparable investments or investors receive the same benefits. For example, two companies operating in the same industry and providing similar services should be treated equally under the MFN obligation, irrespective of their country of origin.

3 *Immediate and unconditional advantage*: The advantage must be extended to all like investments or investors from all BIT partners without any preconditions. This requirement prevents states from imposing additional requirements or conditions that could undermine the principle of non-discrimination. For instance, if a state provides certain regulatory advantages to investors from one country without requiring additional qualifications, it must do the same for investors from all other BIT partner countries.

By ensuring that any benefits provided to investors from one country are also available to investors from any other country that is a party to a BIT with the host state, the MFN obligation fosters a fair and non-discriminatory international investment environment. Adhering to these principles is crucial for states to maintain the integrity and attractiveness of their investment regimes, thereby promoting international economic cooperation and development.

Under an MFN clause, a state commits to granting treatment to investors from another state that is no less favourable than the treatment extended to investors from any third state. The objectives of the MFN standard are to ensure equality and non-discrimination for foreign investors from a particular country in comparison to other investors. This standard is extensively used in investment treaties because it promotes the equality of states by establishing similar treatment in like circumstances, thus avoiding discrimination.[8] By maintaining a consistent application of the MFN principle, states can enhance the predictability and stability of their investment environments, which is essential for attracting and retaining foreign investment.

The content of MFN treatment can vary depending on the differing economic conditions of states. One scholar notes:

> Such standards do not guarantee certainty of treatment to the investor; since they are contingent upon an external set of rules or facts, any

8 Guido Santiago Tawil, 'Most Favoured Nation Clauses and Jurisdictional Clauses in Investment Treaty Arbitration' in Christina Binder et al. (eds), *International Investment Law for the 21st Century: Essays in Honour of Christoph Schreuer* (Oxford University Press 2009) 11–42; See, UNCTAD, 'Most Favoured-Nation Treatment' *United Nations Conference on Trade and Development*, UNCTAD Series on Issues in International Investment Agreement (1999) 13; A.R. Ziegler, 'Most-Favoured-Nation (MFN) Treatment' in August Reinisch (ed), *Standards of Investment Protection* (Oxford University Press 2008) 63.

changes in these external rules or facts will also alter the standards applicable to the foreign investor.[9]

Therefore the practices of states regarding MFN and NT standards in BITs are diverse, reflecting different economic conditions and legal traditions. However, the inclusion of these standards, along with explicit prohibitions against unreasonable or discriminatory actions, is a common strategy to promote non-discrimination and protect foreign investments. Some BITs, in addition to the guarantees of national and MFN treatment, may separately prohibit the impairment of investment by unreasonable or discriminatory action.[10] Many BITs even do not contain MFN treatment.[11]

The MFN clause may limit a host state's capacity to promote human rights extraterritoriality by exerting control over domestic investment conditions[12] as it obligates states to provide foreign investors with treatment that is no less favourable than that given to investors from any third state. This requirement means that any human rights conditions imposed on investors from one country must also be uniformly applied to investors from all BIT partner countries, complicating the implementation of tailored human rights measures. Additionally, the MFN clause can reduce a host state's regulatory flexibility, making it difficult to respond swiftly to human rights violations by specific investors. The need to balance economic objectives with human rights goals further complicates this issue, as states may hesitate to impose stricter human rights conditions if it could discourage foreign investment and impact economic development. Moreover, imposing human rights conditions that are seen as discriminatory could lead to legal disputes under BITs and strain diplomatic relations. For example, in the *CMS Gas Transmission Company v. Argentina* case,[13] Argentina was found to have violated the MFN clause by not extending the same favourable treatment to a US investor as it did to investors from other countries. Similarly, in *Saluka Investments BV v. Czech Republic*, the Czech Republic's failure to provide the same protections to a Dutch investor as provided to other foreign investors led to a finding of MFN violation.[14]

9 Stephen Vasciannie, 'The Fair and Equitable Treatment Standard in the International Investment Law and Practice' (2000) 70 *British Yearbook of International Law* 99, 106.
10 See, Chile-Denmark (1993), Art. 3(1).
11 For instance, China-Japan BIT (1988).
12 Ryan Suda, 'The Effect of Bilateral Investment Treaties on Human Rights Enforcement and Realization' in Olivier De Schutter (ed), *Transnational Corporations and Human Rights* (Hart Publishing 2006) 108.
13 ICSID Case No. ARB/01/8, Award 12 May 2005.
14 UNCITRAL, Partial Award, 17 March 2006.

Fair and Equitable Treatment

While NT and MFN treatment are considered relative standards of treatment, FET is regarded as an absolute standard. The FET standard is a flexible and elusive concept, often leading to numerous interpretations under different circumstances due to its imprecise language. The imprecise nature of language involved in the concept may give rise to numerous interpretations in different circumstances. Although most BITs contain this standard, they do not define it. Despite its growing popularity among the investors, its content and parameters remain ambiguous, uncertain and subject to debate.[15] Its specific meaning often depends on the specific circumstances of each case.[16] The lack of certainty and precision has led to its increasing use as an alternative and more flexible means to protect investors, 'where the test for indirect expropriation is too difficult to achieve'.[17] Sometimes FET may be combined with the provision of full protection and security. Full protection and security are generally interpreted as imposing an obligation on the state to exercise due diligence in protecting foreign investment from injurious activities by the government or by private parties.[18] For instance, in *Tecmed v. Mexico*[19] the tribunal held that Mexico violated the FET standard by failing to provide a transparent and predictable regulatory environment, which ultimately impaired the foreign investment. Similarly, in *CMS Gas Transmission Company v. Argentina*[20] the tribunal found that Argentina's actions during its economic crisis breached the FET standard by creating an unpredictable and unstable investment climate.

The FET standard has been formulated in diverse ways in BITs, leading to a lack of uniformity in its defining elements. Relevant arbitral jurisprudence indicates that four categories of elements can be identified within the FET standard:

1 Vigilance and protection.
2 Due process, including non-denial of justice.
3 Lack of arbitrariness and non-discrimination.
4 Transparency and stability, including the respect of investors' reasonable expectations.[21]

15 See Jean Kalicki and Suzana Medeiros, 'Fair, Equitable and Ambiguous: What Is Fair and Equitable Treatment in International Law?' (2007) 22(1) *ICSID Review: Foreign Investment Law Journal* 25; Christopher Schreuer, 'Fair and Equitable Treatment in Arbitral Practice' (2005) 6 *Journal of World Investment and Trade* 357, 364.
16 *CME v. Czech Republic*, UNCITRAL Case, partial award, September 13, 2001.
17 Katia Yannaca-Small, 'Fair and Equitable Treatment Standard: Recent Developments' in August Reinisch (ed), *Standards of Investment Protection* (Oxford University Press 2008) 111.
18 Rudolf Dolzer and Margrete Stevens, *Bilateral Investment Treaties* (Martinus Nijhoff Publishers 1995) 61.
19 ICSID Case No. ARB(AF)/00/2, Award, on 29 May 2003.
20 ICSID Case No. ARB/01/8, Award, on 12 May 2005.
21 Yannaca-Small (n 17) 118.

The stability of legal framework remains an important component of this treatment.[22] For instance, in *Metalclad v. Mexico*, the tribunal found that the obligation to provide FET under NAFTA entailed the host state to ensure a transparent and predictable framework for business planning and investment.[23] The tribunal concluded that Mexico's failure to provide such a framework constituted a breach of the FET standard. Similarly, in *Occidental v. Ecuador*, the tribunal concluded that the stability of the legal and business framework is an essential element of FET.[24] The tribunal held that Ecuador's actions, which created instability and unpredictability in the legal framework affecting the investment, violated the FET standard.

In the *S.D. Myers v. Canada* case,[25] the tribunal held that Canada's actions, which included banning the export of polychlorinated biphenyl (PCB) waste, were arbitrary and unjust. This ban was found to have been implemented primarily to protect the Canadian PCB disposal industry from US competition rather than for environmental reasons. The tribunal concluded that such arbitrary and unjust treatment violated Canada's commitment to FET under NAFTA.[26] In *Loewen v. United States*[27] the tribunal found that the actions of the Mississippi courts, which imposed a US$500 million punitive damages award against Loewen, resulted in manifest injustice and a lack of due process. The tribunal indicated that such state actions, which create a sense of gross unfairness and procedural irregularities, are sufficient to violate the FET standard.[28] The tribunal emphasized that FET requires not only substantive fairness but also adherence to due process in judicial and administrative proceedings.

In several cases, the tribunal has held that the principle of good faith is not an essential element of FET, therefore violation of the standard would not require the existence of bad faith.[29] For instance, in *Waste Management, Inc. v. United Mexican States*[30] the tribunal noted that a violation of the FET standard does not necessarily require proof of bad faith by the host state. Instead, a breach can occur through actions that are inconsistent with the investor's legitimate expectations, lack transparency or are arbitrary and discriminatory, regardless of the state's intent. The case of *Saluka Investments BV v. Czech Republic* (UNCITRAL, Partial Award, 17 March 2006) further supports this view. The tribunal held that the Czech Republic's actions towards Saluka were not in bad faith but were still

22 See for this point, Peter D. Cameron, 'Stability of Contract in the International Energy Industry' (2009) 27(3) *Journal of Energy and Natural Resources Law* 305–332.
23 ICSID Case No. ARB(AF)/97/1, Award, 30 August 2000.
24 LCIA Case No. UN3467, Award, 1 July 2004.
25 UNCITRAL, Partial Award, 13 November 2000.
26 UNCITRAL Case, First Partial Award, 13 November 2000.
27 ICSID Case No. ARB(AF)/98/3, Award, 26 June 2003.
28 ICSID Case No. ARB(AF)/98/3, Award, 2003.
29 *Loewen v. United States*, ICSID Case No. ARB(AF)/98/3, Award, 2003; *Enron Corporation and Ponderosa Assets, L.P. v. Argentina*, ICSID Case No. ARB/01/3, Award, 22 May 2007.
30 ICSID Case No. ARB(AF)/00/3, Award, 30 April 2004.

in breach of the FET standard because they were unreasonable and discriminatory, disrupting the investor's business operations and legitimate expectations.

The absence of clear guidance on the constitutive elements of FET in BITs and NAFTA, combined with divergent interpretations by tribunals, has led to considerable debate on whether FET is equivalent to the 'minimum standard of treatment' under customary international law or whether it is an autonomous standard. This issue has been at the centre of many arbitral decisions, especially under NAFTA and various BITs, resulting in inconsistent rulings and interpretations. Some arbitral decisions under NAFTA place the FET above and beyond the minimum standard of treatment required under customary international law.[31] For example, in *Pope & Talbot Inc. v. Canada*[32] the tribunal held that FET encompasses more than the traditional international minimum standard. The tribunal concluded that FET includes protection against arbitrary actions, a duty of transparency, and a requirement for states to act consistently, without ambiguity, and with full respect for the investor's reasonable expectations. In contrast, other tribunals have adhered to the view that FET under BITs should be interpreted as synonymous with the minimum standard of treatment under customary international law.[33] In *ADF Group Inc. v. United States*[34] the tribunal explicitly linked FET to the customary international law minimum standard, emphasizing that it did not impose additional obligations beyond those well-established in international law. In many BIT cases, tribunals have taken different interpretative approaches regarding FET. In *Tecmed v. Mexico*[35] the tribunal considered FET as an autonomous standard, interpreting it in light of the object and purpose of the treaty.[36]

To prevent the expansive interpretation of the FET standard and to provide certainty, its scope should be limited to protect foreign investors and their investments from treatment that falls below the minimum international law standard.[37] This approach would ensure that FET remains a safeguard against the most egregious forms of state misconduct while preventing overly broad interpretations that could unduly constrain state sovereignty and regulatory autonomy. Equating the FET with the minimum standard of treatment in international law is not only supported by the intentions of states as evidenced

31 The *Metalclad, S.D. Myers* and *Pope and Talbot* decisions.

32 UNCITRAL, Award on the Merits of Phase 2, 10 April 2001.

33 *Genin v. Estonia*, ICSID Case No. ARB/99/2, Award, June 25; *Lauder v. Czech Republic*, UNCITRAL Case, Final Award; *Occidental v. Ecuador*, LCIA Case No. UN 3467, 1 July 2004.

34 ICSID Case No. ARB(AF)/00/1, Award, 9 January 2003.

35 ICSID Case No. ARB(AF)/00/2, Award, 29 May 2003.

36 *Saluka v. Czech Republic*, UNCITRAL Partial Award, 17 March 2006; *MTD v. Chile*, ICSID Case No. ARB/01/7, Award, 25 May 2004.

37 Todd Weiler, 'Comment on International Law on Investment: The Minimum Standard of Treatment (MST)' (2004, February) 2(1) *OGEL—Oil, Gas and Energy Law Intelligence*, available at www.gasandoil.com/ogel/.

by drafting history of investment agreements, but is also favourable to certainty as to the scope and content of that standard, and a reasonable evolutionary process that does not overly stretch the standard.[38] Because extending the scope of the FET beyond the minimum standard can unduly restrict the host states' ability to regulate foreign investment in their territory,[39] ultimately undermining the States' legitimate role in promoting their social and economic development objectives.[40]

In order to limit the scope of the standard, the NAFTA Free Trade Commission issued a 'Note of Interpretation' in 2001 stating that FET under NAFTA does not require treatment beyond the minimum standard of treatment already required by international law.[41]

A potential means to limit the scope of the treatment is the adoption of the progressive interpretation of the FET, which entails that 'the investor who seeks equity for the protection of their investment must also be accountable under principles of equity and fairness, to the host state's population affected by the investment'.[42] According to this view, FET is not an one-sided concept, rather it should require balancing of competing interests—the interests of the investor and the interest of individuals and social groups who seek remedy against possible adverse impacts of the investment on their life or the environment.[43] Another human rights–based argument is that in calculating damages for breaches of FET, the behaviour of the investor that may have contributed to the losses should be taken into account. Thus an investor should be accountable for breaches of international or national standards which the state is obliged to uphold.[44]

Legitimate expectation as an element of FET can be another avenue through which human rights considerations can find their way into investment

38 J. Roman Picherack, 'The Expanding Scope of the Fair and Equitable Treatment Standard: Have Recent Tribunals Gone Too Far?' (2008) 9(4) *Journal of World Trade and Investment* 255–291.

39 Lorenzo Cotula, *Foreign Investment, Law and Sustainable Development* (IIED 2014) 23.

40 Picherack (n 38) 291.

41 NAFTA Free Trade Committee, comprising 'cabinet-level representatives' of the three NAFTA State parties, with the power to resolve disputes that may arise regarding its interpretation or application. Notes on Interpretation of chapter 11 provisions (3 July 2001), available at www.international.gc.ca/tna-nac/NAFTA-interpr-en.asp, accessed 22 October 2022.

42 Francesco Francioni, 'Access to Justice, Denial of Justice and International Investment Law' (2009) 20(3) *European Journal of International Law* 729, 739.

43 Ibid. 739; see also, C. McLachlan, L. Shore and M. Weiniger, *International Investment Arbitration: Substantive Principles* (Oxford University Press 2007) ('some elements of human rights law may furnish a source of general principle from which the obligation of fair and equitable treatment may be given contemporary content') 206.

44 Iona Knoll-Tudor, 'The Fair and Equitable Standard and Human Rights Norms' in Pierre-Marie Dupuy, Francesco Francioni and Ernest-Ulrich Petersmann (eds), *Human Rights in International Investment Law and Arbitration* (Oxford University Press 2009) 341; see also Peter Muchlinski, 'Caveat Investor? The Relevance of the Conduct of the Investor Under the Fair and Equitable Treatment Standard' (2006) 55 *International and Comparative Law Quarterly* 567–598.

law. While legitimate expectations are of particular importance in the assessment of breach(es) of the FET standard, there can be no legitimate expectations that are contrary to human rights law.[45] The doctrine of legitimate expectations protects investors from arbitrary changes in the legal and regulatory framework of the host state that could negatively affect their investments. This concept is grounded in the notion that investors rely on the stability and predictability of the host state's legal and business environment when making investment decisions. Tribunals have recognized the importance of legitimate expectations in several landmark cases. For instance, in *Tecmed v. Mexico*[46] the tribunal emphasized that Mexico's actions must be consistent with the investor's legitimate expectations and that these expectations should be based on the host state's representations and regulatory framework.

However, the concept of legitimate expectations must be balanced with the host state's duty to uphold and protect human rights. This balance ensures that investor protections do not undermine the state's obligations under international human rights law. In *Bilcon v. Canada* (PCA Case No. 2009–04, Award on Jurisdiction and Liability, 17 March 2015), the tribunal underscored that while investors may have legitimate expectations, these expectations must align with the host state's public policy objectives, including human rights obligations.

Moreover, international investment tribunals have increasingly acknowledged that legitimate expectations cannot override fundamental human rights principles. For example, in *Philip Morris v. Uruguay*[47] the tribunal rejected Philip Morris's claim that Uruguay's tobacco regulations violated its legitimate expectations. The tribunal found that the regulations were a valid exercise of the state's sovereign right to protect public health, aligning with human rights obligations to ensure the right to health. Thus the principle of legitimate expectations in FET can be a conduit for human rights considerations in investment law. Investors cannot reasonably expect the host state to maintain a regulatory framework that conflicts with its human rights obligations. This principle was further reinforced in *Von Pezold v. Zimbabwe*,[48] where the tribunal recognized that the host state's actions, although detrimental to the investor, were necessary to fulfil its human rights obligations towards its citizens.

Investment, Human Rights and Environmental Soft Law Norms

In the absence of legally binding instruments to govern the relationship between investment, human rights, and the environment, many soft law instruments have been adopted over the last decade to address this complex

45 Ursula Kriebaum, 'Human Rights of the Population of the Host State in International Investment Arbitration' (2009) 10(5) *The Journal of World Investment and Trade* 653, 669.
46 ICSID Case No. ARB(AF)/00/2, Award, 29 May 2003.
47 ICSID Case No. ARB/10/7, Award, 8 July 2016.
48 ICSID Case No. ARB/10/15, Award, 28 July 2015.

interplay. These soft law norms, while imposing certain obligations on host states, are primarily formulated as CSR initiatives. This has been reflected in the report of the UN Special Rapporteurs,[49] the UN GC[50] and many corporate human rights policy statements.[51]

The international community's first significant effort to establish CSR standards was the Tripartite Declaration of Principles concerning Multinational Enterprises and Social Policy, adopted by the ILO in 1977.[52] The standards incorporated in the Tripartite Declaration are intended to encourage positive contributions which multinational corporations (MNCs) can make to economic and social progress. The preamble of the declaration proclaims:

> All the parties concerned by this Declaration should respect the Universal Declaration of Human Rights and the corresponding International Covenants adopted by the General Assembly of the United Nations, as well as the Constitution of the International Labour Organisation and its principles, according to which freedom of expression and association are essential to sustained progress.[53]

The Tripartite Declaration provides guidance to governments, companies and worker organizations in areas such as equal opportunities and treatment, working conditions, safety and health, and freedom of association. However, the declaration is non-binding, and 'its implementation has been constrained by its dependency on domestic incorporation by states and on promotion and publication campaigns by non-governmental entities'.[54] The 1977 Tripartite Declaration has been supplemented by the 1998 ILO Declaration on Fundamental Principles and Rights at Work. The 1998 ILO Declaration addresses how most labour rights should be observed by member countries of the ILO. It also offers a list of core standards that should be observed by MNCs in their

49 John Ruggie, 'Guiding Principles on Business and Human Rights: Implementing the United Nations "Protect, Respect and Remedy" Framework' *Report of the Special Representative of the Secretary-General on the Issue of Human Rights and Transnational Corporations and Other Business Enterprises*, Human Rights Council, Seventeenth session, Agenda item 3, Promotion and protection of all human rights, civil, political, economic, social and cultural rights, including the right to development, UN General Assembly, A/HRC/17/31, 21 March 2011.

50 The UN Global Compact, available at https://unglobalcompact.org/, accessed 14 March 2024.

51 Unilever Human Policy Statement, March 2023, available at https://spcommreports.ohchr.org/TMResultsBase/DownLoadFile?gId=37573, accessed 12 March 2024.

52 ILO, 'Tripartite Declaration of Principles Concerning Multinational Enterprises and Social Policy' (1978) 17 *International Legal Materials* 422.

53 ILO Tripartite Declaration of Principles, par. 8, Official Bulletin (Geneva, ILO), 1978, Vol. LXI, Series A, No. 1.

54 Ralph G. Steinhardt, 'Corporate Responsibility and the International Law of Human Rights: The New *Lex Mercatoria*' in Philip Alston (ed), *Non-State Actors and Human Rights* (Oxford University Press 2005) 204.

operations. These standards include the elimination of child labour, the abolition of forced labour, the elimination of discrimination in employment, and the recognition of the right to collective bargaining.

The UN made several attempts to formulate codes of conduct for regulation of MNEs through laying down international standard(s). The UN adopted the Draft Code of Conduct on Transnational Corporations (TNC) in 1983,[55] and it was revised in 1988[56] and 1990.[57] The UN Draft Code of Conduct on Transnational Corporations of 1990, which has wider mandate than the earlier ones, addressed many issues including good faith negotiations of contract and respect for tradition, fundamental freedoms and international standards of human rights. Paragraph 14 of the Draft UN Code states that 'transnational corporations shall respect human rights and fundamental freedoms in the countries in which they operate . . . and shall not discriminate on the basis of race, color, sex, religion, language, social, national and ethnic origin or political or other opinion'.[58] According to the 1990 Draft UN Code's preamble, one of its principal purposes is to minimize the harmful effects of multinationals activities. But the Draft UN Code was never made into enforceable legal instrument by the General Assembly. The main reasons for failure could be attributed to disagreements between developing and developed countries on many issues of transnational investment.

In 2003, the UN Sub-Commission on Human Rights adopted a set of principles governing corporate human rights standards, titled Norms on the Responsibilities for Transnational Corporations and Other Business Enterprises with Regard to Human Rights.[59] The Norms oblige corporations to respect and promote economic, social and cultural rights, like adequate food, health, housing and education. But their implementation is left to the MNCs themselves and subject to periodic monitoring and verification by United Nations, other international and national mechanisms already in existence or yet to be created, regarding application of the Norms. According to one distinguished commentator, 'The Norms seek to synthesize developments in treaty law which expressly or implicitly expand the scope of human rights

55 Draft United Nations Code of Conduct on Transnational Corporations, U.N. Center on Transnational Corporations, Special Sess. (7–18 March 1983 and 9–20 May 1983), U.N. Doc.E/C.10/1982/6(1986).

56 Code of Conduct on Transnational Corporations, UN. ESCOR, Organisational Session for 1988, Provisional Agenda Item 2, at 4, UN Doc. E/1988 39(Add.1) (1988).

57 Development and International Economic Cooperation: Transnational Corporations, U.N. ESCOR, 2d Sec, Agenda Item 7(d), para. 13, U.N. Doc E/1990/94(1990).

58 Ibid.

59 United Nations Economic and Social Council, Commission on Human Rights, Fifty-Fifth Session of the Sub-Commission on the Promotion and Protection of Human Rights, *Norms on the Responsibilities of Transnational Corporations and Other Business Enterprises*, E/CN.4/Sub.2/2003/12/Rev.2 (2003).

obligations to non-state actors such as businesses, and clarify the extent of the obligations that apply directly to businesses.'[60]

The Norms contain several implementation strategies. First, considering the fact human rights obligations will be most effective if internalized as a matter of company policy and practice, the Norms call upon businesses to adopt the substances of the Norms as the minimum standards for their own company codes of conduct or internal roles of operation and to adopt mechanisms for creating accountability within the company. The Norms call upon companies to disseminate their adopted rules amongst employees in an intelligible way.[61] It also encourages business to conduct internal monitoring, to establish complaints mechanisms, to undertake periodic reporting and assessment by an independent verification so that current practices meet the standards in the Norms.[62] Civil society entities, such as NGOs, trade unions and business associations, are urged to adopt the standards and use them as benchmarks for measuring performance, while intergovernmental organizations may also use them in the formulation of their own standards.[63]

The Norms are sui generis in character as they are neither voluntary nor treaty. But a basic principle of the Norms is that they should be respected by all businesses.[64] The Norms do not distinguish between businesses on the basis of the domestic or international nature of their operations, but they do reflect differences between corporations with regard to their ability to influence markets, governments, stakeholders and communities, by providing in the first paragraph:

> States have the primary responsibility to promote, secure the fulfillment of, respect, ensure respect of and protect human rights recognized in international as well as national law, including ensuring that transnational corporations and other business enterprises respect human rights. Within their respective spheres of activity and influence, transnational corporations and other business enterprises have the obligation to promote, secure the fulfillment of, respect, ensure respect of and protect human rights recognized in international law as well as national law, including the rights and interests of indigenous peoples and other vulnerable groups.[65]

60 Philip Alston, 'The "Not-a-Cat" Syndrome: Can the International Human Rights Regime Accommodate Non-State Actors?' in Philip Alston (ed), *Non-State Actors and Human Rights* (Oxford University Press 2005) 33.

61 David Weissbrodt and Muria Kruger, 'Human Rights Responsibilities of Business as Non-State Actors' in Philip Alston (ed), *Non-State Actors and Human Rights* (Oxford University Press 2005) 341.

62 Ibid. 342–343.

63 Alston (n 60) 33.

64 David Weissbrodt and Muria Kruger, 'Norms on the Responsibilities of Transnational Corporations and Other Business Enterprises with Regard to Human Rights' (2003) 97 *American Journal of International Law* 901, 910.

65 Para. 1.

The UN GC launched in 1999 invites companies to commit themselves to a set of nine principles relating to labour rights, internationally proclaimed human rights, and protection of the environment.[66] The GC calls on world business to 'respect the protection of international human rights within their sphere of influence' and 'make sure their own corporations are not complicit in human rights abuses'.[67] The GC urges companies to engage with human rights and environmental issues and to support its principles through adopting 'best practices'. But the Compact is not legally binding instrument and has been criticized on the grounds of lack of a process for monitoring of its observance.[68] Nevertheless, the GC has been successful in initiating a dialogue of corporate responsibility in many parts of the world and it has promoted discussion by and with many MNCs regarding their responsibilities towards protection of human rights in host states. The GC provides a universal framework for action by states, business and civil society.

The OECD adopted a series of codes of conduct for MNCs from 1976 to 2000. The first OECD Guideline on Multinational Enterprises adopted in 1976 deals with disclosure of information by corporation(s), improvement of employment and industrial relations through employee's rights to representation, conforming competition rules to avoid restrictive business practice, and environmental protection. The OECD Guidelines are mainly recommendations by governments to MNEs that operate in or from their territories. But the Guidelines impose obligations upon the states to implement them and to promote compliance with them by MNEs.[69] In 2000 the OECD substantially updated and revised the Guidelines which call upon the corporations to act consistently with the host state's international human rights obligations.[70] The new version states that MNEs should respect the human rights of those affected by their activities consistent with the government's international obligations and commitments. It also contains detailed implementation

66 The nine principles are: Principle 1: respect and support the protection of internationally proclaimed human rights within their sphere of influence; Principle 2: make sure that they are not complicit in human rights abuse; Principle 3: uphold the freedom of association and the effective recognition of the right to collective bargaining; Principle 4: support the elimination of all forms of forced and compulsory labour; Principle 5: support the effective abolition of child labour; Principle 6: eliminate discrimination in respect of employment and occupation; Principle 7: support a precautionary approach to environmental challenges; Principle 8: undertake initiatives to promote greater environmental responsibility; Principle 9: encourage the development and diffusion of environmentally friendly technologies.

67 UN Compact for the New Century, at http://unglobalcompact.org/un/gc/unweb.nsf/content/thenine.htm.

68 'Beyond Voluntarism: Human Rights and the Developing International Legal Obligations of Companies' (International Council on Human Rights Policy, 2002) 157.

69 Steinhardt (n 54) 209.

70 OECD, 'The OECD Guidelines for Multinational Enterprises-Text' available at www.oecd.org/daf/investment/guidelines/mnetext.htm, accessed 9 September 2023.

procedures such as 'follow-up', soft procedures including consultations, good offices, mediation and conciliation, as well as 'clarifications' of the Guidelines themselves.[71]

The above standards are not legally binding on companies, but all provide frameworks for appropriate company behaviour. They are used either as tools by companies themselves to guide performance, or as a benchmark by which governments and other stakeholders may hold companies to account.[72]

In addition, sector-specific voluntary initiatives have also been established to seek greater alignment between international investment with environmental and human rights protection for business, governments, NGOs, trade unions and industry associations. They include the Extractive Industries Transparency Initiative (EITI) (2003), the Kimberly Process Certification Scheme (2002), the Voluntary Principles on Security and Human Rights (2000), the Ethical Trading Initiative 1998, the Fair Labour Association (1999) and the Equator Principles (2002). The ILO Declaration on Social Justice for a Fair Globalization, 2008 also called on non-state entities and economic actors, such as MNEs operating at the global level, to enhance the effectiveness of ILO operational guidelines through respecting, promoting and realizing the right to freedom of association and collective bargaining.

The Human Rights Council of the UN has adopted Framework Principles on Environment and Human Rights which have clearly established linkages between human rights and the environment.[73] This document contains 16 Framework Principles that set out basic obligations of States under human rights law as they relate to the enjoyment of a safe, clean, healthy, and sustainable environment. Principle 12 of these Framework Principles can be applied by the state to discipline environmental behaviour of corporations as it requires States to establish and maintain substantive environmental standards and ensure the effective enforcement of their environmental standards against public and private actors.[74] On the other hand, the nexus between environment and human rights are clearly established by Framework Principle 16, which lays down that States should respect, protect and fulfil human

71 'OECD Guidelines for Multinational Enterprises' *Revision*, 2000, available at http://www.oecd.org/daf/investment/guidelines/index.htm, accessed 23 October 2022.

72 Monash University Castan Centre for Human Rights Law, Human Rights Translated: A Business Reference Guide, Published by United Nations Human Rights, Office of the High Commissioner for Human Rights, 2008, xii.

73 Report of the Special Rapporteur on the issue of human rights obligations relating to the enjoyment of a safe, clean, healthy and sustainable environment, Human Rights Council Thirty-seventh session 26 February–23 March 2018 Agenda item 3, A/HRC/37/59, 24 January 2018, para. 13. The Framework Principles are available at https://www.ohchr.org/Documents/Issues/Environment/SREnvironment/FrameworkPrinciplesUserFriendlyVersion.pdf, accessed 13 October 2023.

74 Principle 11 and 12.

rights in the actions they take to address environmental challenges and pursue sustainable development. In conclusion, soft law norms have played a crucial role in shaping the relationship between investment, human rights and the environment. Through instruments like the ILO Tripartite Declaration, the 1998 ILO Declaration on Fundamental Principles and Rights at Work, the UN GC and the UN Guiding Principles on Business and Human Rights, the international community has provided important frameworks for promoting CSR. However, the challenge remains in transforming these soft law norms into binding obligations to ensure consistent and enforceable standards globally.

International Soft Law Supporting Environmental and Natural Resource Protection in FDI

Significant reform is underway to improve the governance of IIAs and align them with best practices, particularly in the realm of environmental protection. This reform is primarily occurring at multilateral and regional levels, providing a supportive framework for individual IIAs. Several host states critical of their respective FDI experiences, such as Brazil, Australia, South Africa and various Latin American countries, are driving these changes. These countries are either reviewing their participation in IIAs, opposing ISDS arbitration,[75] or withdrawing from treaties like the ICSID Convention.[76]

International Finance Corporation Environmental and Social Performance Standards

The International Finance Corporation (IFC) Sustainability Framework and Environmental and Social Performance Standards[77] provide mechanisms for incorporating social and environmental issues into investment decision-making. Since January 1, 2012, these standards have been mandatory for projects directly financed by the IFC. The IFC's eight performance standards, particularly Performance Standard 6, require projects to consider biodiversity, ecosystem services and sustainable resource management. This standard aligns with the Convention on Biological Diversity and promotes managing biodiversity impacts throughout the project lifecycle. A notable mechanism under Performance Standard 6 is the requirement for a supply chain review for primary

75 See Australian Government, Productivity Commission, Bilateral and Regional Trade Agreements (Productivity Commission, November 2010) section 14.2.

76 Sergey Ripinsky, 'Venezuela's Withdrawal from IISID: What It Does and Does Not Achieve' *Investment Treaty News* (13 April 2012), available at https://www.iisd.org/itn/2012/04/13/venezuelas-withdrawal-from-icsid-what-it-does-and-does-not-achieve/.

77 See International Finance Corporation, 'Environmental and Social Performance Standards' (IFC, 2012), available at http://www.ifc.org/wps/wcm/connect/115482804a0255db96fbffd1a5d13d27/PS_English_2012_Full-Document.pdf?MOD=AJPERES.

commodities sourced from critical habitats, encouraging environmentally responsible supply chains.[78]

Performance Standard 1 emphasizes integrated assessment of environmental and social impacts, risks and opportunities, mandating public participation and community engagement. This includes meaningful consultation with affected communities, grievance mechanisms and ongoing reporting. The World Bank Group's Environmental, Health, and Safety Guidelines (EHS Guidelines) further support these standards by providing industry-specific best practices.

However, challenges remain. The EHS Guidelines lack specific guidance on public participation barriers in natural resource extraction industries. Additionally, the standards are undermined when financial intermediaries, rather than the IFC, oversee compliance, resulting in substandard environmental and social practices in many cases.

Equator Principles

The Equator Principles, a risk management framework adopted by financial institutions, aim to assess and manage environmental and social risks in projects.[79] The third revision of these principles includes ten guidelines covering social and environmental impact assessments, stakeholder engagement, grievance mechanisms and transparency. These principles echo the importance of IFC Performance Standard 6.

Despite growing adoption by 88 financial institutions worldwide, the Equator Principles face criticism for their narrow scope, primarily focusing on project finance and not extending to other financial services. Confidentiality arrangements between institutions and investors also limit transparency, hindering stakeholders' access to critical project information.[80]

Extractive Industries Transparency Initiative

The EITI publishes a global standard for enhancing transparency and civil society participation in managing oil, gas and mineral reserves. The EITI standard requires signatory countries to disclose the processes used to award mining licenses, ensuring effective communication between investors and

78 See International Finance Corporation, 'IFC Performance Standards on Environment and Social Sustainability' (IFC, 2012) 2, available at http://www.ifc.org/wps/wcm/connect/c8f524004a73daeca09afdf998895a12/IFC_Performance_Standards.pdf?MOD=AJPERES.

79 Equator Principles Association, 'Environmental and Social Risk for Projects' (Equator Principles Association, 2011), available at http://www.equator-principles.com/

80 See Manual Worsdorfer, '10 Years of "Equator Principles": A Critical Economic-Ethical Analysis' (Osgoode CLPE Research Paper No. 54/2013) 16; see also Oliver Balch, 'Sustainable Finance: How Far Have the Equator Principles Gone?' *The Guardian* (15 November 2012), available at https://www.theguardian.com/sustainable-business/sustainable-finance-equator-principles.

affected parties. It also mandates transparency in production processes and revenue collection by governments.

Initiatives like the EITI are crucial for aligning IIAs with public participation obligations under international environmental law, preventing conflicts between environmental and investment obligations.[81] They support the application of environmental and investment obligations harmoniously, as emphasized in Principle 10 of the UN Rio Declaration on Environment and Development,[82] which advocates for public access to environmental information and participation in decision-making.

John Ruggie Report on Business and Human Rights

An important international standard on corporate responsibility for human rights has been formulated by John Ruggie, a special rapporteur appointed by the UN on business and human rights.[83] The Guiding Principles on Business and Human Rights formulated by Ruggie were unanimously approved by the UN Human Rights Council in 2011. The Guiding Principles provide a globally recognized and authoritative framework for the respective duties and responsibilities of governments and business enterprises to prevent and address such impacts.[84] The Guiding Principles clarify that all business enterprises have an independent responsibility to respect human rights, and for this purpose they are required to exercise human rights due diligence to identify, prevent, mitigate and account for how they address impacts on human rights.[85] This due diligence process is essential for integrating human rights considerations into business operations and ensuring that companies do not contribute to human rights abuses. Ruggie proposed a conceptual and policy framework that comprises three core principles: the state duty to respect, protect and fulfil human rights; the corporate responsibility to respect human rights and business are required to comply with all applicable laws; and the need for more effective access to remedies.[86]

81 Rosalin Diepevenn, Yulia Levashova and Tineke Lambooy, 'Bridging the Gap Between International Investment Law and the Environment' (2014) 30(78) *Utrecht Journal of International and European Law and the Environment* 145, 154.

82 United Nations Conference on Environment and Development, *Rio Declaration on Environment and Development*, UN Doc A/CONF.151/26 (Vol 1) (12 August 1992), annex 1, principle 10.

83 John Ruggie, 'Guiding Principles on Business and Human Rights: Implementing the United Nations "Protect, Respect and Remedy" Framework' Report of the Special Representative of the Secretary-General on the Issue of Human Rights and Transnational Corporations and Other Business Enterprises, 21 March 2011, Human Rights Council, UN.

84 Corporate Human Rights Due Diligence—Identifying and Leveraging Emerging Practice, available at https://www.ohchr.org/EN/Issues/Business/Pages/CorporateHRDueDiligence.aspx, accessed 23 October 2023.

85 Ibid.

86 John Ruggie (n 83).

State Duty to Protect Human Rights

States are required to take appropriate steps to prevent, investigate, punish and redress human rights abuses through effective policies, legislation, regulations and adjudication. This principle underscores the role of governments in creating a regulatory environment that mandates and incentivizes businesses to respect human rights. However, the state's duty to protect against human rights abuse by the business enterprise is not a new concept. In 1974 the Charter of Economic Rights and Duties of States proclaimed that 'each state has the right to regulate TNCs within its jurisdiction to ensure that they comply with its laws and economic and social policies, and do not intervene in the state's internal affairs'.[87] The human rights treaties, such as the International Covenant on Civil and Political Rights (ICCPR) and the International Covenant on Economic, Social and Cultural Rights (ICESR), do not specifically address state duties regarding business. They impose generalized obligations to ensure the enjoyment of rights and prevent non-state abuse.[88]

According to John Ruggie, the first principle of 'the state duty to protect' human rights may include the responsibility to regulate the behaviour of businesses and other private entities to safeguard the rights of others. The Committee on Economic, Social and Cultural Rights has suggested that state parties take steps to prevent their own citizens and companies' from violating rights in other countries.[89] General Recommendation 23 of the Convention on the Elimination of All Forms of Discrimination against Women has stated that:

> The Committee is conscious that some commercial companies and state enterprises infringe on the rights of indigenous people to their land and resources, culture and historical identity. States should ensure that these communities enjoy sustainable and economic development, protect their rights to own, develop, control, and use their communal lands, territories, and resources.

Both the universal and regional human rights systems emphasize that states have a duty to protect those living within their jurisdiction from human rights violations by non-state actors. The state obligation to protect requires states to take measures that prevent non-state actors from interfering with human rights. Therefore the corporation must comply with the legal regime of the particular state in which they are operating. When violations by non-state

87 G.A. Res. 3281 UN GAOR, 29th Sess. Supp. No. 31, at 50, 52, UN Doc. A/9946 (1974).

88 John Gerard Ruggie, 'Business and Human Rights: The Evolving International Agenda' (2007) 101 *American Journal of International Law* 819, 828.

89 The Committee on Economic, Social and Cultural Rights (CESCR), General Comment No. 15: The Right to Water, UN Doc. E/C.12/2002/11, para. 33, 20 January 2003.

actors occur, the state must take appropriate measures or to exercise due diligence to prevent, investigate and punish the harm and provide appropriate remedies.[90]

The first pillar proposed by Ruggie involves three sets of issues. First, governments need to preserve their ability to meet their international human rights obligations. Second, governments need to take human rights into account when they enter into any agreement with a business entity whether as owners, investors, insurers, procurers or simply promoters. Governments should consider human rights impacts in a range of broader policy areas, including when they sign trade agreements and investment treaties. Such a policy domain that shapes business practices includes commercial policy, investment policy, securities regulation and corporate governance. Third, even when governments are not connected directly to a business venture, they need to foster a corporate culture respectful of human rights at home and abroad. This requires strengthening and enforcing national laws and regulations of the host states and home states to prevent human rights abuses by MNEs.[91]

Corporate Responsibility to Respect Human Rights

Businesses are required to avoid infringing on the human rights of others and to address adverse impacts with which they are involved. This responsibility exists independently of states' abilities or willingness to fulfil their human rights obligations, going above compliance with national laws and regulations protecting human rights. Companies are expected to adopt policies and practices to ensure that they do not cause or contribute to human rights abuses. It also means that they should avoid infringing on the rights of others and should address human rights impacts with which they are involved. Such responsibility of corporations to respect human rights applies to all enterprises regardless of their size, sector, operational context and structure.[92] In all contexts, corporations should comply with all applicable laws and respect internationally recognized human rights, wherever they operate. In general, the social responsibility of corporation(s) now encompasses a wide range of issues including global environmental sustainability, accountability, transparency of corporate entities, the respect for human rights, developmental responsibilities, employment, labour relations, ensuring competition, refraining from restrictive business practices, consumer protection, corporate good governance, and

90 Manisuli Ssenyonjo, 'Non-State Actors and Economic, Social and Cultural Rights' in Mashood A. Baderin and Robert McCorquodale (eds), *Economic, Social and Cultural Rights in Action* (Oxford University Press 2007) 109–135.

91 John Ruggie, 'Statement on the Issue of Human Rights and Transnational Corporations and other Business Enterprises to the Department of Trade and Industry' South Africa, September 4, 2009; see also, John G. Ruggie, 'Presentation of Report to United Nations Human Rights Council' Geneva, 2 June 2009.

92 Ruggie (n 83).

prevention of corruption.[93] In many countries, the corporate responsibilities are incorporated in the domestic laws such as antitrust, consumer protection, labour or environmental laws, and these laws often confer upon corporations positive obligations to comply with defined standards in relation to their conduct with society. The boundaries of CSR are dynamic and may shift over time.

When do human rights obligations apply to corporations? There are various formulations of suggestions regarding the scope of obligations. But mainly, such obligations should apply to spheres of activity and influence of corporations. Some other scholars highlighted the fact that the obligations vary according to the nexus and the leverage that companies have with regard to the abuse.[94]

Access to Remedy

The third pillar of the framework revolves around access to remedies that plays an important role in achieving the goals of the first two pillars. Both states and businesses have roles in ensuring that victims of human rights abuses have access to effective remedies. This includes judicial, administrative, legislative, and other appropriate means. Remedies should be adequate, effective, and prompt in providing redress and ensuring accountability.

John Ruggie has highlighted that as a part of their duty to protect against the corporate violation of human rights, States must take appropriate steps to ensure, through judicial, administrative and legislative means, that when such abuses occur within their territory, those affected have access to an effective remedy.[95] Victims of corporate abuse should have access to remedies that may include both judicial and non-judicial means, and such remedies should be immediate, accessible, affordable, adequate and effective. States are required to take appropriate steps to investigate, punish and redress corporate-related abuse of rights of individuals within their territory.[96] Remedies through non-judicial mechanisms include agencies with oversight of particular standards, the operation of the ombudsman, national human rights institutions or other non-judicial means.[97] But non-judicial mechanisms to address alleged breaches of human rights standards should meet certain principles to be credible and effective.[98]

93 *World Investment Report*, United Nations, New York and Geneva (2003) 164.

94 S.R. Ratner, 'Corporations and Human Rights: A Theory of Legal Responsibility' (2001) 111 *Yale Law Journal* 443–545; N. Jagers, *Corporate Human Rights Obligations: In Search of Accountability* (Intersentia 2002) 79.

95 Ruggie (n 83).

96 Ibid.

97 UN SRSG Report April 2008.

98 UN SRSG Report April 2008, Paragraph 92. Based on a year of multi-stakeholder and bilateral consultations related to the mandate, the Special Representative believes that, at a minimum, such mechanisms must be: (1) legitimate: a mechanism must have clear, transparent

Ruggie has argued that the United Nations Guiding Principles themselves create a set of authoritative benchmarks against which corporate human rights performance can be assessed. A central component of the Guiding Principles is self-reporting of human rights performance by corporations. The adoption of the Guiding Principles marked a significant step towards integrating human rights considerations into international investment frameworks. For instance, investment treaties and agreements can incorporate these principles to ensure that foreign investments do not lead to human rights violations. By embedding human rights due diligence into the fabric of international investment law, states can create a more balanced and fair investment climate. Additionally, the Guiding Principles have influenced various international organizations and national governments in developing policies and regulations that require businesses to uphold human rights standards. The European Union, for example, has integrated aspects of the Guiding Principles into its regulatory framework, mandating that companies disclose non-financial information related to human rights, environmental and social impacts.

The impact of the Guiding Principles extends to the financial sector, where investors are increasingly considering ESG criteria in their investment decisions. This shift is driven by the recognition that respecting human rights and environmental standards is not only a moral obligation but also a factor that can affect the long-term sustainability and profitability of investments.

Conclusion

The intersection of international standards, general principles and norms on investment protection, human rights and environmental sustainability is particularly significant. These standards and norms regulate international investments by ensuring that they do not come at the expense of human rights

and sufficiently independent governance structures to ensure that no party to a particular grievance process can interfere with the fair conduct of that process; (2) accessible: a mechanism must be publicized to those who may wish to access it and provide adequate assistance for aggrieved parties who may face barriers to access, including language, literacy, awareness, finance, distance, or fear of reprisal; (3) predictable: a mechanism must provide a clear and known procedure with a time frame for each stage and clarity on the types of process and outcome it can (and cannot) offer, as well as a means of monitoring the implementation of any outcome; (4) equitable: a mechanism must ensure that aggrieved parties have reasonable access to sources of information, advice and expertise necessary to engage in a grievance process on fair and equitable terms; (5) rights-compatible: a mechanism must ensure that its outcomes and remedies accord with internationally recognized human rights standards; and (6) transparent: a mechanism must provide sufficient transparency of process and outcome to meet the public interest concerns at stake and should presume transparency wherever possible; non-State mechanisms in particular should be transparent about the receipt of complaints and the key elements of their outcomes.

or environmental sustainability. Key principles such as FET, NT and MFN treatment within BITs aim to protect investors while also upholding essential human rights and environmental standards.

For instance, the principle of legitimate expectations within FET can integrate human rights considerations into investment law, ensuring that investor protections do not override fundamental human rights principles. Cases like *Tecmed v. Mexico* and *Philip Morris v. Uruguay* illustrate how tribunals balance investor expectations with the host state's duty to protect public health and human rights. Moreover, the application of NT and MFN standards often includes exceptions that allow host states to implement measures protecting public health, the environment, and social equity, as seen in the South Africa–Tanzania BIT.

The legal character of the various codes, declarations, reports and resolutions on corporate responsibility towards human rights and environmental protection is fundamentally non-binding, as these instruments often use aspirational language or set out broad values rather than enforceable obligations. None of these instruments was intended to create a legally binding framework for corporations. Instead, they have inspired corporate codes of conduct and multi-stakeholder initiatives, which serve to guide the complex relationship between investment, human rights and the environment.

The implementation of these international soft law standards largely depends on active civil society campaigning. However, these soft law standards establish global norms that MNEs can hardly ignore due to the risk of public criticism for non-compliance. For instance, the Tripartite Declaration of Principles concerning Multinational Enterprises and Social Policy, adopted by the ILO in 1977, and the subsequent 1998 ILO Declaration on Fundamental Principles and Rights at Work, set important standards for corporate behaviour, despite their non-binding nature. Similarly, the UN GC and the Guiding Principles on Business and Human Rights formulated by John Ruggie, which were endorsed by the UN Human Rights Council in 2011, provide a globally recognized framework for corporate responsibility. These principles emphasize the state duty to protect human rights, the corporate responsibility to respect human rights and the need for effective access to remedies for human rights abuses.

Despite their non-binding status, these instruments influence national legislation and corporate practices. MNEs often adhere to these standards to avoid public criticism and potential reputational damage. Moreover, these soft law norms serve as guidelines for national legislation and actions, creating a body of norms that contribute to the evolving standard of corporate responsibility in human rights, environmental and labour standards. Efforts to create legally binding norms for corporations are likely to face strong opposition from home states and corporations due to financial interests. Consequently, voluntary initiatives are often preferred to avoid the legal consequences of violating binding norms.

The international community's adoption of these soft law instruments reflects a growing consensus on the importance of corporate responsibility and the need for MNEs to align their operations with global human rights and environmental standards. This evolving body of norms underscores the significance of continued advocacy and active engagement by civil society to ensure that corporations uphold their responsibilities in a globalized economy. By embedding human rights and environmental considerations into the framework of international investment law, these standards and norms help create a balanced approach to economic development. This approach ensures that investments contribute positively to SDGs without undermining the rights of individuals or the health of the planet. The evolving body of international soft law therefore plays a critical role in guiding the complex relationship between investment, human rights and environmental sustainability, promoting a more equitable and sustainable global economy.

5 Human Rights and Environmental Protection

Addressing Substantive Challenges in Regional and Bilateral Investment Agreements

Introduction

IIAs play a crucial role in promoting sustainable development and aiding developing countries in enhancing their capacity to protect natural resources. The World Summit on Sustainable Development (WSSD) emphasized the importance of FDI in achieving natural resource protection, recognizing that investment is essential for improving economic, social, and environmental outcomes. The importance of integrating of human rights considerations in BITs has been emphasized in a UN Report.[1] It has been stated in the report:

> There is currently no international mechanism to consider complaints on all aspects of economic, social and cultural rights. On the other hand, under investment agreements, investors have recourse to international redress against States and States have redress against other States. These risks skewing the balance of protection in favour of investors, which in turn could lead to investment decisions favouring the interests of investors over the human rights of individuals and communities who could remain voiceless in the event of a conflict of interests and rights.[2]

The assertion of integrated human rights is often justified on the basis that the current regime of BITs only empowers foreign investors, which facilitates the perpetuation of inequality between developed and developing countries.[3] It is

1 Economic, Social and Cultural Rights, Human rights, trade and investment, Report of the High Commissioner for Human Rights, Commission on Human Rights, Sub-Commission on the Promotion and Protection of Human Rights, Fifty-fifth session, Item 4 of the provisional agenda, E/CN.4/Sub.2/2003/9 2 July 2003, Economic and Social Council.

2 Ibid, para. 41.

3 Efraim Chalamish, 'The Future of Bilateral Investment Treaties: A De Facto Multilateral Agreement?' (2008–2009) 34 *Brookings Journal of International Law* 2 353; see also, Howard Mann, 'International Investment Agreements, Business and Human Rights: Key Issues and Opportunities' *International Institute for Sustainable Development*, February 2008 (arguing that there is no legal or structural impediment to the imposition of obligations on states under

DOI: 10.4324/9781003164951-6

also because of increasing recognition that many investments have extensive impacts on the enjoyment of human rights by the local communities where the investments are made. Clear and unambiguous language about human rights obligations are needed for establishing a balance between investor rights and the rights of other stakeholders.[4] This would provide investment tribunals with contextual reference for interpreting substantive obligations, such as FET.[5] Imposing human rights obligations on investors and states would also ensure the legal relevance of human rights to the adjudication of investment claims.[6] Integration of human rights obligations can make investment treaties more balanced and can address many of the concerns regarding the legitimacy of investment arbitration. The express reference to human rights and public policy goals in investment treaty and existence of exception clauses by which host states may derogate from investor protections can contribute to the consistent and persuasive reasoning of the tribunal dealing with the dispute in question.[7]

Human rights and environmental obligations in BITs can be formulated in both passive and active ways. A Passive obligation refers to foreign investors refraining from an activity that would violate human or labour rights, damage the environment or constitute corruption. Conversely, an active obligation makes a development contribution.[8] Integration of human rights obligations in BITs can afford arbitral tribunals to hold investors accountable, and to compensate individual victims for violations of human rights. However, any effort of integration should require a review of existing BITs to examine relevant clauses which conflict with the ability of the host states to comply with their human rights obligations and if needed, to renegotiate them.[9] A sunset clause may be incorporated into BITs, allowing them to be revised if it appears that they conflict with the commitments of States towards fulfilling their human

an investment treaty to meet certain basic human rights duties through the implementation of legislation or regulations designed to fully meet their duties under international human rights law) 12.

4 *Human Rights, Trade and Investment Matters*, Amnesty International UK (May 2006) 20.

5 Andrew Newcombe, 'Sustainable Development and Investment Treaty Law' (2007) 8(3) *Journal of World Investment and Trade* 405.

6 Luke Eric Peterson, 'Human Rights and BITs: Mapping the Role of Human Rights in Investor-State Arbitration' Rights and Democracy, International Centre for Human Rights and Democratic Development, Canada (2009) 35.

7 Daniel Kalderimis, 'Investment Treaties and Public Good' *A Paper Presented to Asian International Economic Law Network Inaugural Conference*, 29 June 2009.

8 UNCTAD Report, 'Development Implications of International Investment Agreements' IIA Monitor No. 2 (2007), United Nations, Geneva, 2007.

9 Olivier De Schutter, 'Transnational Corporations as Instrument of Human Development' in Philip Alston and Mary Robinson (eds), *Human Rights and Development: Towards Mutual Reinforcement* (Oxford University Press 2005) 436.

rights obligations.[10] Moreover, future BITs should be drafted in line with the argument of imposition of direct human rights obligation.[11]

In recent years, IIAs have increasingly incorporated provisions to encourage and ensure environmental conservation in developing countries. A notable example of this trend is reflected in the agreements concluded in 2023. Out of 15 IIAs finalized that year, 13 included explicit clauses stating that environmental measures by host state parties should not be relaxed to attract or further investment opportunities. These provisions underscore a growing recognition of the importance of maintaining robust environmental protections while fostering foreign investment, ensuring that SDGs are not compromised. For instance, Article 16 of the Japan-Mexico Economic Partnership Agreement, concluded in 2023, underscores that it is inappropriate to derogate from environmental protection measures to attract investment. This clause explicitly mandates that neither party should waive or reduce existing environmental regulations to encourage the establishment, expansion, or retention of an investor's project within the host state's territory. Such clauses demonstrate a trend towards embedding environmental protection within the framework of investment treaties.

There has also been progress in integrating human rights considerations into IIAs. For instance, Annex II of the Brazilian-Angolan Cooperation Agreement for the Promotion of Investments sets forth that investors must bear human rights norms in their business activities in accordance with the host State's human rights obligations. In the same vein, the Preamble of the 2018 EU-Singaporean Free Trade Agreement provides that parties must have regard to the principles set forth in the UDHR adopted by the General Assembly of the United Nations. These specific references to human rights treaties would allow any adjudicatory body to interpret investment treaties with regard to human rights instruments.

The arbitral jurisprudence also evolves in this direction. For instance, in *Urbaser v. Argentina*[12] the tribunal upheld jurisdiction over the host State's counterclaim for alleged violation of human rights by the foreign investors under the Spanish-Argentine BIT. In this case, Argentina's main argument was that the foreign investors had violated the principles of good faith and *pacta sunt servanda* by failing to comply with the Concession Contract. In this case, the tribunal also addressed, for the first time, Argentina's considerations on the basic human right of access to water services. In particular, the *Urbaser*

10 Olivier De Schutter, 'A Human Rights Approach to Trade and Investment Policies' *A Paper Presented to the Conference on Confronting the Global Food Challenge: Finding New Approaches to Trade and Investment That Support the Right to Food*, held on 24–26 November 2008, Geneva, Switzerland, 15.

11 Ryan Suda, 'The Effect of Bilateral Investment Treaties on Human Rights Enforcement and Realization' Hauser Global Law School Program, Global Law Working Paper 01/05, New York University School of Law, New York.

12 ICSID Case No. ARB/07/26.

tribunal noted that '[t]he BIT has to be construed in harmony with other rules of international law of which it forms part, including those relating to human rights'.

Implied reference to human rights also can be made when state parties make commitment to internationally recognized standards of CSR. For example, the 2017 amendment to the Canada-Chile investment chapter in their FTA provides that:

> The Parties reaffirm their commitment to internationally recognized standards, guidelines and principles of corporate social responsibility that have been endorsed or are supported by the Parties, including the OECD Guidelines for Multinational Enterprises, and each Party should encourage enterprises operating within its territory or subject to its jurisdiction to voluntarily incorporate these standards, guidelines and principles into their business practices and internal policies.

Despite the progress in integrating human rights and environmental protections into investment frameworks, very few IIAs explicitly refer to human rights obligations. An example of an attempt to incorporate human rights is found in Article 7.2.d of the Common Market for Eastern and Southern Africa (COMESA) Agreement, which includes human rights and other social issues within the institutional structure established to implement the Agreement (COMESA Common Investment Area Committee). This provision allows the COMESA Agreement to consider and promote respect for human rights.[13] However, it is important to note that the COMESA Agreement is not yet in force. The lack of explicit recognition of human rights and sustainable development principles in IIAs limits the ability to create enforceable obligations for foreign investors to respect human rights and environmental protections. This absence acts as a counterbalance to the rights granted to investors, highlighting a significant gap in the current framework of international investment law.[14]

13 It reads as follows: 'recommendations to the (COMESA) council on any policy issues that need to be made to enhance the objectives of this Agreement. For example the development of common minimum standards relating to investment in area such as: (i) environmental impact and social impact assessments; (ii) labour standards; (iii) respect for human rights; (iv) conduct in conflict zones; (v) corruption and (vi) subsidies'. See the reference and discussion, Howard Mann, 'International Investment Agreements, Business and Human Rights: Key Issues and Opportunities' *International Institute for Sustainable Development*, February 2008, 10.

14 See generally IISD Model Agreement on Investment for Sustainable Development, International Institute for Sustainable Development; Suda (n 11); Newcombe (n 5) (he argues that at a minimum, some responsibilities to comply with the ILO Tripartite Declaration of Principles of Multinational Enterprises and the OECD Guidelines for Multinational Enterprises would be desirable).

While Chapter 4 of this book has analysed how principles and norms that establish the framework of international investment law, such as NT, are increasingly integrating human rights and environmental protection doctrines, this chapter will examine the mechanisms used within regional and bilateral treaties and their impact on a host state's obligations for environmental protection and human rights. This chapter will focus on treaty interpretation as a tool for balancing and conflict avoidance, highlighting the importance of exception clauses in BITs and applicable laws for integrating environmental protection and human rights into the investment treaty regime.

Integrating Human Rights and Sustainable Development Into Regional and Bilateral Investment Agreements: Practical Considerations

The direct obligation on foreign investors involves consideration of many practical problems. The inclusion of human rights obligations in investment treaties would necessarily require greater human rights expertise on the part of arbitrators, granting these tribunals greater authority as human rights concerns would then be elaborated and interpreted.[15] Arbitrators rarely have clear human rights law expertise or experience in the human rights law field.[16] The introduction of human rights obligations may create major drafting and negotiating problems, including which categories of human rights are considered, how detailed human rights standards should be and the level of political willingness of the parties to BITs to protect, promote and respect human right standards.[17] Criticism is also levelled against integration of human rights issues within an investment treaty on the ground that it can make it too broad and complex. Despite these practical problems, the eventual inclusion of certain commitments to human rights in future BITs cannot be ruled out due to the continued call for greater legitimacy of investment law along with advocacy from NGOs and other civil society groups, plus affected communities for corporate responsibilities.[18]

However, such an integration of human rights obligations in BITs does not mean that arbitral tribunals would become a forum for adjudicating FDI-related human rights claims against investors, rather it would facilitate

15 Luke Eric Peterson and R. Gray Kevin, 'International Human Rights in Bilateral Investment Treaties and in Investment Treaty Arbitration' *A Paper Presented by the International Institute for Sustainable Development (IISD) for the Swiss Department of Foreign Affairs*, 2003.

16 Ibid.

17 Peter Muchlinski, 'Corporate Social Responsibility and International Investment Law' in P. Muchlinski, F. Ortino and Ch. Schreuer (eds), *The Oxford Handbook of International Investment Law* (Oxford University Press 2008) 681.

18 Ibid. 682.

the consideration of human rights norms in investment treaty arbitration.[19] In order to address the potential drawback of inclusion of human rights in BITs, 'NGOs and other international organizations with relevant expertise can be part of the process, either during the tribunal selection or during the hearings, mirroring the NAFTA model of labour and environment side agreements.'[20] They can take part in arbitral proceedings through submission of amicus curiae briefs for raising voice to the concerns of indigenous or local communities, who are hardly represented in such tribunals. Amicus submissions also aim to assist the courts or tribunals by broadening their perspective on controversial issues[21] and interpreting public interest. However, existing arbitral rules and procedure do not allow such amicus curiae submissions, which results in exclusion of much needed third-party representation in arbitral proceedings. Only in a few instances have arbitral tribunals allowed amicus curiae submissions. For example, in *Suez, Sociedad General de Aguas de Barcelona, S.A., and Vivendi Universal, S.A. v. Argentine Republic,* the arbitral tribunal responded to a petition for transparency and participation filed by five international NGOs as amici curiae.[22]

Most importantly, the integration of human rights obligations depends upon on the bargaining strength of the capital importing countries who sign BITs and formulation of language of model BITs. Under the prevailing situation of investment law framework, any binding human rights obligations on investors are highly unlikely as capital exporting countries, which are mostly developed and industrialized states, have the dominant position during the negotiation of a BIT. But at the same time, given the absence of a multilateral treaty on investment, BIT offers the flexibility to impose some responsibilities for violations of human rights.[23]

19 Leyla Davarnejad, 'Strengthening the Social Dimension of International Investment Agreements by Integrating Codes of Conduct for Multinational Enterprises' Global Forum on International Investment, 27–28 March 2008.

20 Chalamish (n 3) 352–353.

21 Katia Fach Gómez, 'Rethinking the Role of Amicus Curiae in International Investment Arbitration: How to Draw the Line Favorably for the Public Interest' (2012) 35(2) *Fordham International Law Journal* 517.

22 *Suez, Sociedad General de Aguas de Barcelona, S.A., & Vivendi Universal, S.A* v. *Arg. Republic,* ICSID Case No. ARB/03/19, Order in Response to a Petition by Five Non-Governmental Organizations for Permission to Make an Amicus Curiae Submission (12 February 2007), http://icsid.worldbank.org/ICSID/FrontServlet?requestType=CasesRH&actionVal=showDoc&docId=DC693_En&caseId=C19 See also, *Methanex Corp. v. United States Case*, 4 I.L.M. 1345, ¶ 1 (NAFTA Arb. 2005); *United Parcel Service of America, Inc. v. Canada,* Decision on Petitions for Intervention and Participation as Amici Curiae, ¶ 63 (NAFTA Arb. 2001); *Glamis Gold Ltd. v. United States,* Award ¶ 11 (NAFTA Arb. 2009).

23 See Chalamish (n 3) (a mechanism that already allows non-state actors such as MNCs to sue host states directly should be normatively justified in imposing responsibilities on the same MNCs, and where appropriate, finding them accountable for human rights violations) 351.

Substantive Provisions of BITs: Implications for Human Rights

To overcome the challenges hindering the greater integration of human rights and environmental protection into IIAs, there are several reform opportunities that could establish a more robust regulatory framework, thereby imposing stronger protections on foreign investors.

Definition of Investment and Investors

In most BITs, the definition of investment is broad and open-ended, encompassing various assets such as physical property, intellectual property, financial instruments, and contractual rights. A broader and open-ended scope of the definition of covered investment in a BIT has implications for the capacity of host states to regulate TNCs on their territories, since this increases the range of protected assets of other provisions in the BIT.[24] Arguably the broader definition expands the discretion of arbitrators to assume jurisdiction over claims, as well as the potential liability of the state in public law.[25] Most of the definition of investment is an asset-based approach. Such a definition not only covers capital but every kind of asset of an investor in the territory of the host country.[26] For instance, in 2021, ICSID reported a record number of cases, reflecting the rising trend of investor-state disputes, often favouring investors. Attempts to limit investment definitions include clauses requiring investments to be made 'in accordance with host state law', as seen in recent BITs like the Canada-Tanzania BIT, which mandates adherence to environmental regulations. ICSID tribunals have upheld these clauses, as demonstrated in cases where investments violating local laws were denied protection, reinforcing the host state's regulatory authority. However, the broad definitions and protective measures can lead to a regulatory chilling effect, discouraging states from implementing necessary regulations due to fear of arbitration. Therefore, while BITs aim to attract foreign investment, they also necessitate a careful balance to ensure host states can effectively regulate in the public interest without undermining their policy space.

There is some attempt to limit the scope of investment. For instance, many BITs contain a clause that investment be made in 'accordance with host state

24 Suda (n 11).

25 Gus Van Harten, *Investment Treaty Arbitration and Public Law* (Oxford University Press 2007) 80 (the broader the definition, the more likely the treaty can credibly be applied to future forms of regulation in the light of technological change or innovation in legal forms and business strategies).

26 For policy implications on broad definition of investment, see Barton Legum, 'Defining Investment and Investor: Who Is Entitled to Claim?' (2006) 22(4) *Arbitration International* 521–526 (the author concluded that broader definition of investor and investment combine effectively to transform the obligations of BIT into an obligation that the host state must consider potentially applicable to all investors) 525.

law'.[27] Consequently, investment protection is extended only to investments 'made in accordance with the laws, policies and regulations of the host state'.[28] Generally, these clauses can be found in the definition of investment, but they can also be inserted in provisions on protection, admission or promotion.[29] Such a clause will obviously provide a greater scope of control of investment by host states. In two recent decisions, ICSID tribunals declined jurisdiction after having found that the investment agreements had been concluded in breach of local law.[30] Thus it is evident that only investment which conforms to the state's regulatory structure will receive protection under such treaties.[31]

Although the nexus between human rights and this provision has not been raised in arbitration, it implies that the foreign investor will be subjected to the general legal framework consisting of tax laws, labour laws, environmental laws and human rights laws and will have to abide by these laws and regulations. This investment provision has the consequences that BITs are not meant to protect investments made in breach of the local laws of the host state.[32] In *Ioannis Karadassopoulos v. Georgia*, the tribunal underscored this limitation by stating:

> Protection of investments made under a BIT is obviously not without some limits. It does not extend, for instance, to an investor making an investment in breach of the local laws of the host state. A State thus retains a degree of control over foreign investments by denying BIT protection to those investments that do not comply with its laws.[33]

Similarly, in *Salini Costruttori S.p.A. and Italstrade S.p.A. v. Morocco*, the tribunal asserted that the provision defining investment in accordance with the law aims 'to prevent the Bilateral Treaty from protecting investments that should not be protected, particularly because they would be illegal'.[34]

27 See for detailed discussion, C. Knahr, 'Investments in Accordance with Host State Law' (2007) 4(5) *Transnational Dispute Settlement*.
28 For instance, the Malaysian Model Treaty, 2002.
29 Article 2 and 3 of the Spain-Ecuador BIT.
30 *Inceysa Vallisoletana S.L. v. Republic of El Salvador* (Inceysa) Award, 2 August 2006, available at http://ita.law.univic.ca/documents/Inceysa_Vallisoletana_en_000.pdf, accessed 23 May 2022; *Fraport AG Frankfurt Airport Services Worldwide v. Republic of the Philippines* (Fraport), Award 16 August 2007, available at http://ita.law.univic.ca/documents/FraportAward.pdf, accessed 12 April 2022.
31 Anna Joubin-Bret, 'Admission and Establishment in the Context of Investment Protection' in August Reinisch (ed), *Standards of Investment Protection* (Oxford University Press 2008) 9–28.
32 See arbitral awards, *Salini v. Morocco*, ICSID case no. ARB/00/4, Decisions on Jurisdiction, 23 July 2001; *Tokios Tokeles v. Ukraine*, ICSID case No. ARB/02/18, Decision on Jurisdiction, 29 April 2004; *Bayindir v. Pakistan*, ICSID case No. ARB/02/3, Decision on Jurisdiction 14 November 2005.
33 ICSID case No. ARB/05/18, Decision on Jurisdiction 6 July 2007, para. 182.
34 Decision on Jurisdiction, 23 July 2001, 6 ICSID Reports 400, para. 46.

So far as an investor is concerned, most BITs define nationality of investors based on situs of incorporation, which effectively allows investors to adopt a 'home state of convenience' and 'treaty-shop' for favourable investment treaty provisions.[35] In other words, investors whose home state has not signed an investment treaty with the host state can elect a home state of convenience in order to bring arbitration proceedings. Many BITs cover indirectly controlled investments through a special definition of 'investor' or 'national' which encompasses companies controlled by their citizens or by companies' organizations under their laws.[36] This flexibility in definition ensures that even where a treaty is not in place between an investor's home country and its intended destination-country, a foreign investment transaction may still be protected by some treaty.[37] Thus, with the proliferation of investment treaties, investors have more treaties that they can use to sue States.

Another way that host states can lose control over investment is by accepting BITs which regulate entry and treatment in the same manner. Generally, BITs focus primarily on the treatment of foreign investments after they have been admitted into the host state. This allows host states to maintain control over the entry of foreign investments into their territories. However, model BITs, such as those of the United States, include provisions applicable to the pre-establishment phase of investments. These provisions 'may affect the capacity of the host state to prioritize certain investments over others and undermine its negotiating power vis-à-vis incoming investors'.[38] Therefore greater clarification on the scope of what constitutes an investment and the identification of foreign investors who benefit from IIAs is crucial. This will help determine which investors and what types of capital should be subject to enhanced human rights and environmental protection obligations imposed by host states.

Protection Against Expropriation

BITs invariably offer protection against both direct and indirect expropriation. However, the provisions within investment treaties often lack a precise definition of indirect expropriation. The broad and open-textured language used in these definitions can encompass a wide range of state activities undertaken for public purposes, which may interfere with an investor's property rights. This expansive interpretation of expropriation, along with the potential requirement

35 Luke Eric Peterson, R. Gray Kevin (n 17) 22.

36 For instance, BIT between Netherlands and Venezuela, 1991 (nationals shall comprise legal persons not constituted under the law of that Contracting Party but controlled, directly or indirectly, by natural person . . . or by legal persons). Art. 1. See also, French, Canadian and US BITs.

37 Peterson (n 6) 18.

38 Lorenzo Cotula, 'Investment Treaties' *Briefing* 2, International Institute for Environment and Development, London, August 2007.

for compensation, can undermine the ability of host states to introduce new legislation aimed at public interest and development goals. Furthermore, it may inhibit states from enforcing their laws or complying with international human rights agreements.[39] This is evident by the recent arbitral jurisprudence that predominantly focuses on the effects of regulations on investors rather than considering the intention, context and purpose behind the regulations.[40] This approach has significant ramifications, as it hampers host states' ability to enforce more stringent human rights and environmental protection measures on foreign investments. The resulting legal ambiguity contributes to regulatory hesitation, leading to a reluctance among regulators to impose necessary protections, thereby causing a regulatory freeze.

A quintessential example of the application of the 'sole effects' test is the *Metalclad* case.[41] In this instance a US investor, Metalclad Corporation, acquired land in Mexico for the purpose of operating a hazardous waste landfill. The company obtained assurances from the federal government that the necessary permits would be granted. However, local authorities later refused to issue the required operating permits, effectively preventing the landfill from becoming operational.

The arbitral tribunal held that the actions of the Mexican government, particularly the local authorities' refusal to grant the operating permits, deprived Metalclad of the ability to use its property for its intended purpose. The tribunal determined that this constituted an act of indirect expropriation, as it had a significant adverse impact on the investment despite the absence of a formal expropriation decree.[42] Another award that should be mentioned in this regard is the *Tecmed* case,[43] which further illustrates the application of the 'sole effects' test. In this case the claimant, a Spanish investor, operated a hazardous waste landfill in Mexico. The Mexican government refused to renew the necessary operating license, citing environmental concerns and public protests that posed threats of civil disturbance. Despite Mexico's justification for its actions based on environmental protection and the need to maintain public order, the arbitral tribunal concluded that these reasons did not justify the effective expropriation of the claimant's investment. The tribunal determined that the denial of the license had significant negative effects on the claimant's investment and its rights, thereby constituting an expropriation.[44]

39 UNCTAD World Investment Report 2003.

40 For instance, the tribunal in *Santa Elena* case concluded: 'the fact that the expropriation was made with the aim of protecting the environment does not have any impact on the legal character of expropriation or the amount of compensation'. *Compania del Desarrollo de Santa Elena v. Costa Rica*, ICSID Case ARB/96/1, Award, 17 February 2000, para. 71.

41 *Metalclad Corporation v. United Mexican States*, ICSID Case No. ARB(AF)/97/1.

42 *Metalclad Corp. v. United Mexican States*, Award, ICSID (Additional Facility) Case No. ARB (AF)/97/1, 30 August 2000, 16 ICSID Rev.-FILJ (2001), 168.

43 *Tecnicas Medioambientales Tecmed S.A. v. Mexico*, Award of May, 2003, 43 ILM 133 (2004).

44 Para. 151 of the Judgement.

The tribunal's decision emphasized that the adverse impact on the investment outweighed the stated environmental and public order concerns. The *SD Myers* case presents a contrasting example where a NAFTA tribunal held that Canada was required to pay damages for blocking the export of hazardous waste to the United States. This decision, like others, underscores the expansive reach of the sole effect doctrine, wherein any government measure affecting an investor's property can be deemed expropriation, despite involving sensitive public interest issues.[45] The regulatory measures that may be challenged as expropriation can include land reform policies and other redistributionist policy initiatives, and affirmative action policies for indigenous communities. In *Tecmed v. Mexico*[46] the ICSID tribunal acknowledged that non-discriminatory measures taken by states in response to public concerns about health and environmental threats could constitute expropriation. However, the tribunal also applied a proportionality test in interpreting FET. It observed that tribunals might take public interests into account and balance them against investor rights when assessing whether there has been a breach of the applicable BIT.

The United Nations High Commissioner for Human Rights has noted that 'to the extent that broad interpretations of expropriation provisions could affect States' willingness or capacity to introduce new measures to promote and protect human rights, then the use and interpretation of expropriation provisions is a cause of concern'.[47] For instance, in *Philip Morris v. Uruguay* the tribunal recognized Uruguay's right to regulate in the public interest, particularly in the area of public health. Uruguay had implemented stringent tobacco control measures, which Philip Morris claimed amounted to expropriation. The tribunal, however, upheld Uruguay's actions, emphasizing the state's right to protect public health. Another pertinent example is the *Vattenfall v. Germany* case, where Vattenfall, a Swedish energy company, challenged Germany's decision to phase out nuclear power following the Fukushima disaster. The tribunal had to balance Germany's right to ensure public safety and environmental protection against the investor's claims of expropriation and unfair treatment.

International law generally acknowledges that measures taken in accordance with a state's police powers are not prohibited. In the context of regulatory takings, it is crucial to distinguish between the concepts of eminent domain and police power, which serve to differentiate government regulations based on their

45 The sole effects doctrine under investment law jurisprudence prescribes that in the assessment of indirect expropriation claims, tribunals should primarily—or exclusively—base their findings on the effect that the disputed measure had on the investment.

46 *Tecnicas Medioambientales Tecmed S.A. v. United Mexican States, ICSID Case No. ARB(AF)/00/2.*

47 Human Rights, Trade and Investment, Report of the High Commissioner for Human Rights, U.N. Economic and Social Council, at 6, U.N. Doc. E/CN.4/Sub.2/2003/9 (2 July 2003).

purposes.[48] The power of eminent domain refers to the authority of a government to acquire private property, whether tangible or intangible, with the obligation to provide just compensation to the owner. This power is considered an inherent attribute of sovereignty and is typically invoked for public purposes such as infrastructure development, urban renewal or national defence. The distinction between eminent domain and police power is prominent in domestic takings laws, such as those found in the constitutional jurisprudence of the United States. The takings clause of the Fifth Amendment to the US Constitution stipulates that private property cannot be taken for public use without just compensation. This principle ensures that while the government retains the right to expropriate property, it must fairly compensate the affected property owners.[49] This principle is considered as an implicit term in contractual obligations.[50]

On the other hand, in the United States, it is widely recognized that general legislation enacted for the protection of public health, safety or general welfare—actions falling under the police power—does not constitute the taking of property, even if such legislation interferes with contract rights.[51] Consequently, in most cases involving legitimate regulations based on police power, the government is not required to provide compensation to the affected private entity. This distinction between eminent domain and police power has also been a key issue in international arbitration, particularly in the Iran-US Claims Tribunal. In the case of *Too v. Greater Modesto Insurance Associates*,[52] the tribunal addressed a claim for compensation following the seizure of a liquor license by the US Internal Revenue Service. The claimant argued that this seizure amounted to expropriation. However, the tribunal rejected the claim, ruling that the action fell within the scope of police power. The Tribunal noted:

> 'A State is not responsible for loss of property or for other economic disadvantage resulting from bona fide general taxation or any other action that is commonly accepted as within the police power of States, provided it is not discriminatory and is not designed to cause the alien to abandon the property or to sell it at a distress price'.[53]

48 James N. Hyde, 'Economic Development Agreements' *Recueil des Cours*, The Hague, 1962 (I) 298.

49 The Fifth Amendment of the US Constitution holds: 'nor shall private property be taken for public use, without just compensation'; it refers to the eminent domain doctrine and the just compensation requirement for taking of property.

50 The contract clause of the United States reads: 'No State shall pass any law impairing the obligations of Contracts.' US Constitution Art. 1, Section 10, Clause 1.

51 F.A. Mann, 'State Contracts and State Responsibility' (1960) 54 *American Journal of International Law* 572; see also, Jan G. Laitos, 'The Public Use Paradox and the Taking Clause' (1993) 13 *Journal of Energy, Natural Resources, and Environment* 9 (on distinction between eminent domain and police power).

52 23 Iran-US Claim Tribunal Report (1989-III), p. 378.

53 Ibid, p. 387. See also *Sedco, Inc. v. National Iranian Oil Co.*, Interlocutory Award, 9 Iran-US Claim Tribunal Report (1985), 248, 275. It was held that an accepted principle

This judgement upheld the states' regulatory power for public cause as a legitimate objective of police power provided that it is not discriminatory.

A Similar decision was taken in other jurisdictions. For example, in the *Saluka Investments* case,[54] the Japanese Bank Nomura invested in a privatized Czech bank in 1998. Its subsidiary, Saluka, brought a claim under the Netherlands–Czech Republic BIT, arguing that the Czech Republic's provision of state aid to rival unprivatized banks rendered its investment valueless. The Czech Republic counterclaimed, attempting to hold Nomura responsible for the state aid later given to the successor of the Czech bank in which Nomura had invested.

Saluka based its claim on the alleged breach of Article 3 of the Netherlands–Czech Republic BIT, asserting that the Czech Republic failed to accord its investment FET. Additionally, Saluka claimed that by violating Article 5, the Czech Republic unlawfully deprived it of its investment without just compensation equivalent to the genuine value of the investment.

The tribunal acknowledged that Article 5 of the Netherlands–Czech Republic BIT reflects customary international law, which states that a country is not required to pay compensation to a foreign investor when it enacts bona fide, non-discriminatory regulations aimed at the general welfare in the normal exercise of its regulatory powers. The tribunal concluded that the Czech Republic did not 'cross that line' and did not breach Article 5. However, it found the Czech Republic liable for violating the FET standard under Article 3 of the BIT. In the case of *Saluka Investments*, the Tribunal held that:

> a state does not commit an expropriation and is thus not liable to pay compensation to a dispossessed alien investor when it adopts general regulations that are commonly accepted as within the police power of States.[55]

The *Continental Casualty* case[56] illustrates how tribunals attempt to balance claims of indirect expropriation against a state's legitimate regulatory powers. In this case, a US investor sued Argentina under the US-Argentina BIT in response to emergency measures Argentina implemented during its financial

of international law that a State is not liable for economic injury which is a consequence of bonafide regulation, 'within the accepted police power of states'. See also, The Restatement (Third) of the Foreign Relations Law of the United States: which states that 'a State need not provide compensation for loss of property or for other economic disadvantage resulting from bonafide general taxation, regulation, forfeiture for crime, or other action of the kind that is commonly accepted as within the police power of states, if it is not discriminatory and is not designed to cause the alien to abandon the property to the state or sell it at a distress price'. 712.

54 *Saluka Investment BV v. Czech Republic* (Saluka case), PCA, UNCITRAL, Partial Award, 17 March 2006.

55 *Saluka Investment BV v. Czech Republic* (Saluka case), PCA, UNCITRAL, Partial Award, 17 March 2006, paras 253–265.

56 *Continental Casualty Company v. Argentina*, ICSID Case No. ARB/03/9, Award 5 September 2008.

crisis. Continental Casualty, through its subsidiary CAN ART in Argentina, provided worker's compensation insurance. The investor claimed that CAN ART's investment portfolio, which included cash deposits, treasury bills and government bonds, was indirectly expropriated due to Argentina's measures to restrict the rescheduling of cash deposits, specify the terms of US dollar deposits, impose restrictions on external transfers and restructure treasury bill obligations. The tribunal accepted Argentina's necessity defence, acknowledging the severity of the financial crisis, and concluded that no indirect expropriation had occurred. However, it emphasized that legitimate governmental regulation could amount to expropriation if it affected an investment in an 'intolerable, discriminatory, or disproportionate' manner.[57] The tribunal acknowledged:

> in different historical and social contexts the line has been drawn differently and that different international tribunals, including arbitration tribunals under various BIT, have relied on different criteria and have given different weight to them, such as those recognizing public interest on the one side and those protecting the integrity of property rights on the other.[58]

This balancing test is also applied by other investment tribunals to assess the proportionality of state measures in relation to their objectives and their discriminatory nature. Such an approach aligns more consistently with the protection of human rights by the host state through bona fide regulation. Additionally, it is recognized that temporary regulations or those that merely reduce the profitability of an investment without shutting it down completely and leaving the investor in control are generally not considered expropriation.[59]

Performance Requirements

Performance requirements are regulatory measures imposed by host states on foreign investors to ensure that their investments contribute to local development. These requirements can include stipulations related to local content, export performance, joint ventures and equity ownership, technology transfer, research and development, and the employment of nationals. The primary goal is to ensure that foreign investments benefit the host economy by fostering local content, creating linkages, transferring managerial techniques, employing local nationals, investing in underdeveloped regions and promoting exports.[60]

57 Ibid.

58 Ibid.

59 *Corn Products v. United Mexican States*, ICSID Case No. ARB (AF)/04/1 (2008).

60 Federico Ortino, 'Non-Discriminatory Treatment in Investment Disputes' in Pierre-Marie Dupuy, Francesco Francioni and Ernest-Ulrich Petersmann (eds), *Human Rights in International Investment Law and Arbitration* (Oxford University Press 2009) 347.

Host states seek to use performance requirements because they are 'an important policy tool to enhance the benefit of inward Foreign Direct Investment (FDI)'.[61] For instance, local content requirements mandate that foreign investors source a certain percentage of their inputs locally, thereby stimulating local industries and creating jobs. Technology transfer requirements ensure that advanced technologies and know-how are shared with local firms, fostering innovation and enhancing productivity within the host country.

However, performance requirements are subject to regulation under agreements like NAFTA and numerous BITs. Recent BITs, particularly those concluded by the United States, often include provisions that partially or entirely prohibit performance requirements. These prohibitions aim to enhance the efficiency of investments by reducing the regulatory burden on investors. However, they can also limit the ability of host states to realize the economic and social rights of local communities. For example, restrictions on local content requirements can disadvantage local suppliers and businesses that are unable to compete with foreign firms operating under less stringent regulations.[62] Prohibiting performance requirements may confer an undue advantage to foreign investors over domestic businesses, which may face stricter regulations regarding sourcing production materials. This can exacerbate inequalities and limit the developmental benefits of FDI. Additionally, maintaining flexibility in the use of performance requirements, such as employment or local content mandates, is crucial for promoting the rights of cultural or linguistic minorities and implementing affirmative action schemes to enhance employment opportunities for disadvantaged or under-represented groups.

A recent example illustrating these dynamics is the CPTPP, which includes provisions that limit the use of performance requirements among its member states. While these limitations aim to create a more investment-friendly environment, they also restrict the policy space available to host countries to leverage FDI for broader developmental goals.

The Umbrella Clause

Umbrella clauses in investment treaties are designed to afford legal protection to foreign investments in various ways. Generally, these clauses aim to transform contractual commitments made by host states into international obligations, thereby enabling foreign investors to bring claims directly before international arbitral bodies without resorting to national courts. A typical umbrella clause usually obligates the contracting state to observe contractual

61 Aaron Cosbey, 'International Investment Agreements and Sustainable Development: Achieving the Millennium Development Goals' International Institute for Sustainable Development, September 2005, available at http://www.iisd.org.

62 UNESC Report at 31(b).

commitments under the investment agreements.[63] In other words, umbrella clauses turn contractual obligations into international obligations. As a result, a foreign investor can bring related claims directly before an international arbitral body obviating the necessity of filing a claim with national courts. Many multilateral and BITs make provision for umbrella clauses to protect the State's contractual commitment to the foreign investor.[64] For instance, Article 10 of the ECT provides: 'Each contracting party shall observe any obligations it has entered into with an investor or an investment of an investor of any other contracting party.'[65] Similarly, BITs may also provide for the umbrella clause. A typical example of an umbrella clause in a BIT is:

> Each contracting party shall observe any obligation arising from a particular commitment it may have entered into with regard to a specific investment of nationals or companies of the other contracting parties.[66]

Although investment arbitration tribunals under BITs usually have jurisdiction over disputes under treaty, they sometimes exercise jurisdiction to adjudicate breaches of investment-related State contracts by virtue of the umbrella clause.[67] The question arises whether the umbrella clause obligates the host state to observe the state contract as well as the treaty obligation, or does it only apply to treaty obligations rather than contractual obligations under investment agreements. It is sometimes contended that by virtue of the umbrella clause under these treaties, the obligation to comply with the contract becomes an international obligation, and the conflict between the contract commitments of the state and its sovereign prerogatives is resolved in favour of the primacy of the contractual obligations. Consequently, this provision would make a breach of a contractual

63 See for detailed discussion on the subject, Thomas W. Walde, 'The "Umbrella" Clause in Investment Arbitration: A Comment on Original Intentions and Recent Cases' (2005) 6 *The Journal of World Investment and Trade* 183–236. See also, the OECD study on umbrella clause "Interpretation of the Umbrella Clause in Investment Agreements" (October 2006) (Working Papers on International Investment, no. 2006/3), available at www.oecd.org/investment.

64 See, Maria Cristina Griton Salias, 'Do Umbrella Clauses Apply to Unilateral Undertakings?' in Christina Binder et al. (eds), *International Investment Law For the 21st Century: Essays in Honour of Christoph Schreuer* (Oxford University Press 2009) 490–496. (Where it is stated that the umbrella clause is applicable to obligations assumed unilaterally by host states. It follows that, where a treaty for the protection of investments containing an umbrella clause is applicable, the violation of a unilateral undertaking, made through legislation or otherwise, would amount to a violation of the treaty.) 495.

65 The Energy Charter Treaty is available at https://www.energycharter.org/fileadmin/DocumentsMedia/Legal/1994_ECT.pdf.

66 UK-Philippines Bilateral Investment Treaties (1981) Art. 3(3).

67 Anthony Sinclair, 'Bridging the Contract/Treaty Divide' in Christina Binder et al. (eds), *International Investment Law For the 21st Century: Essays in Honour of Christoph Schreuer* (Oxford University Press 2009) 92–104.

or other obligation towards an investor at the same time a breach of the investment treaty.[68] Thus the legal relationship between the investor and the state becomes internationalized through the incorporation of the umbrella clause in the treaty.[69]

The argument that the incorporation of an umbrella clause elevates a contractual claim against the host state to an international treaty claim remains contentious and lacks definitive support from arbitral tribunals constituted under the relevant BITs. The issue was first raised in the case of *SGS v. Pakistan*[70] and *SGS v. Philippines*.[71] Article II of the Switzerland-Pakistan BIT provided: 'either Contracting Party shall constantly guarantee the observance of commitments it has entered into with a respect to the investments of the investors of the other Contracting Party', and Article X(2) of the Philippines-Switzerland BIT stated: 'each Contracting Party shall observe any obligation it has assumed with regard to specific investments in its territory by investors of the other Contracting Party'. Both tribunals refused to entertain purely contractual claims despite the presence of an umbrella clause, as they were concerned about opening the floodgates to numerous contractual claims if such cases were permitted. Consequently, the inclusion of an umbrella clause in BITs merely codifies the existing principle of *pacta sunt servanda* (agreements must be kept) within treaty law. The presence of an umbrella clause in a BIT does not transform the legal nature of an investment contract into that of an international treaty claim.[72] This distinction maintains the separation between contractual obligations and treaty protections, ensuring that not all breaches of contract automatically escalate to treaty violations. Therefore an umbrella clause reinforces the sanctity of investment contract, though it does not elevate the contract to the status of treaty.

Arbitral tribunals have exhibited expansive but inconsistent interpretations of umbrella clauses, particularly regarding a state's failure to fulfil obligations to a claimant's local subsidiary. These divergent decisions significantly impact the application of umbrella clauses and the level of protection afforded to investors. For instance, the tribunals in the *Azurix* and *Siemens* cases refused to apply the umbrella clause to contracts entered into by the claimant's subsidiaries. Conversely, the tribunals in the *CMS, Enron* and *Sempra* cases found

68 F.A. Mann, 'British Investment Treaties for the Promotion and Protection of Investments' (1981) 52 *British Year Book of International Law*241, 246; G. Schwarzenberger, *Foreign Investments* (Stevens 1969).

69 Ibid.

70 *SGS v. Pakistan* (2003) (ICSID Case No. ARB/01/13).

71 *SGS v. Philippines* (2004) (ICSID Case No. ARB/02/6).

72 See also James Crawford, 'Treaty Contract in Investment Arbitration' *The 22nd Freshfields Lecture on International Arbitration*, London 29 November 2007 (proposing an integrationist model of umbrella clause which allows it to be operative and form the basis for a substantive treaty, but it does not convert a contractual claim into a treaty claim.).

that the respondent state breached the umbrella clause by failing to fulfil its contractual obligations to the claimant's local subsidiaries.[73]

In the arbitral award of *LG&E v. Argentine Republic*, the tribunal applied the umbrella clause to the government's legislative guarantees of investment protection. These guarantees included promises of a reasonable return on investment, protections against currency exchange and inflation, and assurances against unilateral changes as outlined in the Gas Law and its regulations.[74] The tribunal held that the legislative guarantees under the Gas Law and its regulations on investment protection were not legal obligations of a general nature, but they were specific obligations in relation to LG&E's investment in Argentina, meaning their abrogation would be a violation of the umbrella clause.[75] The tribunal further observed that the Gas Law and its regulations became obligations within the meaning of the umbrella clause in the investment treaty, which targeted foreign investors and applied specifically to their investments.[76] According to these arbitral awards, the umbrella clauses can be interpreted to give effect to the State's contractual commitments to the foreign investors by elevating such commitments to the level of treaty obligation. The broad interpretation given by the arbitral tribunals in these cases supports the expanded view of investor rights at the expense of the state right to regulate human rights or environmental matters under international law.[77] In such cases, a contractual obligation by the host state on environmental or human rights matters could become the subject of investment dispute.

The arbitral tribunal in the *El Paso Energy* case warned that the broad interpretation of the umbrella clauses would have 'far reaching consequences, quite destructive of the distinction between national legal orders and the international legal orders',[78] because a broad interpretation of umbrella clause can open the floodgates for an abuse of investment arbitration for the purpose of enforcing mere contract claims. The indeterminate scope of umbrella clauses can lead to a varying nature of their interpretation and an expanded notion of investment and rights of investors. The divergent interpretations of umbrella clauses underscore the need for clearer guidelines and consistent application to ensure predictability and balance in the protection of investments. Moreover, it is essential to strike a balance between investor protection and the regulatory autonomy of host states, particularly in areas such as human rights and environmental regulation.

73 Nick Gallus, 'An Umbrella Just for Two? BIT Obligations Observance Clause and the Parties to a Contract' (2008) 24(1) *Arbitration International* 157, 159.

74 ICSID Case No. ARB/02/1(Award of 3 October 2006), available at: www.investment-claims.com.

75 Para. 174.

76 Para. 175.

77 Howard Mann, 'International Investment Agreements, Business and Human Rights: Key Issues and Opportunities' *International Institute for Sustainable Development*, February 2008, 33.

78 Para. 82.

Transfer of Funds

Nearly all BITs guarantee investors the right to transfer their investments and any returns into a freely convertible currency. This right is crucial for ensuring that foreign investors can repatriate their profits, dividends and other returns without encountering restrictive barriers imposed by the host state. While these provisions are vital for fostering an attractive investment climate, they can pose significant challenges for host states, particularly during periods of economic instability. Allowing free transfers can lead to massive capital flight during economic crises, exacerbating the host country's financial problems.

To address these challenges, recent BITs often incorporate provisions that limit the right to free transfers under specific conditions. These limitations aim to balance protecting investor rights with safeguarding the host state's economic stability. Some restrictions are necessary to address balance of payments difficulties arising from exceptional economic or financial circumstances, support local industries and enhance the training and employment of nationals.

Exceptions Clauses in BITs: Gateways to Human Rights or Environmental Protection?

A noteworthy trend in modern IIAs is the increasing inclusion of non-precluded measure (NPM) clauses. These clauses allow states to adopt necessary measures for public policy objectives, such as national security, public health and environmental protection, without breaching their treaty obligations. This evolution signifies a significant shift in the objectives of IIAs, reflecting a growing commitment to sustainable development and the protection of fundamental rights alongside economic interests.

One key method for endorsing non-trade values, similar to the free trade exceptions found in Article XX of the GATT, is through the incorporation of general exceptions in FTAs. These exceptions are designed to ensure that FTAs do not undermine the protection offered by domestic environmental and labour laws.[79] By referring to these general exceptions, FTAs provide a safeguard that allows states to maintain their domestic regulations without breaching their trade obligations. This approach not only preserves the regulatory autonomy of states but also aligns trade policies with broader social and environmental goals.

Generally, NPM clauses in BITs share four elements.[80] First, the NPM clauses require a link between the measures adopted by the host state that might breach the treaty and the permissible objectives in the provision. Second, they define the breadth or scope of the NPM clause's application vis-à-vis the other

79 See for instance, Chile-Korea FTA, Art. 20.01.

80 William W. Burke-White and Andreas Van Staden, 'Investment Protection in Extraordinary Times: The Interpretation and Application of Non-Precluded Measures Provisions in Bilateral Investment Treaties' (2008) 48 *Virginia Journal of International Law* 309, 329.

treaty provisions. Third, they list the permissible objectives in pursuit of which measures deviate from other substantive treaty provisions not precluded by the BIT. Finally, these terms determine whether states or investors will bear the costs of state action in exceptional circumstances.

The comprehensiveness of these clauses varies; some apply to the entire treaty while others are limited to specific provisions. NAFTA,[81] along with its side agreements on labour and environmental standards, has set a precedent for incorporating non-trade values into trade agreements. This model requires parties to adopt and maintain domestic laws and policies that ensure high labour and environmental standards. Following this precedent, subsequent trade agreements have integrated similar provisions, albeit with variations. For instance, the Canada-Colombia Free Trade Agreement exemplifies this approach through Article 1703,[82] which outlines mutual obligations concerning environmental protection. Key elements include commitments to conserve, protect and improve the environment for the benefit of present and future generations, and a pledge not to derogate from domestic environmental laws to encourage trade or investment.

Furthermore, the agreement emphasizes the conservation and sustainable use of biological diversity, the protection of traditional knowledge, the development and enforcement of environmental laws, transparency, public participation in environmental matters and bilateral cooperation on environmental issues of common interest. Non-derogation provisions are another critical tool used in FTAs to uphold non-trade values. These provisions explicitly prevent states from lowering their human rights, social and environmental standards to promote trade or attract foreign investment. Such clauses are now a recurrent feature in modern FTAs. This clause underscores that trade and investment should not come at the expense of environmental protection.

In contrast, the Canada-Panama FTA employs more detailed language, stating:

> The Parties recognize that it is inappropriate to encourage investment by relaxing domestic health, safety, or environmental measures. Accordingly, a Party should not waive or otherwise derogate from, or offer

81 The North American Agreement on Environmental Cooperation Between the Government of Canada, the Government of the United Mexican States and the Government of the United States of America (NAEEC) and the North American Agreement on Labor Cooperation Between the Government of Canada, the Government of the United Mexican States and the Government of the United States of America (NAALC). See in particular, NAALC, Art. 2 and NAAEC, Art. 3.

82 Canada-Colombia FT A, Art. 1702. Similar language is founds in the FT A between the Republic of Albania and the EFTA STATES (Iceland, the Principality of Liechtenstein, the Kingdom of Norway, the Swiss Confederation) (2009), Art. 24.2: 'The Parties . . . recognise that it is inappropriate to encourage investment by relaxing health, safety or environmental standards' available at https://investmentpolicy.unctad.org/international-investment-agreements/treaty-files/2581/download, accessed 4 August 2024.

to waive or otherwise derogate from, such measures to encourage the establishment, acquisition, expansion, or retention in its territory of an investment of an investor.[83]

This provision not only prohibits the reduction of standards but also establishes a mechanism for dialogue if one party believes the other is engaging in such practices, thereby fostering cooperation and mutual accountability.

These approaches reflect a broader trend within FTAs to balance economic objectives with social and environmental responsibilities. By embedding non-derogation provisions and general exceptions, FTAs ensure that trade liberalization does not erode critical domestic policies aimed at protecting the environment, labour rights and human rights. This trend underscores the recognition that sustainable development and trade policies must be harmonized to create an inclusive and responsible global trading system. The significance of these provisions extends beyond mere regulatory formalities; they embody a commitment to uphold and advance public policy goals within the context of international trade. The inclusion of such clauses ensures that economic growth facilitated by FTAs does not come at the expense of social equity or environmental sustainability. Instead, it promotes a model of development that is holistic and aligned with the principles of sustainable development. Moreover, these clauses have practical implications for how countries negotiate and implement FTAs. They necessitate a careful consideration of domestic regulatory frameworks and international obligations, encouraging states to adopt a more integrated approach to policymaking. This approach not only enhances the legitimacy of FTAs but also supports the broader objectives of global governance, including the promotion of sustainable development, human rights and environmental protection.

The fundamental purpose of these exception clauses is to recognize that the property rights of investors may need to yield to other competing interests. According to Kalderimis, 'A general exception provision would lend a greater coherence and legitimacy to the interpretation process.'[84] These provisions aim to preserve sufficient policy space for host countries to pursue developmental or other objectives while maintaining compliance with treaty obligations.[85] NPM clauses seek to protect state freedom of action in certain domains of public policy from the restrictions or limitations that would otherwise be imposed by obligations created by a BIT.[86] The permissible objectives

83 Canada-Panama FTA, Art. 9.16. An early example using similar language is NAFTA, Art. 1114.

84 Daniel Kalderimis, 'Investment Treaties and Public Good' *A Paper Presented to Asian International Economic Law Network Inaugural Conference*, 29 June 2009, 10.

85 See also, International Investment Agreements: Trends and Emerging Issues, 'UNCTAD Series on International Investment Policies for Development' UN New York and Geneva, 2006, 23–25.

86 Burke-White and Staden (n 80) 332.

covered by NPM clauses include national and international security, public order, public health, public morality, taxation, financial system stability, economic emergency and other similar concerns. The exception clauses can be incorporated in substantive provisions of investment protection. Many recent BITs have started to spell out the exceptions to NT and MFN treatment under such treaties. In 2022 and 2023, several new IIAs were signed and a significant number were terminated. For instance, at least 18 new IIAs were signed, 24 entered into force, and 60 were terminated during this period.

The interpretative implications of GATT-like exceptions in investment arbitration have yet to be fully explored. These exceptions were not prominently considered in investor-state arbitration until the Argentine financial collapse of 2001–2002. Argentina faced several arbitrations where the issue of NPMs was raised. Argentina argued it should be exempt from liability due to the state of necessity or emergency resulting from its severe economic, social and political crisis. In the *CMS, Enron* and *Sempra* cases,[87] the tribunals found the NPM clauses inapplicable. For example, the tribunal in CMS acknowledged the severity of the Argentine crisis but concluded it did not result in total economic and social collapse, thus the treaty would still impose liability. In contrast, the tribunal in LG&E delved into the details of the Argentine crisis, noting the sharp declines in GDP, private competition, domestic prices and asset values in the last quarter of 2001, alongside rapidly rising unemployment and poverty, with unemployment at 25% and nearly half the population living below the poverty line. Based on this analysis, the LG&E tribunal applied the NPM clause and relieved Argentina of liability during the period of its applicability.

The LG&E tribunal also rejected the notion that Article XI of the Argentine-US BIT, which contains the NPM clause, was only applicable in circumstances amounting to military action or war. Instead, it recognized the broader context of severe economic and social emergencies as valid grounds for invoking the clause:

> To conclude that such a severe economic crisis could not constitute an essential security interest is to diminish the havoc that the economy can create on the lives of an entire population and the ability of the Government to lead. When a State's economic foundation is under siege, the severity of the problem can equal that of any military invasion.[88]

87 *CMS Gas Transmission Co. v. Argentine Republic*, ICSID Case No. ARB/01/8, Award of May 12, 2005 (CMS Award); *Enron Corporation Ponderosa Assets, L.P. v. Argentine Republic*, ICSID Case No. ARB/01/3, Award of May 22, 2007 (Enron Award); *Sempra Energy International v. Argentine Republic*, ICSID Case No. ARB/02/16, Award of Sept. 28, 2007 (Sempra Award).

88 Para. 238.

Thus the interpretation of these exception clauses by arbitral tribunals does not offer a coherent analysis of their legal implications. Rather, it could be argued that these tribunals undertook a contradictory approach in interpreting these clauses. One implication of the exception clause is that the relevant investment protection provision may not be invoked to challenge the special preferences or policies adopted by the host states for historically disadvantaged groups. In other words, no compensation would be due since any expropriation takes place by measures under this provision by states.[89] Implied references to human rights may be included in NPM clauses where host States are authorized to take measures 'to protect human rights' without breaching any provision of the investment treaty. Article 17 of the Canada-Cameroon BIT, for example, provides that 'each of the Parties may adopt or enforce a measure necessary: (i) to protect human, animal or plant life or health'. Incorporating exception clauses into BITs would create greater space for the state to impose measures addressing environmental issues. In turn, this could create sufficient scope for the states to adopt regulatory measures in future.

Conclusion

The intersection between international human rights law, environmental protection and international investment law is expanding. This is an area of continuing convergence, yet challenges remain. Practically, this chapter has highlighted that adequately incorporating human rights and environmental protections into IIAs requires greater expertise in drafting and negotiating these issues, adjudicating human rights and sustainable development disputes within the context of IIAs, and the political willingness of the parties to BITs to protect, promote, and respect human rights standards. There are also political difficulties in addressing systemic negotiating imbalances between developed and developing countries in the context of protecting human rights and environmental protection standards in BITs.

Addressing these concerns requires reform towards substantive provisions contained in IIAs. Clarification of the scope and content of human rights and environmental protection obligations for foreign investors, as expressed through clarification on the definition of investors, protections against expropriation, performance requirements, clarification of umbrella clauses and provisions regulating the transfer of capital are important in relieving the problems that arise with the practical issues associated with greater convergence of human rights and environmental protection.

89 See, Andrew Newcombe, 'Canada's New Model Foreign Investment Protection Agreement' August 2004, available at: https://www.international-arbitration-attorney.com/wp-content/uploads/2014/08/205arbitrationlawCanadianFIPA_001.pdf, accessed 17 March 2024.

6 Investor-State Dispute Settlement

Harmonizing Investment Protection With Human Rights and Sustainability

Introduction

The ISDS system addresses disputes between foreign investors and host states, arising from investment contracts or terms of IIAs between the host state and the investor's home state. ISDS is based on thousands of BITs and regional investment agreements rather than a single multilateral treaty. As of April 2024, UNCTAD reported 3368 international investment treaties of which 2589 are in force. ISDS allows foreign investors to directly bring claims against host states, seeking damages for government actions or inactions that constitute breaches of investment treaty obligations. This system enables investors to enforce investment treaty obligations through arbitration without involving their home state or first exhausting domestic remedies. IIAs often include arbitration clauses, providing a legal basis for adjudicating investor-state claims before international courts and tribunals. Most arbitration takes place under the rules of the ICSID Convention and its Additional Facility, though some BITs permit other arbitral bodies.

ISDS continues to be a significant mechanism within the international investment regime, offering investors a means to protect their investments while prompting ongoing debates about its impact on state sovereignty and the need for reforms to ensure fairness and balance between investor protection and public interest. As of April 2024, there have been 1184 known treaty-based ISDS cases. However, ISDS has faced criticism for its perceived pro-investor bias, high costs, and lack of transparency. Critics argue that ISDS undermines the requirement for exhausting domestic remedies, a standard in other international law fields like human rights and environmental law.[1]

1 G. Van Harten and A.Y. Vastardis, 'Critiques of Investment Arbitration Reform: An Introduction' (2023) 24(3) *The Journal of World Investment & Trade* 363–371; Anil Yilmaz Vastardis, 'Investment Treaty Arbitration as Justice Bubbles' in Thomas Schultz and Federico Ortino (eds), *Oxford Handbook of International Arbitration* (Oxford University Press 2020) 617; Maria Laura Marceddu and Pietro Ortolani, 'What Is Wrong with Investment Arbitration? Evidence from a Set of Behavioural Experiments' (2020) 31 *European Journal of International Law* 405, 407; Sergio Puig and Gregory Shaffer, 'Imperfect Alternatives: Institutional Choice

DOI: 10.4324/9781003164951-7

Other criticisms include the confidentiality of proceedings and the potentially high compensation awards.[2] Proceedings are generally not public unless the parties agree or the treaty mandates transparency. The system also faces criticism for perceived limited mechanisms against awards, potential lack of arbitrator independence, and interference with state sovereignty on human rights, environmental and national security issues. ISDS has also been accused of lacking sensitivity towards communities affected by large investment projects, who cannot assert their rights within the ISDS framework. Critics such as Ladan Mehranvar highlight how investment-affected rights holders' access to justice can be undermined or denied within the ISDS mechanism.[3]

Furthermore, the ISDS system has faced scrutiny for its lack of consistency in arbitral decisions. Without a binding precedent system, different tribunals can reach contradictory conclusions on similar issues, creating legal uncertainty and undermining the rule of law. This inconsistency is problematic, particularly when dealing with the same investment treaty or identical state measures. The well-known *CME v. Czech Republic* and *Lauder v. Czech Republic* cases exemplify this issue, where separate tribunals rendered contradictory awards on essentially the same dispute.[4] The ISDS mechanism's interference with states' regulatory autonomy is another significant ground of criticism.[5] Arbitral decisions can impact a state's ability to legislate on matters such as environmental protection, public health, and national security. This regulatory chilling effect deters states from implementing necessary regulations for fear of potential ISDS claims and hefty compensation awards. This concern has led to calls for

---

and the Reform of Investment Law' (2018) 112 *American Journal of International Law* 361; Michael Waibel and others, *The Backlash Against Investment Arbitration: Perceptions and Reality* (Kluwer Law International 2010).

2 Ibid.

3 Ladan Mehranvar, with Jessica Hennings, Robin Marie Kelly, Lena Raxter and Ana Toimil, 'How the International Investment Law Regime Undermines Access to Justice for Investment-Affected Stakeholders'. New York: Columbia Center on Sustainable Investment (CCSI), January 2024; these include those instances in which (1) investment tribunals favour the laws that protect investors' economic interests over the laws and rules that protect human rights or community interests; (2) the regime denies or limits the participation of investment-affected communities and organizations, even in the limited amicus curiae role they may play in ISDS proceedings; (3) ISDS awards either directly or effectively undermine legal outcomes obtained by local communities or organizations in other fora; (4) investment tribunals minimize or gloss over the violence and repression created or amplified by foreign investors or host states toward such communities and individuals in their deliberations; and (5) an ISDS claim, or the threat of a claim, can be used by foreign investors to unduly restrict legitimate domestic regulation in host countries. p. 8. See also Lorenzo Cotula and Nicolás Perrone, 'Reforming Investor-State Dispute Settlement: What About Third-Party Rights?' February 2019, 2, available at http://pubs.iied.org/17638IIED; David Schneiderman, 'Local Resistance: At the Margins of Investment Law' (2022) 19(6) *Globalizations* 897, 899.

4 https://www.iisd.org/itn/en/2018/10/18/cme-v-czech-republic-lauder-v-czech-republic/.

5 https://globalarbitrationreview.com/guide/the-guide-investment-treaty-protection-and-enforcement/first-edition/article/suitability-of-isds-societal-challenges.

reform, including proposals for more transparent and consistent ISDS procedures and the establishment of a permanent international investment court.

In response to these criticisms, there have been various proposals for ISDS reform. Suggestions include improving transparency, enhancing arbitrator independence and impartiality, and establishing an appeals mechanism to ensure consistency in arbitral decisions.[6] Additionally, some scholars and policymakers advocate for integrating human rights and environmental considerations into the ISDS framework to ensure that investment protection does not come at the expense of broader public interests.[7]

Investor-State Dispute Settlement: Issues With Legitimacy and Coherence

Traditionally, the protection of investments and investor rights has been the dominant paradigm in investment law.[8] The current framework often views human rights primarily through the lens of protecting the property rights of investors. However, recent arbitral jurisprudence has begun to consider non-investment obligations from other areas of international law. These obligations are sometimes used as reference points or invoked as defences for regulatory actions in investment arbitrations. This trend indicates that non-investment and investment obligations are becoming increasingly intertwined. The potential conflicts between these obligations need to be addressed in future BIT negotiations and investment arbitrations. As international investment law evolves, it must accommodate, resolve and elaborate on these complex issues.[9] This evolution is essential for creating a balanced system that effectively reconciles the protection of investor rights with the need to uphold human rights

6 Piero Bernardini, 'Reforming Investor-State Dispute Settlement: The Need to Balance Both Parties' Interests' (2017) 32 *ICSID Review* 38; M. Langford, M. Potestà, G. Kaufmann-Kohler and D. Behn, 'UNCITRAL and Investment Arbitration Reform: Matching Concerns and Solutions: An Introduction' (2020) 21(2–3) *The Journal of World Investment & Trade* 167–187.

7 Alessandri Arcuri and Federica Violi, 'Human Rights and Investor-State Dispute Settlement: Changing (Almost) Everything, So that Everything Stays the Same?' (2019) 3 *Diritti umani e diritto internazionale* 579; Barnali Choudhury, 'Democratic Implications A Rising from the Intersection of Investment Arbitration and Human Rights' (2009) 46(4) *Alberta Law Review* 983; S. Steininger, 'What's Human Rights Got to Do with It? An Empirical Analysis of Human Rights References in Investment Arbitration' (2018) 31(1) *Leiden Journal of International Law* 33–58; Reiner Clara and Christoph Schreuer, 'Human Rights and International Investment Arbitration' in Pierre-Marie Dupuy, Ernst-Ulrich Petersmann and Francesco Francioni (eds), *Human Rights in International Investment Law and Arbitration* (Oxford University Press 2009).

8 See, Ignaz Seidl-Hohenvelderm, *International Economic Law* (3rd edn, Kluwer Law International 1999) (chapters 12 and 13 deal with human rights of economic value and property rights of aliens).

9 Vaughan Lowe, 'Changing Dimension of International Law' University of Oxford Faculty of Law Legal Studies Research Paper Series, Working Paper No 4/2007, March 2007, available at http://papers.ssrn.com/Abstract=970727, accessed 17 May 2023.

and other public interest concerns. Most BITs are drafted in ways that are extremely narrow in their formulation, focusing only on rights of investors.[10] This narrow formulation results in exclusion of human rights values and concerns from the broader landscape of the international investment law that gives rise to legitimacy crisis and the fragmented approach to treaty interpretation.

Legitimacy Issues

BITs are often negotiated without public oversight, and the insulated nature of these negotiations can neglect broader regulatory concerns impacting the community. Consequently, BITs are frequently criticized for their lack of transparency and perceived bias towards investor interests.[11] The extensive protections afforded to foreign investors, combined with the expanding scope of their rights, have led many to view these treaties as excessively one-sided.[12] This imbalance is evident in the fact that investment agreements typically do not include mechanisms for addressing investor misconduct that may affect the rights of individuals or groups in the host territory.[13] Additionally, the substantive obligations outlined in these treaties, along with their broad interpretation by arbitral tribunals, can restrict states' abilities to regulate social and environmental issues and fulfil their duties to protect and promote human rights.[14] This point has been succinctly stated by the UN Special Representative on Business and Human Rights:

> Recent experience suggests that some treaty guarantees and contract provisions may unduly restrain the host Government's ability to achieve its legitimate policy objectives, including its international human rights obligations. That is because under threat of binding international arbitration, a foreign investor may be able to insulate its business venture from new laws and regulations, or seek compensation from the Government for the cost of compliance.[15]

10 Luke Eric Peterson, 'International Human Rights in Bilateral Investment Treaties and Investment Treaty Arbitration' *International Institute for Sustainable Development*, 2003, 35.

11 G. Van Harten, *Investment Treaty Arbitration and Public Law* (Oxford University Press 2008) 159.

12 See, N.J. Schrijver, 'A Multilateral Investment Agreement from a North-South Perspective' in E.C. Nieuwenhuys and M.M.T.A. Brus (eds), *Multilateral Regulation of Investment* (Kluwer Law International 2001) 17–33.

13 *Human Rights, Trade and Investment Matters*, Amnesty International UK (May 2006) 20, available at http://www.jussemper.org/Newsletters/Resources/HRTradeInvestmentMatters.pdf, accessed 23 April 2023.

14 M. Sornarajah, *The International Law on Foreign Investment* (2nd edn, Cambridge University Press 2004) 259; See also Aaron Cosbey, 'International Investment Agreements and Sustainable Development: Achieving the Millennium Development Goals' *International Institute for Sustainable Development*, September 2005, available at http://www.iisd.org (the study concluded that in a number of ways, BITs can frustrate the achievement of the MDGs).

15 Report of the Special Representative of the Secretary-General Business and Human Rights, A/HRC/11/13 (23 April 2009), paras 29–31.

This restraint can happen in several ways. Primarily, investors may invoke provisions within BITs to challenge regulations inspired by human rights that they perceive as detrimental to their investments. Additionally, investors can challenge host state laws and policies aimed at implementing human rights obligations under the state's constitution and international human rights treaties.[16] This ability of investors to contest such regulations can significantly undermine the enjoyment and enforcement of human rights within the host state.[17] The investment regime thus has the potential to adversely impact human rights, posing a significant challenge to balancing the protection of investors with the public interest. On one hand, investors require protection against arbitrary or discriminatory measures by host states. On the other hand, there is a pressing need to ensure that these protections do not impede the host states' ability to regulate in the public interest, particularly concerning human rights.[18]

ISDS proceedings are generally opaque, secretive and exclusive. The problem of legitimacy has become a contentious issue in international investment law. For Thomas Frank, legitimacy must be rooted in a framework of formal requirements in order for a system of rules to have the fairness that society expects.[19] According to him, the requirements for legitimacy include determinacy, symbolic validation, coherence and adherence.[20] The crisis of legitimacy of investment treaty and investor-state arbitration stems from both substantive and procedural biasness.[21] The legitimacy crisis in ISDS is multifaceted, rooted in both substantive and procedural biases. Addressing these issues requires a holistic approach that considers the interplay between investment protection and public policy goals, ensures greater transparency and accountability, and incorporates human rights and regulatory concerns into the investment law framework.

Substantive bias arises from the fact that first, investment treaties often fail to balance the rights of investors with corresponding obligations. This imbalance creates a situation where investors are afforded extensive protections without

16 Ryan Suda, 'The Effect of Bilateral Investment Treaties on Human Rights Enforcement and Realization' *Hauser Global Law School Program, Global Law Working Paper 01/05*, New York University School of Law, New York.

17 Ibid.

18 The World Investment Report of 2003 stated: 'For developing countries, the most important challenge in future IIAS is to strike a balance between the potential contribution of such agreements to increasing FDI flows and the preservation of the ability to pursue development oriented FDI policies that allow them to benefit more from them—that is, the right to regulate in the public interest. This requires maintaining sufficient policy space to give governments the flexibility to use such policies within the framework of the obligations established by the IIAs to which they are parties.'

19 See, Thomas M. Frank, *Fairness in International Law and Institutions* (Oxford University Press 1995).

20 Thomas M. Frank, *The Power of Legitimacy among Nations* (Oxford University Press 1990) 49.

21 Abdullah Al Faruque, 'Mapping the Relationship between Investment Protection and Human Rights' (2010) 11(4) *The Journal of World Investment and Trade* 539, 544.

being subject to equivalent responsibilities. The vagueness and indeterminacy of the standards of investment protection further exacerbate this issue, leading to unpredictability and incoherence in the application of investment treaties.[22] Moreover, investment treaties frequently inadequately address the regulatory needs of host states. This inadequacy manifests in several ways. Host states may find their ability to regulate in the public interest, such as in environmental protection, public health and labour rights, constrained by the fear of triggering investor claims. For instance, in the case of *Philip Morris v. Uruguay*, Uruguay's tobacco control measures were challenged under a BIT, illustrating how regulatory actions intended to protect public health can be contested by foreign investors.[23] BITs also create disparity in protection of property rights in host states by affording a greater level of protection to the foreign investors than it does to domestic investors.[24] As many developing countries do not offer effective means of protecting property rights, simply because their legal systems do not recognize such rights or to the extent that property rights are recognized, the judicial infrastructure is incapable or unwilling to enforce those rights.[25] For instance, in *Siemens v. Argentina*,[26] the German multinational

22 See, M. Sornarajah, 'A Coming Crisis: Expansionary Trend in Investment Treaty Arbitration' in Karl P. Sauvant (ed), *Appeals Mechanism in International Investment Disputes* (Oxford University Press 2008); Susan D. Franck, 'The Legitimacy Crisis in Investment Treaty Arbitration: Privatizing Public International Law through Investment Decisions' (2005) 73 *Fordham Law Review* 1521, 1523; Ari Afilalo, 'Towards a Common Law of International Investment: How NAFTA Chapter 11 Panels Should Solve Their Legitimacy Crisis' (2004) 17 *Georgetown International Environmental Law Review* 51. See also UN High Commissioner for Human Rights on potential danger to human rights obligation 'of allowing recourse to strong dispute settlement provisions under investment agreements in the absence of similarly strong accountability mechanisms for human rights issues arising in the context of investment' at 55. For the counter argument, see Charles N. Brower and Stephan W. Schill, 'Is Arbitration a Threat or a Boon to the Legitimacy of International Investment Law' (2008–2009) 9 *Chicago Journal of Investment Law* 471–498) (claiming that investment arbitration is legitimate and effective dispute settlement, while admitting that legitimate concern of public interest should be accommodated in the current system of international investment protection, argue that it does not require a fundamental redesign of the entire system); Moritz Renner, 'Towards a Hierarchy of Norms in Transnational Law?' (2009) 26(4) *Journal of International Arbitration* 533–555 (The regulatory aspects of host states are only insufficiently represented in both in the general principles and the more specific treaty instruments of international investment law. The conflicts arising out from this state of affairs have led to sometimes problematic and often inconsistent developments in ICSID arbitral practice.) 545.

23 *Philip Morris Brands Sarl, Phillip Morris Products S.A. and Abel Hermanos S.A. v. Oriental Republic of Uruguay*, ICSID Case No. ARB/10/7.

24 Tom Ginsburg, 'International Substitute for Domestic Institutions: Bilateral Investment Treaties and Governance' (2005) 25 *International Review of Law and Economics* 107, 114.

25 Christopher M. Ryan, 'Meeting Expectations: Assessing the Long-term Legitimacy and Stability of International Investment Law' (2007–2008) 29 *University Pennsylvania Journal of International Law* 725–761.

26 *Siemens A.G. v. Argentine Republic*, ICSID case no. ARB/02/8.

received significant compensation for the termination of its contract, while domestic contractors received no such protections under local law.

From the substantive point of view, the investment arbitration process has also been criticized as a coercive technique to bind the host state to dispute settlement since individual investors can trigger the compulsory arbitration of disputes under all BITs.[27] This is largely due to the structure of BITs and other investment agreements, which often allow investors to trigger compulsory arbitration without the need for the consent of the host state at the time of the dispute. This unilateral right to initiate arbitration can put significant pressure on host states, particularly in situations where regulatory actions are challenged. For instance, in *Philip Morris v. Australia*, the tobacco company challenged Australia's plain packaging laws under a BIT between Australia and Hong Kong, despite the overwhelming public health evidence supporting the legislation.[28] The initiation of arbitration by Philip Morris was seen as a coercive attempt to force Australia to retract its regulations, showcasing how investors can leverage BIT provisions to challenge sovereign regulatory measures. Although Philip Morris ultimately lost the case, the process itself imposed significant legal and financial burdens on Australia.

Furthermore, the investment arbitration gives a comprehensive jurisdiction to arbitrators to determine the legality of sovereign acts and to award public funds to investors that sustain loss as a result of government regulation.[29] This expansive jurisdiction raises concerns about the erosion of state sovereignty and the prioritization of investor interests over public policy objectives. The extensive jurisdiction of arbitrators also affects the regulatory autonomy of host states. The fear of potential arbitration claims can create a 'regulatory chill', where states may hesitate to implement or enforce regulations that could be perceived as detrimental to foreign investments. A pertinent example is the case of *Vattenfall v. Germany*.[30] Vattenfall, a Swedish energy company, filed a claim against Germany under the ECT, seeking compensation for Germany's decision to phase out nuclear power following the Fukushima disaster. The arbitration tribunal had the authority to scrutinize Germany's sovereign decision, which was made in the interest of public safety and environmental protection. The tribunal eventually ruled in favour of Vattenfall, awarding substantial compensation. This case illustrates how investment arbitration can

27 Kenneth J. Vandevelde, 'Investment Liberalisation and Economic Development: The Role of Bilateral Investment Treaties' (1998), 36 *Columbia Journal of Transnational Law* 522 (an investor could use the arbitration provision to pressure the host state into making concessions in the same way that businesses will threaten litigation as a coercive negotiation tactic).

28 *Philip Morris Asia Limited v. Commonwealth of Africa*, UNCITRAL, PCA Case No. 2012–12.

29 Van Harten (n 1) (the author takes the view that the system of investment arbitration's mixture of private nature and public law undermines accountability and openness in judicial decision-making).

30 *Vattenfall A B and others v. Federal Republic of Germany*, ICSID Case no. ARB/12/12.

challenge and potentially penalize states for regulatory actions aimed at protecting public interests.

The power of arbitrators to award substantial sums from public funds to investors poses significant financial risks for host states. These awards can result from regulatory actions that are deemed to negatively impact the value of foreign investments, even when such actions are undertaken in the public interest. This financial liability can be particularly burdensome for developing countries with limited resources. In *Occidental v. Ecuador*, Occidental Petroleum[31] was awarded $1.77 billion, one of the largest awards in ISDS history, after Ecuador terminated an oil contract for breaches of the agreement by the company. The financial strain of such awards can have profound economic implications, diverting public funds from critical social and developmental programs to compensate foreign investors.

Procedural bias arises due to the lack of accountability and legal coherence in interpretations, non-recourse to the domestic legal system, the broad rendering of the arbitrability of disputes, increased cost, ad hoc nature of arbitral tribunals, confidentiality of the procedures and lack of appellate body.[32] A major procedural issue is the lack of accountability and consistency in the interpretations of arbitral awards. Arbitrators, often appointed on an ad hoc basis, may deliver inconsistent rulings on similar issues, leading to legal uncertainty. This inconsistency undermines the predictability of the ISDS system, making it difficult for states and investors to understand the rules and their applications. For instance, the cases involving Argentina during its financial crisis illustrate this problem. Different tribunals reached varying conclusions on similar facts and legal standards. In *CMS v. Argentina, Enron v. Argentina* and *Sempra v. Argentina*, the tribunals concluded that Argentina could not rely on the necessity defence to justify its measures. However, in *LG&E v. Argentina*, a different tribunal allowed Argentina to invoke the necessity defence. These contradictory decisions create a fragmented legal landscape, reducing the credibility and reliability of the ISDS system.

31 *Occidental Petroleum Corporation and Occidental Exploration and Production Corporation v. Republic of Ecuador*, ICSID case No. ARB/06/11.

32 See, Jose E. Alvarez and Kathryn Khamsi, 'The Argentine Crisis and Foreign Investor: A Glimpse into the Heart of the Investment Regime, 72 (International Institute for Law and Justice, IILJ Working Paper 2008/5, 2008), available at http://www.iilj.org/publications/docuemtns/2008_5.AlvarezKhamsi.pdf, accessed 12 June 2022; see also, Asha Kaushal, 'Revisiting History: How the Past Matters for the Present Backlash against the Foreign Investment Regime' (2009) 50(2) *Harvard International Law Journal* 491; See also, Steven R. Ratner, 'Corporations and Human Rights: A Theory of Legal Responsibility' (2001) 111 *Yale Law Journal* 443, 459 (Bilateral investment treaties are heavily skewed in favour of foreign investors. Beyond the substantive rights noted above, the BITs and NAFTA also provided investors a critical procedural right- to institute international arbitration without the consent of the host state to the individual arbitration and thereby bypass domestic courts entirely.).

The purpose-built ad hoc arbitration tribunals appointed by parties are not designed to address complex issues of public policy that may come into play in investor-state disputes.[33] Lack of standing for third parties such as NGOs and civil society in investment arbitration also precludes it from public scrutiny. ISDS often bypasses domestic legal systems, allowing foreign investors to take disputes directly to international arbitration without first seeking resolution through local courts. This can undermine the sovereignty of host states and diminish the role of domestic legal institutions in handling investment disputes.

BITs allow the foreign investors the unfettered right to initiate direct action against their host governments as most BITs do not require the exhaustion of local remedies before initiating arbitration. This right can be exercised without any obligation to seek amicable resolution. This privilege creates an imbalance between the rights of foreign investors and the regulatory autonomy of host states. Even when BITs include such provisions, they are often restricted, such as imposing time limits for local remedies. This limitation can lead to a lack of integration between international arbitration and domestic legal systems, further contributing to the perception of procedural bias. The case of *Ethyl Corporation v. Canada* illustrates this point. Ethyl Corporation challenged Canada's ban on the gasoline additive MMT under NAFTA's ISDS provisions without first seeking resolution through Canadian courts. Canada eventually settled the case, lifting the ban and compensating the company. This case demonstrates how BIT provisions can enable foreign investors to bypass domestic legal processes and challenge sovereign regulatory decisions directly.

One of the most contentious aspects of BITs is the provision that allows foreign investors to claim compensation not only for actual losses but also for lost future profits when government regulations affect their investments. A prominent case illustrating this issue is *Philip Morris v. Uruguay*. In this arbitration, Philip Morris International challenged Uruguay's stringent tobacco control regulations, which were enacted to protect public health. The company claimed that these regulations violated Uruguay's obligations under the Switzerland-Uruguay BIT by effectively expropriating its investments and causing significant financial losses, including future profits. Many poor developing countries have no resources and expertise to contest the claims in arbitration, which often involves complex legal issues.[34] The high costs of arbitration, including legal fees, tribunal expenses, and potential compensation awards, can be crippling for poorer countries. An extreme aspect of the legitimacy crisis can be manifested through a withdrawal of States from the BIT arbitration procedure, as well as the termination and renegotiation

33 Faruque (n 21) 545–546.

34 See Luke Eric Peterson, *All the Roads Lead Out of Rome: Divergent Paths of Dispute Settlement in Bilateral Investment Treaties* (Routledge 2004) 11–12.

of BITs.[35] In fact, more countries are reviewing their BIT regimes to reflect new concerns related to human rights, the environment and social issues.[36] In 2013, South Africa announced its intention to terminate several BITs and replace them with domestic legislation that would balance investor protection with the state's right to regulate in the public interest. The Protection of Investment Act, enacted in 2015, aims to ensure that foreign investments are protected while allowing the government to pursue its social and economic policies without undue interference from arbitration claims.

Similarly, Ecuador has terminated numerous BITs as part of a broader strategy to regain control over its regulatory space. In 2017, Ecuador withdrew from 16 BITs, arguing that the treaties were skewed in favour of foreign investors and limited the government's ability to implement policies for public welfare. Ecuador's actions reflect a growing trend among developing countries to reassess their participation in the international investment regime.

The current structure of the ISDS system has garnered extensive criticism for its perceived lack of sensitivity to states' human rights obligations and public interest considerations. Reforming the system is necessary to address these criticisms and enhance the legitimacy of ISDS mechanisms. The procedural concerns associated with ISDS have been widely documented, highlighting issues such as lack of accountability, legal coherence, and transparency. The ad hoc nature of arbitral tribunals, confidentiality of proceedings, and the absence of an appellate body contribute to the opacity and inconsistency of ISDS decisions. Thus there is a demand for wider reform in the current structure of investment protection and dispute settlement process in an effort to make the investment regime more sensitive to a state's human rights obligations and public interest.[37] Making more regulatory space in BITs, establishing effective linkage between human rights and treaty regime, establishing permanent international investment court,[38] state-to state arbitration mechanisms instead of current investor-state arbitration and addressing procedural concerns may enhance the acceptance of investor-state arbitration in particular and BITs in general. The tension between investment protection and public goals can be reconciled by introducing an appellate process.[39]

35 Some Latin American countries such as Bolivia have withdrawn from the ICSID, while Ecuador has announced that consent to ICSID arbitration is no longer available for certain categories of disputes.

36 For instance, South Africa is currently reviewing its BIT regime. See for detailed analysis: Bilateral Investment Treaty Policy Framework Review: Government Position Paper of Republic South Africa, Pretoria, June 2009. See also, Recent developments in international investment agreements (2007–June 2008), IIA MONITOR No. 2 (2008), United Nations, Geneva, 2008.

37 Suda (n 16).

38 Van Harten (n 1).

39 Ernst-Ulrich Petersmann, 'Human Rights, International Economic Law and "Constitutional Justice"' (2008) *European Journal of International Law* 769, 797 (as supervision of arbitral

A WTO-style appellate system in investment arbitration can help in resolving the frequent contradictions in the legal reasoning of arbitral awards and can enhance the perception of legitimacy of the arbitral system.[40] An appellate body would provide a forum for reviewing and correcting erroneous decisions, contributing to greater legal coherence and predictability. Encouraging the use of alternative dispute resolution (ADR) mechanisms, such as negotiation and mediation, in investment disputes could offer a more cost-effective, timely and flexible means of resolving conflicts. ADR mechanisms such as negotiation and mediation for resolving investment disputes are increasingly incorporated in BITs to meet the growing criticism against arbitration, which is viewed as costly, lengthy and complex.[41] Only a few BITs make provisions for consultation for settlement of a dispute before submission to an arbitral body.[42] The creation of a permanent international investment court could enhance the consistency and transparency of ISDS decisions. Such a court would replace ad hoc tribunals and provide a more stable and predictable forum for resolving investment disputes.

Fragmentation and Coherence

Fragmentation of investment law can occur in both a narrow and broad sense. In a narrow sense, fragmentation can occur from inconsistent interpretations by investment arbitral tribunals. Inconsistent decisions generally arise under three typical scenarios.[43] First, different tribunals can interpret the same stand-

awards by ICSID annulment committees is essentially limited to jurisdictional errors, procedural improprieties, or serious violation of public policies).

40 Ibid.

41 See, Valentina Sara Vadi, 'Reconciling Public Health and Investor Rights: The Case of Tobacco' in Pierre-Marie Dupuy, Francesco Francioni and Ernest-Ulrich Petersmann (eds), *Human Rights in International Investment Law and Arbitration* (Oxford University Press 2009) 452–486. For instance, the Japan-Philippines Economic Partnership Agreement 2006 which as a joint trade-investment treaty grants investors a broad range of protection, does not provide investors a right to international arbitration. Rather the Agreement provides that the Parties shall continue to negotiate for a mutually acceptable dispute resolution procedure and that, in the absence of an agreement, an investor may submit a dispute to "international conciliation or arbitration" only after receiving the express consent of the state-parties to the Agreement (Article 107). The Agreement is available at www.mofa.go.jp/region/asia-paci/philippine/epa0609/index.html, accessed 27 May 2022.

42 Article 8 of The Agreement Between the Government of the Hong Kong Special Administrative Region of the People's Republic of China and the Government of the United Arab Emirates for the Promotion and Reciprocal Protection of Investments, available at https://investmentpolicy.unctad.org/international-investment-agreements/treaty-files/5865/download, accessed 19 July 2022; Article 9 of the Agreement between the Government of Australia and the Government of the Republic of Indonesia concerning the Promotion and Protection of Investments (Jakarta, 17 November 1992) Entry into force: 29 July 1993.

43 Susan D. Franck, 'The Legitimacy Crisis in Investment Treaty Arbitration: Privatising Public International Law Through Inconsistent Decisions' (2005) 73 *Fordham Law Review* 1521, 1545–1546.

ard within the same treaty in varying ways, leading to divergent outcomes. This lack of uniformity undermines the predictability and reliability of investment law. Second, different tribunals organized under different treaties can come to different conclusions about disputes involving the same facts, related parties, and similar investment rights.[44] These types of cases will typically involve investments that have been structured to take advantage of multiple investment treaties so that, when a dispute arises, claims can be brought by related corporate entities under different treaties.[45] This practice can lead to forum shopping and inconsistent arbitral awards, further fragmenting the legal landscape.

For example, in Argentinian financial cases (*CMS v. Argentina, Enron v. Argentina, LG&E v. Argentina* and *Sempra v. Argentina*), four arbitral tribunals were confronted with the same facts, but they reached different conclusions.[46] The tribunals in the *CMS v. Argentina, Enron v. Argentina* and *Sempra v. Argentina* cases concluded that Argentina was not entitled to rely upon the necessity and NPMs defences, whilst the tribunal in the *LG&E v. Argentina* case concluded that Argentina is entitled to invoke the NPMs defence and that the necessity defence is potentially applicable. Argentina applied to annul the award in the *CMS v. Argentina* case and the Annulment Committee criticized the tribunal's finding that Argentina was not entitled to rely on the NPMs defence but acknowledged it had limited power to review the award.[47] According to William Burke White,

> [t]he fact that four Tribunals, when confronted with the same facts, evidence, and argumentation would reach very different interpretations of the law and diametrically opposite holdings is, itself, sufficient to call into question the legitimacy and viability of the ICSID arbitral system.[48]

44 Ibid.

45 Ibid.

46 *CMS Transmission Co. v. Argentine Republic*, ICSID Case No. ARB/01/8, Award, 12 May 2005 (hereinafter *CMS Award*), available at http://icsid.worldbank.org/ICSID/FrontServlet?requestType=CasesRH&actionVal=showDoc&docId=DC504_En&caseId=C4; *LG&E Energy Corp. v. Argentine Republic*, ICSID Case No. Arb/02/1, Decision on Liability, 3 October 2006, available at http://icsid.worldbank.org/ICSID/FrontServlet?requestType=CasesRH&actionVal=showDoc&docId=DC627_En&caseId=C208; *Enron Corp., Ponderosa Assets, L.P. v. Argentine Republic*, ICSID Case No. Arb/01/3, Award, 22 May 2007, available at http://ita.law.uvic.ca/documents/Enron-Award.pdf; *Sempra Energy Int'l v. Argentine Republic*, ICSID Case No. Arb/02/16, Award, P 391, 28 September 2007, available at http://ita.law.uvic.ca/documents/SempraAward.pdf.

47 *CMS Gas Transmission Company v. Argentine Republic* (ICSID Case No. ARB/01/8) (Annulment Proceeding) Decision of the Ad Hoc Committee on the Application for Annulment of the Argentine Republic, available at https://www.italaw.com/sites/default/files/case-documents/ita0187.pdf.

48 W. Burke-White, 'The Argentine Financial Crisis: State Liability Under BITs and the Legitimacy of the ICSID System' (2008) 3 *Asian Journal of WTO & International Health Law and Policy* 199.

Finally, different tribunals organized under different investment treaties will consider disputes involving a similar commercial situation and similar investment rights but will come to opposite conclusions. Even when dealing with similar commercial situations and investment rights, tribunals under different treaties can render opposite decisions. This inconsistency undermines the coherence of international investment law, making it difficult for investors and states to anticipate legal outcomes.

In a broader sense, interpretation and development of investment law without consideration of human rights law and policy has led to the fragmentation between investment law and international law. The fragmentation of international law arises from the development of specialized and autonomous rules, institutions and adjudicating bodies, resulting in the isolation of different branches of international law. The International Law Commission (ILC) study on the fragmentation of international law highlights the need for systemic integration to address the relationship between treaty-based rights and obligations and those arising under other treaties or customary international law. Systemic integration involves a reasoning process that harmonizes various legal norms, creating a coherent and meaningful whole.[49] In the context of BITs, the focus on investor rights often overlooks the broader regulatory concerns of host states, particularly in areas related to human rights. Investors can use BIT provisions to challenge human rights–inspired regulations and laws aimed at implementing international human rights obligations. This ability to contest such regulations can undermine the enforcement of human rights within the host state. This is of increasing significance as the number of both BITs and investment arbitration arising under those treaties has exploded.[50] There is an emerging consensus that human rights law should play a greater role in strengthening legitimacy of the investment law by shaping the investment rule making. Recent treaties and model agreements, such as the Netherlands' Model Investment Agreement, explicitly link investment protection with sustainable development and human rights, reflecting this emerging consensus.

Improving Legitimacy and Coherence Through the Text of a BIT

Conflicts of norms may arise under international investment law in some situations due to the different interpretations of the same treaty by different

49 International Law Commission, 'Fragmentation of International Law: Difficulties Arising from the Diversification and Expansion of International Law' Report of the Study Group, of the International Law Commission, UN Doc A/CN.4/L682, 13 April 2006.

50 Until February 2024, the total cumulative number of known treaty-based cases reached 1303. These disputes were filed with ICSID (or the ICSID Additional Facility) (182), under the arbitration rules of the United Nations Commission on International Trade Law (UNCITRAL) (80), the Stockholm Chamber of Commerce (14), the International Chamber of Commerce (5) and ad-hoc arbitration (5).

tribunals and prioritization of one norm over another. Specifically, two situations may arise regarding conflicts of norms. First, the investment treaty or investment contract may be in conflict with the existing regulatory regime in host state at the time of conclusion of such treaty. Second, states may undertake new human rights obligations through ratification or accession to a human rights treaty during the lifetime of an investment treaty or investment contract. In the case of a dispute arising out of such situations, the question may arise before an investment tribunal or court whether treaties and contracts can override human rights standards or impair the power of the state to legislate in the field of human rights protection. In this regard, a balanced approach is crucial and a harmonious interpretation is needed so that private interests of foreign investors are aligned with the societal objectives of protection of human rights. Such an approach is evident as in some arbitral tribunals have acknowledged the necessity of balancing public and private interests in investment treaties5. For example, the tribunal in *CMS v. Argentina* argued:

> the right of the host states to adopt its economic policies together with the rights of investors under a system of guarantees and protection are at the very heart of this difficult balance, a balance which the ICSID Convention was careful to preserve.[51]

Although the investment treaties may not expressly contain such balancing, the general concepts of investment protection contain within them considerable flexibility.[52] This flexibility allows arbitrators to balance public and private interests, ensuring that treaty protections leave a significant margin for the exercise of state sovereignty.[53] This balancing act is crucial for international tribunals to preserve greater policy space for governments to fulfil their human rights obligations while protecting the legitimate expectations of foreign investors. For instance, in *Impreglio v. Argentina*, the tribunal recognized that while governments have regulatory space, a violation of investors' legitimate expectations could occur in instances of drastic or unreasonable modifications.[54] The prevailing imbalance in international investment law often accords more rights to investors than imposing corresponding obligations on them.[55] This imbalance can be explained by the relative bargaining power of the parties to a BIT. Developing countries often lack expertise and bargaining

51 *CMS Gas Transmission Co. v. Republic of Argentina*, ICSID Case No. ARB/01/8, 12 May 2005, para. 499.

52 Campbell McLachlan QC, Laurence Shore and Matthew Weiniger, *International Investment Arbitration: Substantive Principles* (Oxford University Press 2007) 23.

53 Ibid.

54 *Impregilo S.p.A. v. Argentine Republic* (ICSID Case No. ARB/07/17) para. 291.

55 Leyla Davarnejad, 'Strengthening the Social Dimension of International Investment Agreements by Integrating Codes of Conduct for Multinational Enterprises' *A Paper Presented at OECD Global Forum on International Investment*, 27–28 March 2008.

power in investment regulation rulemaking. The UNCTAD has highlighted this issue in its World Investment Report 2021, noting that:

> Asymmetries in bargaining power put weaker economies at a disadvantage in the negotiations of bilateral agreements. Although this applies in all negotiating situations, it is particularly relevant in agreements between large developed countries and small and poor developing ones. When bilateral agreements go beyond a narrow coverage, the principal objective of investor protection is often complemented with liberalization clauses related to the right of establishment and expanded lists of restricted performance requirements.

To address this imbalance, a balanced approach should be sought by enhancing the development dimension of investment agreements. According to an UNCTAD study, there are three key aspects to this approach.[56] For developing countries, promoting policy coherence is crucial for enhancing the development dimension of investment agreements. Policy incoherence often results from diverse investment agreements based on the various model agreements of developed country partners.[57] Developing countries must integrate these agreements into their economic development policies effectively. Due to capacity constraints, frequent policy changes, and weak bargaining power, developing countries face serious challenges in establishing coherent economic and development policies.[58] Therefore building internal capacity and ensuring policy coherence in investment agreements are essential steps for developing countries to attract and retain foreign investment while respecting human rights and public goals.

Second, an important aspect of promoting development dimension is how to balance the rights and interests of foreign investors with those of the host country, and how to ensure regulatory flexibility for host countries.[59] Ensuring regulatory flexibility for host countries can be accommodated through stronger emphasis on public policy in investment treaties. This ensures that investment protection does not come at the expense of other legitimate public interests. Third, the development dimension of investment agreements can be strengthened through giving more space for pursuing public interest goals. This can be achieved through reservations, exceptions, temporary derogations, transitional arrangements and institutionalized monitoring and consultations mechanisms.[60]

56 UNCTAD Report, 'Development Implications of International Investment Agreements' IIA Monitor No. 2 (2007), United Nations, Geneva.

57 Ibid.

58 'International Investment Agreements: Trends and Emerging Issues' UNCTAD Series on International Investment Policies for Development, UN New York and Geneva, 2006, 71.

59 UNCTAD Report (n 56).

60 Ibid.

The preceding discussion clearly provides clear testimony to the assertion that the investment regime should strike a balance between investment protection and human rights. But the most important challenge of balancing test remains *how* to strike a balance between legitimate expectation of the foreign investors and legitimate measures of the host states. The balancing of conflicting norms is necessitated by the fact that investment treaties should contribute to sustainable development of host states.[61] This raises the fundamental issue that international legal norms in the spheres of foreign investment and human rights should lead to convergence rather than divergence.[62]

Improving Legitimacy and Coherence Through Interpretation: Recognizing the Human Rights and Sustainable Development Contexts

The exponential growth of BITs with diverse treaty language and various formulations of substantive obligations indicates the need for consistency and coherence in their interpretation. In fact, arbitral awards have provided a number of inconsistent awards and diverse interpretation of substantive obligations of BITs, which effectively contributes to fragmentation of treaty interpretation. In the context of an increasing number of BITs and resultant increase of investment disputes, the issue of policy coherence is now more important than ever before. This raises questions about how to ensure a harmonized and coherent approach to the treaty interpretation is adopted.[63] The role of interpretation is increasingly recognized in harmonizing conflicting interests of the parties to the investment disputes because interpretation is not only a part of the implementing process of a treaty but also plays a fundamental role in avoiding antinomies between different treaty regimes.[64] A holistic approach should be adopted by arbitrators taking into account human rights law and relevant customary international law in interpreting relevant investment treaty provision(s) to prevent fragmentation of international law.

The role of interpretation in the context of investment protection and human rights obligations of the host states can be approached in the following way: first, in interpretation of investment treaties, particular attention is given to the object and purpose of the treaty as expressed in the preamble. It has been

61 Faruque (n 21) 549.

62 See, Shyami Fernando Puvimanasinghe, *Foreign Investment, Human Rights and the Environment: A Perspective from South Asia on the Role of Public International Law for Development* (Martinus Nijhoff Publishers 2007); see on the interface between sustainable development and the governance of investment, Lyuba Zarsky, *International Investment for Sustainable Development: Balancing Rights and Rewards* (Earthscan 2004).

63 C. Schreuer, 'Diversity and Harmonization of Treaty Interpretation in Investment Arbitration' (2006) 3(2) *Transnational Dispute Management.*

64 Valentina Sara Vadi, 'Reconciling Public Health and Investor Rights: The Case of Tobacco' in Pierre-Marie Dupuy, Francesco Francioni and Ernest-Ulrich Petersmann (eds), *Human Rights in International Investment Law and Arbitration* (Oxford University Press 2009) 470.

argued that 'preambular statements in investment treaties cannot simply be conflated with a general preference for the interests of the investor over those of the host state. The overall objective in fact requires a balanced approach'.[65] The preamble of a BIT can be interpreted in consistency with human rights obligations if it contains reference to human rights. Although preambles do not create any legally binding obligations, these can be used in guiding the interpretation of treaties where there is ambiguity in language. Article 31 of the Vienna Convention states that the preamble constitutes part of the context of an argument. The presence of any public interest goal or development objectives in the preamble of an investment treaty can strengthen the human rights arguments by the host state or by tribunal.[66]

Second, interpretation of an investment treaty could also be approached from the perspective of conflict of norms. The scope of potential conflicts between international norms occurs because all norms of international law do not have the same status. Some of them protect important and universal values, such as the prohibition of genocide, which constitute jus cogens or peremptory norms that do not allow derogation. It means these norms have a hierarchical standing that is higher than other norms.[67] Thus in case of a conflict between two norms, in some instances, the primacy of human rights should be recognized.[68] Even within the sphere of human rights, some human rights which are called non-derogable have hierarchy over others. For instance, Article 4(1) of the ICCPR allows for derogation in emergency situations. However, some human rights, such as right to life or freedom from torture or slavery, can never be suspended or limited, even during times of national emergency. Indeed, an ICSID tribunal sitting under NAFTA in the *Methanex* case stated that:

> as a matter of international constitutional law a tribunal has an independent duty to apply interpretive principles of law or *jus cogens* and not give effect to parties' choice of law that are inconsistent with such principles.[69]

65 C. McLachlan, 'Investment Treaties and General International Law' (2008) 57(2) *International Comparatively Law Quarterly* 361, 371.

66 Ernst-Ulrich Petersmann, 'Human Rights, Constitutionalism, and "Public Reason" in Investor-State Arbitration' in Christina Binder et al. (eds), *International Investment Law for the 21st Century: Essays in Honour of Christoph Schreuer* (Oxford University Press 2009) 877–893.

67 J. Pauwelyn, *Conflict of Norms in Public International Law: How WTO Law Relates to Other Rules of International Law* (Cambridge University Press 2003) 32 (defines conflict of norm when two norms are in a relationship of conflict if one constitutes, has led to, or may lead to, a breach of the other) 175–176.

68 Marcos A. Orellana, 'Science, Risk and Uncertainty: Public Health Measures and Investment Disciplines' in Philippe Kahn and Thomas Walde (eds), *New Aspects of International Investment Law* (Martinus Nijhoff Publishers 2007) 718–719.

69 *Methanex Corporations v. United States of America* (Final award of the Tribunal on Jurisdiction and Merits of 3 August 2005) ICSID Case, Part IV, chapter 11.

Conflict of norms can be avoided by drafting treaties more clearly (ex ante),[70] adopting generally accepted presumptions against conflict[71] and using treaty interpretation as a conflict avoidance tool. In order to avoid conflict, a contextual approach of interpretation should be preferred instead of a textual one. The principle of an effective treaty interpretation in consideration of 'other relevant rules of international law' may be useful in solving the conflict of norms.[72] Thus treaty interpretation can play an important role in balancing conflicting norms.

A balancing approach to treaty interpretation is already evident in some arbitral awards. For example, an arbitral tribunal succinctly observed:

> The protection of foreign investments is not the sole aim of the Treaty, but rather a necessary element alongside the overall aim of encouraging foreign investment and extending and intensifying the parties' economic relations. That in turn calls for a balanced approach to the interpretation of the Treaty's substantive provisions for the protection of investments, since an interpretation which exaggerates the protection to be accorded to foreign investments may serve to dissuade host states from admitting foreign investments and so undermine the overall aim of extending and intensifying the parties' mutual economic relations.[73]

Third, in order to achieve coherence and unity of international law and systemic integration in the interpretation of an investment treaty, the central role of international law should be recognized in view of the public nature of the rights involved in such a treaty.[74] The concept of systemic integration is based on the premise that investment treaties are not self-contained regimes as they are creatures of international law and governed by it.[75] General principles of international law inform the content of the specific treaty norm and of

70 Pauwelyn (n 58) 237–268 (Conflict prevention which is termed as ex ante means that conflict of norms be avoided at the negotiation stage of new norms. Conflict may then be prevented by one norm explicitly stating that derogates from, or is an exception to, another norm. One norm can also make an explicit reference to, or incorporate the conditions of, another norm. Conflict may further be avoided by drafting treaties more clearly or negotiating new treaties with other treaties in mind.).

71 Ibid. ('Every new norm is created within the context of pre-existing international law and the presumption is that this new norm builds upon and further develops existing law') 240.

72 Ibid. 244–253.

73 *Saluka Investments BV (The Netherlands) v. Czech Republic* (Partial Award) (UNCITRAL 2006) para. 300.

74 Charles N. Brower, 'Whither International Commercial Arbitration: The Goff Lecture 2007' (2008) 24(2) *Arbitration International* 181.

75 McLachlan (n 65). See also, Zachary Douglas, 'The Hybrid Foundations of Investment Treaty Arbitration' (2003) 74(1) *The British Yearbook of International Law* 151 (to treat international law as a self-contained legal order in the sphere of foreign investment is plainly untenable). 152.

States' obligation more generally.[76] Systemic integration requires harmonious interpretation of international law, which is essential for preserving the coherence and unity of international law.[77] Achieving such a purpose will obviously require the consideration of non-investment law, including general principles of international law, human rights norms and customary international law in applying and interpreting investment law.[78]

Article 31(3)(C) of the Vienna Convention on the Law of Treaties may serve as the legal basis for consideration of human rights in the process of the interpretation of investment treaties. This provision reflects a principle of integration and emphasizes both the unity of international law in the sense that rules should not be considered in isolation of general international law.[79] It requires that in the interpretation of a treaty, there shall be taken into account, together with the context, any relevant rules of international law applicable in the relations between the parties. The ICJ in the *Oil Platform case* emphasized that under the general rules of treaty interpretation, as reflected in the 1969 Vienna Convention on the Law of Treaties, interpretation must take into account 'any relevant rules of international law applicable in the relations between the parties'.[80] In its first case, *Asian Agricultural Products Ltd. v. Republic of Sri Lanka*, the ICSID tribunal explained that a BIT

> is not a self-contained close system limited to provide for substantive material rules of direct applicability, but it has to be envisaged within a wider judicial context in which rules from other sources are integrated through implied incorporation methods, or by direct reference to certain supplementary rules, whether of international law character or of domestic law nature.[81]

The expression 'relevant rules of international law' must include international human rights law as applicable in interpretation of investment treaties. The human rights law can be used by investment tribunals as part of relevant rules of international law to determine the generic terms of treaties to achieve the harmonization of treaty interpretation.[82] Indeed, many provisions of BITs are

76 McLachlan (n 65).

77 See, Anne van Aaken, 'Fragmentation of International Law: The Case of International Investment Protection' University of St. Gallen Law School, Working Paper No. 2008–1, available at http://ssrn.com/abstract=1097529, accessed 23 June 2023.

78 Petersmann (n 57) 892.

79 Philippe Sands, 'Treaty, Custom and the Cross-fertilization of International Law' (1998) 10 *Yale Human Rights and Development Law Journal* 3.

80 See, *Case Concerning Oil Platforms (Iran v. United States of America)*, Judgement, 6 November, 2003, ICJ Reports 2003, at para. 41.

81 *Asian Agricultural Products Ltd. v. Republic of Sri Lanka* (Award) (ICSID) (1990), 4 ICSID Report 245, 257.

82 See for analysis on this point, Bruno Simma and Theodore Kill, 'Harmonizing Investment Protection and International Human Rights: First Steps Towards A Methodology' in

defined by other sources of international law insofar as they make direct and general reference to international law as a source of binding obligations.[83] For example, FET clauses sometimes are defined with reference to customary international law or international law.

In *Saluka Investments BV (the Netherlands) v. the Czech Republic* the tribunal concluded that in interpreting the provisions of treaties such as BITs or FTAs, account has to be taken of any relevant rules of international law, including general customary international law, applicable in the relations between the parties.[84] This demonstrates that international investment law should not operate in isolation from the rest of the rules of international law, rather the investment tribunal 'should take into account other competing principles of international law'. Therefore, applicable law governing BITs needs to include human rights and environmental protection, and the dispute settlement procedure needs to recognize standing of third parties to provide evidence through amicus briefs.

Conclusion

Although the ISDS system is an integral part of the international investment law regime, it has been widely criticized for its lack of legitimacy, consistency and transparency. Civil society has particularly highlighted issues such as the unpredictability of arbitration outcomes and inadequate transparency, noting that the system's focus on confidentiality and privacy prevents public access to the dispute resolution process. To address these criticisms, comprehensive reform of the ISDS system is essential. Reforms should aim to enhance transparency in proceedings and ensure that ISDS tribunals adhere to norms related to human rights, environmental protection, and other public interest goals. This would make their decisions more coherent and align the system with broader legal and policy objectives.

In addition, the legitimacy crisis in ISDS can be significantly mitigated through several key reforms. These include improving procedural aspects such as the establishment of a permanent international investment court and an appellate mechanism to ensure consistency in arbitral decisions. Additionally, enhancing arbitrator independence and allowing third-party participation in the dispute resolution process can address concerns about confidentiality

---

Christina Binder et al. (eds), *International Investment Law for the 21st Century: Essays in Honour of Christoph Schreuer* (Oxford University Press 2009), 678–707 ('The practice of referring to external rules to determine the meaning of generic terms would seem to be fruitful field for the harmonization of human rights and international investment law') 703.

83 See Joshua Robbins, 'The Emergence of Positive Obligations in Bilateral Investment Treaties' (2005–2006) 13 *University of Miami International & Comparative Law Review* 403–473 (argues that BITs combines multiple incorporating devices including separate treaties, other sources of international law or domestic law).

84 *Saluka* case.

and lack of accountability. Integrating human rights and environmental considerations into the ISDS framework is crucial. This integration ensures that investment protection does not come at the expense of public interest goals, thereby fostering a balanced approach that respects both investor rights and state sovereignty. Encouraging the use of ADR methods, such as negotiation and mediation, can also provide more flexible, cost-effective, and timely means of resolving investment disputes.

In summary, addressing both substantive and procedural biases within the ISDS system through comprehensive reforms is vital for restoring its legitimacy. By ensuring greater transparency, accountability and alignment with human rights and environmental norms, the ISDS framework can become a more balanced and fair mechanism for resolving investment disputes, supporting sustainable development and respecting fundamental legal principles.

7 Business and Human Rights

The Interplay Between Labour Standards, Investment and Human Rights

Introduction

The nexus between labour, investment and human rights is now well established, with international labour standards being integral to the domestic labour laws of many countries. However, despite these standards, many internationally recognized labour rights and standards can be ignored or violated, particularly within the operations of MNCs and foreign investors in the manufacturing sector. Core labour rights and standards, such as minimum wages, freedom of association and collective bargaining, are often denied by authoritarian regimes or governments with poor human rights records. A socially responsible company cannot overlook these core labour rights issues.

The most important labour standards that MNEs must observe are (1) freedom of association and effective recognition of the right to collective bargaining; (2) elimination of all forms of forced or compulsory labour; (3) effective abolition of child labour; (4) elimination of discrimination in respect of employment; (5) encouragement of human capital formation; and (6) observance of effective health and safety regulations.[1] Most of the labour standards mentioned above are found in ILO codes, the GC and OECD Guidelines. The OECD Guideline on Multinational Enterprises 1976 and the UN GC 1999 put emphasis not only on the elimination of child labour and forced labour but also made provisions for the societal integration of released children or labourers through vocational training, schooling for children, access to medical care and counselling, and assistance in developing income generation.[2] Conversely, there is also a well-established opposing view that foreign investments operating under investment treaties actually enhance labour

1 Illias Bantekas, 'Corporate Social Responsibility in International Law' (2004) 22 *Boston University International Law Journal* 309, 332.

2 See Guide to the Global Compact: A Practical Understanding of the Vision and Nine Principles 51, UN Global Compact (2002), available at http://www.unglobalcompact.org/content/public_Documents/gcguide.pdf, accessed 12 July 2023.

DOI: 10.4324/9781003164951-8

standards and the protection of labour rights in host states.[3] These differing views demonstrate how the relationship between labour and investment is often contested and ambivalent.

The origin of this contested and ambivalent approach arises from the inherent tensions between the Global North and Global South. Developed nations typically aim to improve working conditions in developing countries by incorporating international minimum labour standards in investment and trade agreements and imposing trade sanctions for breaches. In contrast, developing nations resist these impositions due to fears of losing market competitiveness.

A significant case study illustrating the implementation of labour standards within global supply chains is the Sialkot football industry in Pakistan, which faced international scrutiny for using child labour. In response, a coalition of stakeholders, including the ILO, UNICEF, Save the Children UK, and local manufacturers, formed the Atlanta Partnership to eliminate child labour from this sector. This partnership established comprehensive measures, including formal registration and monitoring of football stitchers, social protection programmes, and the creation of football-stitching centres. Despite these efforts, the intervention also had unintended negative socio-economic impacts. While the elimination of child labour was achieved, the new production structure marginalized semi-skilled, part-time, and seasonal football stitchers, particularly those in remote areas. This led to reduced family income and lower food security and social participation levels. Conversely, skilled male football stitchers benefited from higher wages and better working conditions. The interaction between international trade law and human rights further complicates this relationship. While corporations drive international trade, states bear the responsibility for implementing human rights protections. International trade law could potentially incorporate obligations for corporations to respect human rights, including labour rights, within their operations. However, incorporating human rights into trade law is contentious, with critics arguing it could undermine the trading system's fundamental attributes.

This chapter delves into these complexities, examining the potential and challenges of enforcing comprehensive labour standards in global supply chains and exploring the role of international trade and foreign investment law in enhancing human rights protections. This chapter analyses intersection of labour standards and foreign investment, delves into how labour rights have been incorporated in investment treaties and trade agreements, and investigates the extent to which incorporation of these rights has improved labour governance in developing countries. The chapter concludes with a discussion on the need for balanced approaches to ensure equitable and positive outcomes for all stakeholders involved.

3 Bonnie Penfold, 'Labour and Employment Issues in Foreign Direct Investment: Public Support Conditionalities' Working Paper No. 95, ILO, available at https://www.ilo.org/wcmsp5/groups/public/@ed_emp/@emp_ent/@multi/documents/publication/wcms_101040.pdf, accessed 19 November 2022.

The Labour and Investment Nexus: A Race to the Bottom?

The labour-investment nexus has gained increasing significance in recent years, particularly as many investment and trade agreements now integrate considerations of labour, human rights and environmental issues. This nexus is frequently a focal point in the discourse surrounding globalization. Trade and investment are pivotal modalities of globalization, often criticized for allegedly weakening domestic labour protections, labour rights and national trade union movements, a phenomenon commonly referred to as the 'race to the bottom'.[4] This type of scenario, which remains a major threat of globalization, is explicated by the fact that many developing countries have relaxed national regulatory standards, reduced labour rights and social services and cut many employment benefits in order to remain internationally competitive.[5] This trend is driven by the competitive pressures of globalization, where countries promise low labour costs and minimal trade union presence to entice foreign investors. Consequently, this leads to deteriorating labour rights, poor working conditions, low unionization rates and increasingly authoritarian labour relations.

In fact, many developing countries attract foreign investment, especially in labour-intensive sectors such as the ready-made garment industry, with promises of low labour costs and no trade unions. These conditions collectively result in a race to the bottom, a scenario generally reflected by worsening conditions in labour rights leading to poor working conditions, low unionization and authoritarian labour relations. Recent data and literature further elucidate this issue. According to a 2023 report by the ILO, over 60% of the workforce in developing countries operates in informal sectors, often characterized by lack of social protections and poor working conditions. Studies also highlight how MNCs leverage these conditions to minimize costs and maximize profits, exacerbating the race-to-the-bottom phenomenon.

Over the last few decades, with low labour standards and weak union representation, many developing countries have become very attractive to potential foreign investors and MNCs.[6] The claim is that developed countries that open their borders to trade with and offer FDI to developing countries are forced to reduce their labour standards in order to keep up with the increased competition. Barbara J. Fick noted such competition among developing countries for FDI, and the desire to further strengthen domestic economies through trade and exports led to the growing influence of MNCs over domestic labour

4 See for details, Joseph Stiglitz, *Globalization and Its Discontents* (W.W. Norton 2002).

5 Eric Neumayer and Indra De Soysa, 'Globalisation, "Women's Economic Rights and Forced Labour"' (2007) 30(10) *The Journal of World Economy* 1510–1535; Robert Blanton and Shannon L. Blanton, 'Labour Rights and Foreign Direct Investment: Is There a Race to the Bottom?' (2012) 38(3) *Journal of International Interactions* 267–273.

6 Alejandro Donado and Klaus Wälde, 'Globalization, Trade Unions and Labour Standards in the North' Employment Working Paper No. 119 ILO (2012) XI.

policies.[7] It is asserted that as a result of competition, some developing countries responded more to these external economic pressures than by adhering to the international labour standards developed by ILO. In 2003, the UN High Commissioner for Human Rights noted that governments have lowered environmental and human rights standards (including labour standards, freedom of expression and freedom of association) to attract foreign investment. While there is little direct evidence to support such race-to-the-bottom arguments, the ILO acknowledges that downward pressure on labour and environmental standards exists as a result of foreign investment, and it is difficult to judge the extent to which foreign investment is inhibiting the socially optimal raising of labour standards.[8]

A more recent example can be seen in Ethiopia's industrial parks. In an effort to attract foreign investment, Ethiopia established several industrial parks, offering incentives such as tax breaks and low-cost labour. According to a 2022 report by Human Rights Watch, these parks have attracted numerous international garment manufacturers. However, the report highlights significant labour rights violations, including low wages, poor working conditions and suppression of union activities. This example illustrates the ongoing relevance of the race-to-the-bottom phenomenon, as Ethiopia's strategies to attract FDI have led to compromised labour standards. An OECD study found 'some governments in non-OECD countries have restricted labour rights (especially in export processing zones) in the belief that doing so would help attract inward foreign direct investment from both OECD and non-OECD investors'.[9]

However, this trend is not limited to developing countries. Deregulation of labour in order to attract FDI is not exclusively done by developing countries but also by developed countries.[10] Deregulation of labour has led to a flexible labour market, and MNCs generally target their direct investments in countries with relatively low production costs in order to seek cost advantages and thus obtain higher returns on their investments. Recent data from the World Bank and other international bodies highlight the scale of this issue. According to the World Bank's 2023 report, FDI inflows to developing countries have increased by 25% over the past decade, with a significant portion directed towards sectors with lower labour costs. This underscores the ongoing attractiveness of these countries to MNCs seeking cost advantages and higher returns on investments.

7 Barbara J. Fick, 'Introduction' in Barbara J. Fick (ed), *International Labour Law* (Edward Elgar 2015) xiii.

8 OHCHR, 'Human Rights, Trade and Investment' E/CN.4/Sub.2/2003/9 (2 July 2003) para. 13.

9 OECD, 'Trade, Employment and Labour Standards: A Study of Core Workers' (1996) *Rights and International Trade* 123.

10 R. Zandvliet and R. Trade, 'Investment and Labour: Interactions in International Law' 2019, available at https://scholarlypublications.universiteitleiden.nl/access/item%3A2977132/view, accessed 15 March 2024.

The general assumption that lowering domestic standards can attract foreign investment is not based on the empirical data.[11] Even a few experts such as Dani Rodrik assert that lowering labour rights may be a hindrance, rather than an attraction, for foreign investors.[12] A possible explanation for this is that the costs of high labour standards are offset by externalities that create conducive trade or investment climate.[13] For example, the right to freedom of association and collective bargaining contribute to political and social stability, and the eradication of child labour and occupational discrimination positively affects a country's human capital.[14] Recent data and case studies illustrate this nuanced relationship between labour standards and foreign investment. A 2023 report by the ILO found that countries with stronger labour protections tend to attract more sustainable and long-term foreign investment. Investors are increasingly valuing stable, predictable, and socially responsible business environments, which high labour standards help to create.

For example, Costa Rica has successfully attracted substantial foreign investment while maintaining robust labour standards. The country's commitment to labour rights, including freedom of association and comprehensive social protections, has not deterred investment. Instead, it has helped Costa Rica develop a reputation for stability and sustainability, attracting companies like Intel and Boston Scientific, which value these factors.

Labour Rights in Bilateral Investment Treaties

Earlier investment agreements rarely contained provisions related to labour standards, nor did they impose any obligations on host states or investors regarding social matters. Yet, recent BITs of some countries contain provisions addressing social issues including labour rights and the labour welfare of what is typically known as 'social clause'.[15] Some BITs contain labour-related

11 William W. Olney, 'A Race to the Bottom? Employment Protection and Foreign Direct Investment' (2013) 91(2) *Journal of International Economics* 191–203.

12 Dani Rodrik, 'Labour Rights in International Trade: Do They Matter and What Do We Do about Them?' in Robert Lawrence, Dani Rodrik and John Whalley (eds), *Emerging Agenda for Global Trade: High Stakes for Developing Countries* (Johns Hopkins Press for the Overseas Development Council 1996) 35.

13 David Kucera, 'Core Labour Standards and Foreign Direct Investment' (2002) 141 *International Labour Review* 31, 63; Simon Deakin, 'The Contribution of Labour Law to Economic and Human Development' in Guy Davidov and Brian Langille (eds), *The Idea of Labour Law* (Oxford University Press 2011) 173–174.

14 Kucera (n 14) 37.

15 *Social clause* in BIT refers to provisions for labour rights and human rights to be observed by foreign investors. For example, Article 24 of the Pan-African Investment Code (PAIC) uses conditional verbs ('should') to encourage investors to comply with internationally recognized human rights legislation. Article 17 of the Argentina-Japan Bilateral Investment Treaty of 2018 requires host States to encourage investors to implement CSR principles into their internal policies on a voluntary basis.

provisions in their preambles.[16] The introduction of references to labour rights and issues in the preamble of BITs is non-binding in nature since preambles do not contain any operational provisions and as such, they do not create any legally binding obligations. However, such references to labour rights have some interpretative value and can be invoked before international courts and tribunals for interpretation. Moreover, inclusion of labour-related provisions in preambles of modern BITs clearly marks a departure from earlier treaty practice and signal contracting parties' clear intent to respect labour rights or international labour standards as a fundamental value.[17] A 2022 review by ILO found that about 30% of new BITs include references to labour standards. This trend signals a departure from earlier treaty practices and reflects a growing recognition of labour rights as fundamental values. For example, the 2018 Canada-Senegal BIT explicitly mentions labour rights in its preamble, indicating a clear intent by the contracting parties to uphold international labour standards. The earlier BITs did not address the labour, environment and human rights issues.

Advocates of social clauses in trade agreements argue that these provisions are essential to effectively promote workers' rights in developing countries. These countries often use low labour standards as a tool to attract more trade and investment in an increasingly competitive global economy, leading to a race-to-the-bottom situation. Experts assert that social clauses are necessary to discourage developing countries from weakening worker protections or failing to enforce labour laws to expand exports or attract FDI.[18] In this way, the 'social clause' acts as a legal provision in an international trade agreement that seeks to eliminate the worst forms of worker exploitation in exporting countries.[19] Under such clauses, importing developed countries can prevent exporters with unacceptable labour standards from receiving preferential trade terms under systems like the generalized system of preferences (GSP) or MFN status. Developed countries can also impose punitive trade sanctions, such as higher tariffs or outright bans, against violators.[20]

Reflecting the development of social clauses, many modern investment agreements now include references to labour standards and welfare issues. This trend began with developed countries, including the United States, Canada and Australia, which have addressed labour welfare and rights in their BITs. Gradually, some developing countries have also included labour standards and human rights issues within their BITs. For example, the India Model

16 Mozambique/United States, 1998, preamble.

17 Bertram Boie, 'Labour Related Provisions in International Investment Agreements' Employment Sector Employment Working Paper No. 126, ILO (2012) 12.

18 See, Günseli Berik and Yana van der Meulen Rodgers, 'Options for Enforcing Labour Standards: Lessons from Bangladesh and Cambodia' (2010) 22 (1) *Journal of International Development* 56–85.

19 Ibid.

20 Ibid.

BIT of 2015 provides that investors are subject to 'internationally recognized standards of corporate social responsibility'.[21] Similarly, the Southern African Development Community Model BIT Template imposes on investors the duty to respect human rights in the workplace, in the community and in the host state where the investment is made.[22] The same provision expands upon this obligation by referencing the ILO Declaration on Fundamental Principles and Rights of Work, and by underlining that foreign investment must be made and managed in accordance with international environmental and human rights obligations.[23] Furthermore, the Morocco-Nigeria[24] BIT of 2016 requires foreign investors to conduct their businesses with a mindset of pursuing sustainable development and fostering the well-being of local communities, in addition to carrying out a social and environmental impact assessment on the basis of the relevant domestic legislation.[25] Under this BIT, investors are obligated to adhere to the ILO's Tripartite Declaration on Multinational Investment and Social Policy (2006)[26] and to uphold the highest possible standards of CSR.

According to SADC Model Bilateral Investment Treaty Template of South Africa, '[i]nvestors and their investments shall act in accordance with core labour standards as required by the ILO Declaration on Fundamental Principles and Rights of Work, 1998'.[27] It further provides that 'investors and their investments shall not [establish,] manage or operate Investments in a manner inconsistent with international environmental, labour and human rights obligations binding on the Host State or the Home State, whichever obligations are higher'.[28] The Morocco-Nigeria BIT 2016 imposes the obligation of undertaking social and environmental impact assessments, respecting international labour and human rights standards, and upholding anti-corruption practices.[29]

21 Model Text for the Indian Bilateral Investment Treaty (Bilateral Investment Treaty Between the Government of the Republic of India and . . .) (2015) art. 12, available at http://investmentpolicyhub.unctad.org/Download/TreatyFile/3560, accessed 22 June 2022.

22 S. African Dev. Cmty, 'Model Bilateral Investment Treaty Template with Commentary Art. 15' (2012), available at https://www.iisd.org/itn/wp-content/uploads/2012/10/sadc-model-bittemplate-final.pdf, accessed 22 June 2022.

23 Ibid.

24 Reciprocal Investment Promotion and Protection Agreement, Morocco-Nigeria, art. 24, 3 December 2016, available at http://investmentpolicyhub.unctad.org/Download/TreatyFile/5409 (hereinafter *Morocco-Nigeria BIT*) (requiring investors and host states to assess the potential impact of an investment on the local community).

25 Morocco-Nigeria BIT, art. 24. It is also worth recalling that several other recent IIAs provide for similar clauses. See, e.g., Brazil-Mozambique ACFI, art. 14.

26 The Declaration is available at https://www.ilo.org/wcmsp5/groups/public/---ed_emp/---emp_ent/---multi/documents/publication/wcms_094386.pdf, accessed 23 July 2022.

27 Article 15.2.

28 Article 15.3 of SADC Model Bilateral Investment Treaty Template with Commentary, Southern African Development Community, July 2012, Article 15.

29 *Morocco-Nigeria* BIT 2016, art 14, 15, 17.

BITs may also contain 'non-lowering of standards' provisions that prohibit states from derogating from labour standards in order to attract more investment from MNC investors.[30] These clauses generally aim to prevent host states from lowering their environmental or labour standards as an incentive to attract foreign investment. For instance, the US Model BIT 2012 includes two provisions preventing lowering of standards, one addressing environmental standards and the other labour standards. Specifically, Article 13 of the US Model BIT prohibits signatory states from lowering their labour standards to draw in more investments. The 2012 US Model BIT, the 2002 Belgium Model BIT, and the 2008 Austria Model BIT all contain such non-lowering clauses. The Belgium Model BIT 2002 stipulates that it is 'inappropriate to encourage investment by relaxing domestic labour legislation'.[31] Similarly, the US Model BIT takes this approach. The Austrian Model BIT applies the non-lowering of standards clause to domestic labour legislation and references 'internationally recognized labour rights'.[32] Article 5 of the Austrian Model BIT calls upon state parties to ensure that they do not 'waive or otherwise derogate from, or offer to waive or otherwise derogate from, such laws in a manner that weakens or reduces adherence to the internationally recognized labour rights'.

These provisions of model BITs do not commit states to realizing the appropriate level of labour rights. Instead, these provisions provide that the existing level(s) of protection shall not be lowered by the contracting parties when dealing with investors and their investments.[33] Direct reference to internationally recognized labour standards in BITs can produce a more beneficial impact on improving domestic labour standards compared to non–lowering of standards clauses because direct reference can stipulate a defined labour standard to be followed by the host states. Direct reference to international labour standards can be used by the courts or tribunal as an interpretative tool to advance labour rights. The 2008 Austrian Model BIT introduces the concept of 'employment' in its preamble while recognizing the relevance of international labour rights. This agreement effectively stipulates that the treatment of investors by the contracting parties will 'contribute to the efficient utilization of economic resources', the 'creation of employment opportunities', and the 'improvement of living standards'.[34]

This new trend of incorporating labour standards in BITs aligns with the view that investors have a duty to respect human rights within their sphere of

30 On non-lowering of standards, see, John Ruggie, Just Business 182–84 (2013) Megan Wells Sheffer, 'Bilateral Investment Treaties: A Friend or Foe to Human Rights?' (2011) 39 *Denver Journal of International Law and Policy* 483, 484.

31 Article 6.

32 Austria Model BIT, available at https://edit.wti.org/document/show/e169ce6e-482f-48dd-9a67-2387ecd194f3.

33 Bertram Boie, 'Labour Related Provisions in International Investment Agreements' Employment Sector Employment Working Paper No. 126, ILO (2012) 14.

34 The preamble of the 2008 Austria Model BIT.

operations in host states. These investments should not assist in, or be complicit in, the violation of human rights by others in the host state. The emergence of new generation BITs has been influenced by factors such as the rise of state-owned enterprises from emerging and transitional economies, greater governmental participation in directing national economies, and the adoption of sustainable development-oriented investment policies.[35] These new generation BITs aim to reassert the state's sovereign power and right to regulate social issues.

Despite these advancements, the labour provisions in BITs remain largely rhetorical. They do not legally bind host states to safeguard and uphold workers' rights, nor do they hold MNCs liable for directly or indirectly causing labour rights violations.[36] Mere references to ILO standards or non-binding declarations in BITs do not significantly improve the domestic labour laws of developing countries, many of which fall short of international standards. While international labour law frameworks place an onus on states to enforce labour standards, no such onus is imposed on companies to adhere to basic CSR norms in their operations. This gap allows MNCs to evade compliance through practices such as subcontracting.[37] For instance, the European Union's recent trade agreements with Vietnam and Japan include chapters dedicated to sustainable development, which encompass labour rights. These agreements emphasize the importance of adhering to ILO conventions and promoting CSR. However, the enforcement mechanisms remain weak, with compliance largely dependent on the political will of the involved parties.

Labour Provisions in Trade Agreements

Generally, labour provisions in trade agreements include international labour standards on employment, wages, working conditions, any domestic system of protection given to workers under national law, and agreement relating to cooperation and monitoring of the observance of labour standards.[38] While labour provisions in WTO or other multilateral treaties are largely symbolic and less pronounced due to resistance of the developing countries, such provisions have been frequently included in bilateral trade agreements. As of 2016,

35 UNCTAD, 'Investment Policy Framework for Sustainable Development' New York and Geneva, 2015, at chapter 1; 'UNCTAD's Reform Package for the International Investment Regime' New York and Geneva, 2018, at 22–23.

36 Sharon Hang, 'Investing in Human Rights: Using Bilateral Investment Treaties to Hold Multinational Corporations Liable for Labour Rights Violations' (2014) 37 *Fordham International Law Journal* 1215, 1223.

37 Ronald C. Brown, 'Promoting Labour Rights in the Global Economy: Could the United States' New Model Trade and Investment Frameworks Advance International Labour Standards in Bangladesh?' (2016) 155(3) *International Labour Review* 383–403.

38 'Singapore WTO Ministerial Declaration Regarding Labour Standards' adopted on 13 December 1996, available at https://www.wto.org/english/thewto_e/minist_e/min96_e/wtodec_e.htm, accessed 13 March 2024.

136 countries had at least one trade agreement that included labour provisions.[39] The EU, United States, Canada and Australia are pioneers in concluding trade agreements that incorporate labour standards in recent years. Currently, labour provisions or labour standards are found in trade agreements between developed and developing countries and have been included in trade agreements concluded between developing countries themselves. This reflects a shift of attitude of developing countries towards labour issues in trade arrangements, which demonstrate that many developing countries have abandoned their opposition to a trade-labour linkage in the trade agreements.[40]

Labour provisions in trade agreements differ considerably with consequent varied legal implications. Labour provisions may include a commitment for states to adhere to internationally recognized labour standards in reference to core labour standards, or to respect important ILO documents, such as the 1998 ILO Declaration on Fundamental Principles and Rights at Work and ILO Conventions. Such references to these international labour protection instruments could either progressively raise the level of protection of the national labour laws or reduce the impact of the non-lowering of labour regulation standards with a view to promoting exports or investment. The application of labour provisions in trade agreements may be restricted to labour issues concerning trade relations between the parties, or may even apply more broadly to all labour issues within and between the parties, regardless of the extent to which labour provisions are linked to trade activities.[41] The most prominent feature of the majority of labour rights provisions in trade instruments is the mutual commitment of contracting parties to the enforcement of existing national labour legislation.[42]

Labour provisions may be mandated to be included in trade agreements by national law. For example, the US Trade Act 2002 obliges any new American FTAs to protect fundamental workers' rights and the environment.[43] Although some trade agreements contain social issues, such social clauses are mostly only declaratory, not legally binding.[44] All this language is located in the non-binding preamble portions and is not subject to any remedy. One

39 International Labour Organization, *Handbook on Assessment of Labour Provisions in Trade and Investment Agreements* (ILO 2017) 11 (ILO Handbook).

40 James Harrison, 'The Labour Rights Agenda in Free Trade Agreements' (2019) 20 *Journal of World Investment & Trade* 705–725.

41 Franz C. Ebert and Anne Posthuma, 'Labour Provisions in Trade Arrangements: Current Trends and Perspectives' *International Labour Organization* (International Institute for Labour Studies), 2011, 2–3.

42 Rene-Claude Droiin, 'Promoting Fundamental Social Rights Through International Framework Agreements: Practical Outcomes and Present Challenges' (2010) 31 *Comparative Labour Law and Policy Journal* 591.

43 The US 2003 Trade Policy Agenda, available at www.ustr.gov/reports/2003.html, accessed 12 January 2024.

44 Bonnie Penfold, 'Labour and Employment Issues in Foreign Direct Investment: Public Support Conditionalities' Working Paper No. 95, International Labour Office—Geneva, 2.

notable example is the CPTPP, which includes robust labour provisions. The CPTPP, which involves 11 countries including Canada, Japan and Australia, incorporates enforceable labour standards, ensuring that member countries maintain acceptable conditions of work. This agreement reflects a collective effort to uphold labour rights across a diverse group of countries, setting a high standard for future trade agreements.

The majority of labour provisions in trade agreements now refer to ILO instruments, mostly in the form of the ILO 1998 Declaration on Fundamental Principles and Rights at Work,[45] which is non-binding in nature. Reference to such non-binding documents in trade agreements has very limited effectiveness to raise labour standards. As regards enforcement, the principles of the Declaration do not expressly define the rules of conduct for breach of the Declaration. According to Orbie and Roozendaal, although labour standards have become an almost routine feature of trade agreements, their effectiveness is not clear.[46] Whilst a large proportion of trade agreements contain references to labour concerns in their preambles, these provisions are not included in the substantive part of such non-binding agreements. For example, the US bilateral trade and investment frameworks do not obligate the country to adopt substantive standards that are ultimately enforceable even though these frameworks function to advance labour standards.[47] According to a report by the ILO, there has been a significant increase in the number of trade agreements with labour provisions. By 2018, more than 80 trade agreements included labour provisions, compared to just four in 1995. This trend highlights a global recognition of the importance of labour standards in trade policy.

Integration of Labour Provisions in Trade Agreements: The United States Model FTA and Global Trends

The United States Model Free Trade Agreement was pioneering in embedding labour provisions and enforcement mechanisms within its trade agreements. This model has set a precedent, influencing the inclusion of labour rights in bilateral agreements between the United States and other countries. Starting in the early 1990s, the United States introduced a clause in the preamble of its FTAs stating: 'Recognizing that the development of economic and business ties can promote respect for internationally recognized worker rights; and agreeing that these objectives can be achieved without relaxing health, safety, and environmental measures of general application.'[48] This clause laid

45 Ibid. 30.

46 Jan Orbie and Gerda Van Roozendaal, 'Labour Standards and Trade: In Search of Impact and Alternative Instruments' (2017) 5(4) *Politics and Governance* 2183–2463.

47 Ronald C. Brown, 'Promoting Labour Rights in the Global Economy: Could the United States' New Model Trade and Investment Frameworks Advance International Labour Standards in Bangladesh?' (2016) 155(3) *International Labour Review* 383–403.

48 Mozambique/United States, 1998, preamble.

the foundation for the integration of labour standards in trade agreements, marking a significant shift towards incorporating social dimensions in trade policy. Since then, many developed countries have incorporated labour standards in bilateral and regional trade agreements.

NAFTA, now replaced by the United States–Mexico–Canada Agreement (USMCA), was one of the first significant trade agreements to include labour provisions. The USMCA, for instance, requires Mexico to enhance its labour laws, ensuring workers' rights to unionize and bargain collectively. This agreement represents a robust framework for enforcing labour standards and demonstrates US leadership in this area.

A growing number of countries are including labour rights provisions in trade agreements. For example, the European Union, African, Caribbean and Pacific (ACP) Partnership Agreement (a trade preference program) covers some 79 countries and includes labour rights obligations. This agreement ensures that labour standards are upheld in exchange for trade benefits, promoting sustainable development and fair labour practices in these regions.

The United States also has preferential agreements with some 140 developing countries with labour rights conditionality. These agreements require partner countries to adhere to internationally recognized labour standards, providing a framework for improving working conditions and protecting workers' rights. In addition, the EU has bilateral agreements with over 15 countries with labour rights provisions, while the United States has some 20 FTAs with labour standards conditionality. Canada includes labour rights obligations in side agreements to its FTAs.[49]

Labour Standards, Human Rights, and GATT Article XX(a): Protection of Public Morals

The GATT provides a framework for integrating social policies within trade agreements. Article XX of GATT allows for exceptions to trade obligations for measures necessary to protect public morals, human, animal or plant life or health, and to secure compliance with GATT-consistent laws. These exceptions can justify trade measures that address labour standards and human rights concerns.

Article XX(a) of the GATT allows members to enact measures necessary to protect public morals, even if these measures contravene other GATT obligations. However, the interpretation of what constitutes 'public morals' is complex and varies across different cultural, social and legal contexts. The lack of a clear definition has led to uncertainty in its application.

49 Susan Ariel Aaronson and Michele Rioux, 'Striking a Proper Match? Strategies to Link Trade Agreements and Real Labour Rights Improvements' available at https://www.ids.trade/files/news/2008/GLG%20Report.pdf, accessed 15 March 2024.

Inhumane Treatment and Human Rights

One pertinent example is Australia's stance in the Tuna-Dolphin case,[50] where it argued that Article XX(a) could justify measures addressing the inhumane treatment of animals, provided these measures apply equally to domestic and foreign products. This perspective can extend to human rights, suggesting that Article XX(a) could similarly justify trade actions against the inhumane treatment of individuals. If inhumane treatment of animals can fall under public morals, it logically follows that the protection of human beings should also be included. Thus, trade measures aimed at preventing gross human rights violations, such as forced labour or child exploitation, could be defended under Article XX(a).

Moral Standards and Human Rights

Another approach to integrating human rights into Article XX(a) is to recognize certain human rights as moral standards. International covenants on human rights, widely accepted by the global community, can be viewed as embodying these standards. In the *United States—Gambling and betting services* case, the WTO Panel defined 'public morals' as the standards of right and wrong conduct maintained by or on behalf of a community or nation.[51] These standards, while variable, are essential for societal functioning and can justify the inclusion of human rights considerations in trade measures.

The Appellate Body in the same case upheld this interpretation, acknowledging that WTO members should have the autonomy to define and apply public morals within their territories according to their cultural, ethical and religious values. Given that human rights are universally recognized as benchmarks for moral conduct,[52] violations of these rights can be deemed morally reprehensible, thus justifying trade measures under Article XX(a).

50 GATT Panel Report, 'United States—Restrictions on Imports of Tuna, DS21/R, BISD 39S/155' (1991), available at https://www.wto.org/english/tratop_e/dispu_e/gatt_e/91tuna.pdf

51 Report of the Panel, United States—Gambling and betting services, WTO Doc. WT/DS285/R, paras. 6.465–6.468 and 6.461 (10 November 2004); Office of the High Commissioner for Human Rights, Human Rights and World Trade Agreements: Using General Exceptions Clauses to Protect Human Rights, Document No. HR/Pub/05/5 (New York and Geneva, 2005).

52 Thomas Cottier, 'Trade and Human Rights: A Relationship to Discover': Part I: The State of International Economic Law' (2002) 5(1) *Journal of International Economic Law* 111, at 114.

Convergence of Labour Standards Within Trade Agreements: Reactions

This trend to incorporate labour standards into trade agreements has been met with mixed reactions. On one side, developing countries argue that adhering to higher labour standards could erode their competitive advantage. Opponents of integrated labour standards argue that low standards do not necessarily imply low wages, nor does competitiveness necessarily depend upon low wages or weak labour standards.[53] Protectionism has been found to be the most cited argument against the application of international labour standards. The argument for protectionism is often put forward by developing countries that claim the insertion of social clause(s) actually penalizes developing countries for taking full advantage of their comparative advantages (particularly low wages) to compete in world manufacturing.[54] Developing countries often rely on lower labour costs to maintain a competitive edge in the global market. The argument against stringent labour standards is that they could undermine this advantage, leading to reduced economic growth and fewer job opportunities. This perspective finds support in the WTO's 1996 Singapore Ministerial Declaration, which states:

> We reject the use of labour standards for protectionist purposes and agree that the comparative advantage of countries, particularly low-wage developing countries, must in no way be put into question.

On the other hand, NGOs and some developed countries contend that trade liberalization should consider fundamental human rights, including core labour rights.[55] Social dimensions of trade or investment agreements help avoid a race-to-the-bottom scenario in developing countries to attract foreign investment. According to Tsogas, 'One of the most widely noted justifications for the establishment of a social dimension as part of any trade agreement is to avoid "social dumping".'[56] 'The basic principle is that no partner in a trade agreement should derive competitive advantage from inadequate labour standards.'[57] Without social clauses in trade agreements, increased international competition might lead to 'a destructive downward spiral in the

53 George Tsogas, 'Labour Standards in International Trade Agreements: An Assessment of the Arguments' (1999) 10(2) *International Journal of Human Resource Management* 351–375.

54 S. Islam, 'Something for Everyone' (1994) 157(16) *Far Eastern Economic Review* 82.

55 Brian Bereusson and Cynthia Estlund, *Regulating Labour in the Wake of Globalization: New Challenges, New Institution* (Hart Publishing 2008) 169.

56 George Tsogas, 'Labour Standards in International Trade Agreements: An Assessment of the Arguments' (1999) 10(2) *International Journal of Human Resource Management* 351–375.

57 R.J. Adams and L. Turner, 'The Social Dimension of Freer Trade' in M.L. Cook and H.C. Katz (eds), *Regional Integration and Industrial Relations in North America* (ILR Press 1994) 82, 83.

conditions of work and life of working people all over the world'.[58] The insertion of social clauses in investment agreements also ensures a level playing field in the global economy as it helps governments to avoid the temptation of lowering labour standards in the hope that this could give them a greater comparative advantage in international trade and investment.

Practical Implications and Future Directions

To effectively use Article XX(a) for protecting human rights through trade measures, it is essential to establish a clear connection between the moral justification and the trade policy. This requires satisfying the Chapeau of Article XX, ensuring that measures are not applied in a discriminatory or protectionist manner. The policy must genuinely aim to protect public morals, aligning with international human rights norms.

Recent developments, such as USMCA, which includes robust labour provisions, and the EU's trade agreements with similar commitments, illustrate a growing trend towards integrating human rights into trade policies. These agreements reflect a broader recognition of the need to balance economic interests with social justice.

Incorporating human rights into trade agreements through mechanisms like Article XX(a) offers a pathway to enforce labour standards while respecting national sovereignty and cultural diversity. It acknowledges that trade policies should not only facilitate economic growth but also uphold fundamental human rights, preventing exploitation and promoting fair labour practices.

Labour Provisions in Unilateral Systems of Trade Preferences

Labour rights provisions are increasingly found in unilateral trade instruments such as the GSP. The GSP is a unilateral trade instrument that offers reduced tariffs or duties to a select group of developing countries. This system is permissible under the Enabling Clause of the WTO, which allows for an exception to the MFN principle on the condition that 'the beneficiaries are developing countries and that there are objective criteria for differentiating among categories of developing country recipients'.[59]

Such GSP systems provide a substantive legal procedure and establish unprecedented unitary enforcement mechanisms, whereby trade sanctions may be applied for labour violations. Generally, these mechanisms aim to reform the institutional and legislative frameworks governing labour rights.

58 Ibid.

59 Labour rights in Export Processing Zones with a focus on GSP+ beneficiary countries, Directorate-General For External Policies Policy Department, available at http://www.europarl.europa.eu/RegData/etudes/STUD/2017/603839/EXPO_STU(2017)603839_EN.pdf.

Labour Provisions in the US GSP

The United States has been a principal advocate of conditional labour provisions in its bilateral and regional trade agreements. The US GSP establishes conditionality based on adherence to labour standards by candidate countries for such preferences. Specifically, the US GSP stipulates that a candidate country 'must have taken or is taking steps to afford internationally recognized worker rights'.[60] The first agreement that linked labour provisions to economic consequences was the 1994 North American Agreement on Labour Cooperation (NAALC), a side agreement to NAFTA concluded between the United States, Canada and Mexico. The NAALC includes references to 11 basic labour principles, including the prohibition on forced labour. The NAALC calls on all three governments to improve performance regarding all these rights and standards. However, the NAALC does not establish a set of international labour rights and standards but mainly commits the signatories to enforce their national labour law.[61]

Labour Provisions Within the European Union's GSPs

In 1995, the European Union also introduced conditional labour provisions into its GSP, adopting a twofold 'carrot-and-stick' approach that involves both incentives and sanctions in the event of 'systematic and serious violations' of labour provisions.[62] Currently, the EU has three GSP schemes. One of these is the Special Incentive Arrangement for Sustainable Development and Good Governance (GSP+).[63] Introduced in 2005, the EU's GSP+ scheme provides trade concessions to beneficiary countries and obliges them to ratify and effectively implement key international conventions on human rights and labour rights. This grants additional trade preferences to 'vulnerable' beneficiary countries that have ratified and effectively implemented a range of international conventions, including the eight fundamental conventions of the ILO known as core labour standards.[64]

60 Generalized System of Preferences Handbook on the Scheme of the United States of America, available at https://unctad.org/system/files/official-document/itcdtsbmisc58rev3_en.pdf, accessed 10 February 2023.

61 The Evolving Debate on Trade & Labour Standards, IOE Information Paper, International Organisation of Employers, Geneva (March 2006), 5.

62 Tonia Novitz, 'The European Union and International Labour Standards: The Dynamics of Dialogue between the EU and the ILO' in Philip Alston (ed), *Labour Rights as Human Rights* (Oxford University Press 2005).

63 See, Generalized System of Preferences, European Union, available at https://ec.europa.eu/trade/policy/countries-and-regions/development/generalised-scheme-of-preferences/, accessed 7 August 2023.

64 Ibid.

The GSP+ scheme was reformed in 2012, and was applied as of 1 January 2014 and covers a ten-year period.[65] In order to qualify, a country must meet the following criteria: (1) it must be considered 'vulnerable' according to its level of export-oriented economic diversification; (2) it must have ratified and effectively implemented the 27 core international conventions in the fields of human and labour rights, the environment and good governance designated by the EU; and (3) it must accept the reporting requirements imposed by those conventions and cooperate with EU monitoring procedures.[66] Under the GSP, both the EU and the United States can offer increased export market access to LDCs at reduced tariff rates or duty-free, conditional on the exporting country's achievement of certain requirements such as improved labour standards.

Impact and Effectiveness of Sanction-Based Labour Provisions

Sanction-based labour provisions act as a potentially powerful instrument for the implementation of labour standards. Labour provisions involving sanctions may influence countries' behaviour in a number of ways. Apart from their immediate economic effects, which in themselves may constitute a considerable disincentive to violate labour standards, the application of sanctions in the case of the breach of a labour provision is likely to affect the reputation of the country in violation, and thus harm its economic and political relations with other countries.[67]

The United States has a long tradition of using sanction-based trade policy to promote social objectives in the exporting country. A sanction-based mechanism was applied by the United States against Bangladesh when the United States revoked Bangladesh's trade preferences after the *Rana Plaza* incident in order to put economic pressure on the country to adopt and adhere to international labour standards.[68] In 2013, President Obama suspended Bangladesh's trade benefits under the GSP due to insufficient progress by the government of Bangladesh in granting workers internationally recognized rights. This decision followed an extensive review under the GSP program of worker rights and safety in Bangladesh, during which the US government encouraged the Bangladeshi government to implement needed reforms. This action highlights how trade sanctions can be used to pressure countries to adopt and adhere to international labour standards.

65 GSP Regulation (EU) No. 978/2012.

66 Ibid.

67 Benjamin Richardson and James Harrison, 'Labour Rights in Export Processing Zones with a Focus on GSP+ Beneficiary Countries' *Directorate-General For External Policies Policy Department, European Parliament*, available at http://www.europarl.europa.eu/RegData/etudes/STUD/2017/603839/EXPO_STU(2017)603839_EN.pdf, accessed 9 September 2022.

68 The full text of the Sustainability Compact for Bangladesh can be found at: http://trade.ec.europa.eu/doclib/docs/2013/july/tradoc_151601.pdf, accessed 3 June 2023.

Criticisms of GSP Schemes

Some developing countries like Bangladesh have reaped significant benefits in the form of enhanced competitive strength in the EU market and the consequent higher export earnings.[69] However, GSP schemes are not without criticisms. The GSP has not functioned as an effective mechanism to improve working conditions due to other obstacles that prevent eligibility of low-income countries for GSP benefits.[70] Other obstacles include non-participation of an LDC in multilateral trading systems. For example, an LDC will not enjoy GSP if it is not a member of the WTO.

Another criticism of the current trade agreements regime is that most of them do not require a Party's labour laws to comply with the rights established in the ILO's fundamental conventions. As mentioned earlier, most trade agreements contain rhetorical language regarding labour provisions. For example, the state parties are merely required to 'strive to ensure' compliance with these rights and similarly strive not to weaken them to attract trade or investment.[71] A Party's breach of these commitments could not be challenged in dispute settlement.[72] But there is neither a commitment from Parties to the agreement to sign and ratify the ILO's core conventions nor a commitment to effectively implement them once in force.[73] This is particularly necessary in view of the fact that many countries have not ratified many of the ILO fundamental conventions.[74] This has created a compliance gap in international labour standards.

Despite the progress made in integrating labour provisions into trade agreements, several challenges remain. One significant challenge is ensuring compliance with these provisions. Many countries have not ratified ILO fundamental conventions, creating a gap in international labour standards. Furthermore, the rhetorical language in many trade agreements, which merely requires countries to 'strive to ensure' compliance with labour rights, is insufficient to guarantee effective implementation.

Another challenge is the potential for trade agreements to be used as tools for protectionism. Critics argue that incorporating labour provisions into trade agreements can be a guise for protectionism, disadvantaging developing countries that rely on lower labour costs for their competitive edge. This concern underscores the need for a balanced approach that promotes fair labour practices without undermining the economic development of low-income countries.

69 Mustafizur Rahman, 'Proposed revisions in the EU-GSP Scheme: Implications for Bangladesh' *The Daily Star*, 24 October 2021.
70 Berik and van der Meulen Rodgers (n 19).
71 James (n 55) 716.
72 Ibid.
73 Ibid.
74 Ibid.

Conclusion

The exploitative working conditions prevalent in the industries of developing countries have significantly influenced the evolution of BITs, prompting the integration of labour governance mechanisms within trade and investment agreements. Many developed countries, along with the European Union, have strategically employed trade and investment policies to drive enhancements in labour protections in developing nations through the incorporation of labour rights provisions in these agreements. This approach addresses some of the adverse impacts of globalization and shapes the social dimensions of this process.

The integration of labour provisions within FTAs and BITs has yielded several successes in improving workplace conditions and labour rights in certain developing countries. For instance, labour provisions embedded in the United States' FTAs have compelled partner countries such as Bahrain, Colombia, Morocco and Oman to implement significant labour law reforms prior to the ratification of these agreements. These reforms demonstrate the potential effectiveness of incorporating labour rights into trade agreements to foster better labour conditions globally.

However, despite these achievements, the overall effectiveness of FTAs in aligning national labour laws with the ILO fundamental labour rights remains limited. The enforcement of these laws by governments and the respect for these laws by enterprises operating within the countries covered by these agreements also present significant challenges. While compulsion through legal mechanisms is a crucial aspect, persuasion via cooperation and initiating constructive dialogue are equally important in ensuring compliance with international labour standards in developing countries.

The limitations in the effectiveness of FTAs are often due to the largely rhetorical nature of labour provisions within these agreements. Many of these provisions do not legally bind host states to protect and uphold workers' rights, nor do they hold MNCs accountable for directly or indirectly contributing to labour rights violations. For example, the European Union's recent trade agreements with Vietnam and Japan include chapters dedicated to sustainable development encompassing labour rights. However, the enforcement mechanisms remain weak, with compliance largely dependent on the political will of the involved parties.

Furthermore, the use of the GSP as a unilateral trade instrument to enforce labour rights presents both opportunities and challenges. While GSP schemes like the EU's GSP+ provide trade concessions to countries that ratify and effectively implement key international conventions on human rights and labour rights, criticisms remain. These schemes often fail to function effectively due to obstacles that prevent low-income countries from becoming eligible for GSP benefits, such as non-participation in the multilateral trading system. Additionally, many trade agreements do not mandate compliance with the ILO's fundamental conventions, resulting in a compliance gap in international labour standards.

The potential for trade agreements to be utilized as tools for protectionism also poses a significant challenge. Developing countries often view stringent labour standards as a threat to their competitive edge in the global market, fearing that such standards could lead to reduced economic growth and fewer job opportunities. This concern is underscored by the WTO's 1996 Singapore Ministerial Declaration, which rejects the use of labour standards for protectionist purposes and affirms that the comparative advantage of low-wage developing countries should not be undermined.

In summary, while the integration of labour provisions in trade and investment agreements has shown some promise in improving labour conditions, significant challenges remain in ensuring effective compliance and addressing the potential for protectionist misuse. A balanced approach that combines legal enforcement with cooperative dialogue and respects the economic realities of developing countries is essential for achieving sustainable improvements in global labour standards. The ongoing efforts to integrate labour rights into trade policies reflect a broader recognition of the need to balance economic interests with social justice, promoting fair labour practices and preventing exploitation in the global economy.

8 Promoting Sustainable Forest Management Through International Trade and Investment

Introduction

SFM presents a useful framework for forest managers and policymakers to promote social and ecological conservation goals for forestry resources and takes a more holistic approach is realizing the benefits of forest ecosystems that is not just limited to economic benefits. However, successfully implementing SFM requires a realization that forest resources operate in a much larger framework of international trade in timber resources, whereby it has historically treated both social and ecological benefits associated with forest ecosystems as an externality. To further promote SFM that is achievable and aligned with the global export of timber products, there needs to be greater recognition and exploration between international trade and SFM, including the supporting investment that can facilitate greater SFM across forest actors. This is a prevalent question for developing countries, which are not only the sites of some of the world's most valuable forest resources but are also vulnerable to economic exploitation and face capacity constraints when implementing and enforcing SFM.

This chapter examines this intricate relationship between forest trade, international investment and SFM. This chapter will consider how global trade and investment patterns influence forest resources, highlighting the dual role of international investment as both a potential threat and a vital support to SFM. By analysing the current trends in forest exploitation and conservation, the chapter will discuss the mechanisms that can align economic gains with environmental sustainability. This chapter will then consider how IIAs, corporate practices and supporting governance frameworks seek a balance between economic development with the forest conservation. This chapter will also explore how innovative financial instruments and market-based approaches can be used to incentivize sustainable management practices. Finally, this chapter will deliver policy recommendations for enhancing the relationship between international trade laws, investment strategies and SFM to ensure the long-term health and productivity of forest ecosystems worldwide.

DOI: 10.4324/9781003164951-9

Current Trends in SFM: A Greater Need to Integrate Sustainable Trade and Investment

SFM is the practice of managing forests in a way that preserves their ecological functions, biodiversity and productivity for present and future generations. SFM is vital for providing future employment opportunities for rural communities within developing countries, as well as providing co-benefits in the form of greater ecosystem services, including better water quality, soil conditioning and carbon sequestration. Forests play a key role in the global carbon cycle by locking carbon into surrounding soil, biomass, dead wood and leaf litter.[1] In addition, SFM supports a range of cultural activities, including indigenous spiritual and cultural expression, and aesthetic values that are central to local communities. By requiring forest managers to engage and consult with local communities, communities can preserve their sense of identity and exercise their human rights to cultural and religious expression that are inherently tied with their forest landscapes.

SFM does not occur in a vacuum: consumer demand and the international marketplace for timber products play act as a key consideration for SFM policymakers and practitioners. Developing countries are often the sites of significant timber resources and yet have limited capacity to implement SFM and are vulnerable to economic overexploitation to meet the demand from consumers who are often located in developed or advanced economies. Whilst timber licensing regimes and permits play an important role in limiting overexploitation, as will be discussed in this chapter, developing countries remain vulnerable to illegally harvested lumber. Trade restrictions related to such wood pose challenges in terms of compliance and enforcement.

To implement more ecologically and socially enhancing methods to manage forest landscapes, large amounts of capital are required. SFM finance is vital, especially in developing countries, which often lack the access to capital and face serious capacity constraints which prevent sustainable practices from being realized at scale. SFM finance primarily comes through two key sources: public bodies and private actors.[2] Public bodies can provide funds domestically through grants or tax incentives or can provide finance to foreign forest managers either bilaterally or through development agencies as a form of overseas development assistance (ODA). Mobilizing funds from international sources, such as the Green Climate Fund, can enable sustainable forest managers to obtain access to grants, loans or guarantees for projects that reduce greenhouse gas emissions from deforestation and forest degradation (REDD+) or enhance forest carbon stocks through conservation, sustainable management and restoration (REDD++). In addition, payments for ecosystem

1 Yude Pan et al., 'A Large and Persistent Carbon Sink in the World's Forest' (2011) 333 *Science* 988–993.

2 B. Singer, 'Financing Sustainable Forest Management in Developing Countries' (2016) 18(1) *International Forestry Review* 96–109.

services (PES) are important investment vehicles which reward landowners for conserving and enhancing forest resources that provide benefits to society. PES can create incentives for forest protection and restoration, as well as generate alternative sources of income and compensate for the opportunity cost associated for forgoing agricultural or timber production.

Generally, there is overall consensus that the majority of sustainable forest finance is derived from public, domestic sources.[3] When looking at investment into nature-based solutions more broadly, which includes investment into other related sectors such as agriculture, private investment only accounts for 17% of total capital invested into nature-based solutions.[4] Of the public bodies that do invest into SFM, this varies from central, provincial and local governments, reflecting the polycentric nature of forestry governance and how forest management is operationalized between different levels of government and non-government stakeholders.[5] Public funds also play an important function in diversifying against risk associated with prevailing economic conditions and competing priorities. The COVID-19 pandemic witnessed a significant boost in ODA.[6] Whilst this can be attributed to an increase in health-related expenditure to combat the pandemic, historically, ODA has been the most stable source of external finance for developing countries and is not necessarily tied to the donor's gross national income.[7] Over the past decade, multilateral organizations are providing a greater proportion of support to developing countries than donor countries are providing directly through bilateral arrangements.[8] Conversely, the COVID-19 pandemic created a strong headwind for private investors, and there was a significant decline of all private

3 Sara Lofqvist, Rachael Garrett and Jaboury Ghazoul, 'Incentives and Barriers to Private Finance for Forest and Landscape Restoration' (2023) 7 *Nature Ecology and Evolution* 707, 711–712; United Nations Environment Programme, *State of Finance for Nature 2021* (United Nations 2021) 18, available at https://www.unep.org/resources/state-finance-nature-2021#:~:text=If%20the%20world%20is%20to,which%20comes%20from%20public%20sources, accessed 29 May 2023.

4 United Nations Environment Programme, *State of Finance for Nature. Time to Act: Doubling Investment by 2025* (United Nations 2022) 8, available at https://wedocs.unep.org/20.500.11822/41333, accessed 29 May 2023.

5 See generally, Marius Lazdinis, Per Angelstam and Helga Pulzl, 'Towards Sustainable Forest Management in the European Union Through Polycentric Forest Governance and an Integrated Landscape Approach' (2019) 34(7) *Landscape Ecology* 1737–1749.

6 World Bank, 'Defying Predictions, Remittance Flows Remain Strong During COVID-19 Crisis' (World Bank 2021), available at https://www.worldbank.org/en/news/press-release/2021/05/12/defying-predictions-remittance-flows-remain-strong-during-covid-19-crisis?cid=ECR_E_NewsletterWeekly_EN_EXT&deliveryName=DM104029, accessed 3 June 2023.

7 Yasmin Ahmad and Eleanor Carey, 'Development Co-Operation During the COVID-19 Pandemic: An Analysis of 2020 Figures and 2021 Trends to Watch' in *Development Co-operation Profiles* (OECD Publishing 2021), available at https://doi.org/10.1787/e4b3142a-en, accessed 3 June 2023.

8 Ibid.

flows of investment into developing countries at this time.[9] This underscores that public finance, especially the support of multilateral organizations and development agencies, insure against capital flight that occurs during economic downturns and provide sustainable forest managers greater certainty to undertake medium- and long-term planning.

However, notwithstanding the anomaly of ODA growth associated with the COVID-19 pandemic, ODA saw its highest levels of growth during the 2000s.[10] Despite this high-water mark, public finance alone cannot address the vast investment that is required. Private investment, including philanthropy, is needed to provide capital, technology, innovation and market access that is required for forest products to be produced in a sustainable manner. Private investment can occur through domestic investment or via FDI. Furthermore, public-private partnerships can facilitate the involvement of private actors in forest restoration, by sharing risks, costs and benefits, as well as providing technical expertise and innovation. Market-based mechanisms, including certification, are another tool which can unlock private investment into SFM. There are various mechanisms that can be used to deploy private capital, but the biggest challenge is how to scale private sector investment by several orders of magnitude so that the global community can realize SFM.[11]

To date, most private investment goes towards environmentally destructive practices.[12] Each year, almost US$1.8 trillion is spent into environmentally destructive practices, including fossil fuel extraction or overexploitation of freshwater resources.[13] Of this US$1.8 trillion, almost US$520 billion is spent directly towards unsustainable agricultural practices that contribute to soil erosion, water pollution, deforestation, greenhouse gas emissions and biodiversity loss.[14] This indicates a significant ambition gap between the increased rhetoric for greener corporate credentials and where actual capital is being invested to realize these goals. SFM finance requires a nuanced approach which embraces cross-sectoral approaches. It is more than about financing sustainable timber production; it also includes approaches which fund related activities in soil and water rehabilitation, agriculture, biodiversity conservation and climate change adaptation. Cross sectoral approaches also ensure that relevant stakeholders,

9 Ibid.

10 Organisation for Economic Co-operation and Development (OECD) Report, 'Six Decades of ODA: Insights and Outlook in the Covid-19 Crisis' available at https://www.oecd-ilibrary.org/sites/5e331623-en/index.html?itemId=/content/component/5e331623-en&_csp_=b14d4f60505d057b456dd1730d8fcea3&itemIGO=oecd&itemContentType=chapter, accessed 19 August 2024.

11 United Nations Environment Programme (n 4).

12 Ibid.

13 Doug Koplow and Ronald Steenblik, *Protecting Nature by Reforming Environmentally Harmful Subsidies: The Role of Business* (Earth Track 2022), available at https://www.earthtrack.net/document/protecting-nature-reforming-environmentally-harmful-subsidies-role-business, accessed 3 June 2023.

14 Ibid.

including forest communities, local governments and non-government organizations, receive adequate support and consultation before implementing decisions which impact on forest landscapes. As a result, policy coordination is a key aspect in achieving effective sustainable forest finance. Decision makers are continually challenged to ensure that cost externalities are equitably allocated, and that scarce funds are not being deployed into activities that undermine the efforts of sustainable forest managers. Subsidies and incentives which encourage destructive activities only serve to weaken the value of money and effort that is used to preserve forest landscapes, enhance forest communities and protect biodiversity. Whilst a public-private typology is an overt simplification with many institutions and development agencies, such as the World Bank offering hybrid or blended models that mix different donors and sources of funding,[15] this typology provides a useful model to illustrate existing financing patterns and state of play in SFM.

International Agreements, Corporate Practices and Supporting Governance Frameworks: A Need for Policy Coherence and Coordination

Underlying the dynamic relationship between international trade, investment and SFM is a suite of international agreements, practices and institutions which drive SFM policy. Developed countries like the United States and China have engaged in bilateral treaties under the Forest Law Enforcement and Governance (FLEG) programs in Southeast Asia and Africa. However, whilst these initiatives are admirable for addressing the underlying causes of illegally harvested timber, these treaties link aid to trade agreement obligations that grant exclusive rights to a developing country's natural resources. The European Union has taken a different approach with its Forest Law Enforcement, Governance, and Trade (FLEGT) program. FLEGT incorporates trade as a parameter to enhance international compliance. It tackles key issues associated with illegal logging, including uncollected taxes, reduced profitability of legal trade, and deforestation. Notably, FLEGT's timber licensing scheme could have broader implications, potentially leading to international conflicts through trade disputes before the WTO. While this system may serve as a model for other multilateral trade agreements, the prevalence of bilateral treaties may impact its effectiveness. Interestingly, WTO oversight could even constrain European SFM policies, especially if the strict measures against illegal timber imports clash with GATT principles.

In this respect, there are several GATT obligations which have important interactions with SFM. Import restrictions for non-sustainable products,

15 See for instance, World Bank, *Nature and Development Brief: Scaling up Finance for Nature* (World Bank 2022) 5, available at https://thedocs.worldbank.org/en/doc/b08b82598c0bb418ec7f73a49ff3fdfd-0320012022/original/3-Nature-Finance.pdf.

including non-timber products that have an unsustainable impact on forest landscapes (e.g. palm oil production) could constitute as a breach of the WTO principle of the elimination of quantitative restrictions (GATT Article XI). Whilst SFM policymakers imposing such restrictions could argue that the application of such a measure is necessary to protect human, animal or plant life or health, or that it relates to the conservation of an exhaustible natural resource—which are valid exemptions under GATT Article XX(b) and (g)—these are untested propositions. Furthermore, the application of process and production methods (PPMs) such as the use of forest certification, which is discussed in more detail below, could also constitute a breach of GATT Article I which requires Members to accord MFN treatment to any other like product of other WTO Members regarding tariffs and regulation of exports and imports. Because the WTO remains in an institutional crisis given that the United States continues to block the appointment of Appellate Body judges, this is a highly uncertain area of international trade law whereby it remains doubtful that such matters would be resolved in the immediate future.

REDD+ is an essential part of SFM. Developed by the United Nations Framework Convention on Climate Change, REDD+ encourages developing countries to take action in two key areas. First, by slowing, halting, and reversing forest loss and degradation, REDD+ aims to decrease greenhouse gas emissions (GHGs). When forests are cleared or degraded, they can become a source of GHG emissions by releasing stored carbon. Halting deforestation is a cost-effective measure with a clear impact on reducing global GHG emissions. Second, REDD+ promotes the conservation, management and expansion of forests to increase the removal of GHGs from the atmosphere. Forests play a fundamental role in climate change mitigation by absorbing CO_2 from the atmosphere and storing it in biomass and soils. The Food and Agriculture Organization of the United Nations (FAO) supports developing countries in their REDD+ processes, helping them turn their political commitments (as represented in their nationally determined contributions) into action on the ground.

The Need for Greater Policy Coherence

SFM investment risk can also be attributed to an unstable policy and regulatory environment which may diminish returns. Findings from stakeholder interviews and actor perceptions have continually cited a lack of intersectoral coordination and coherence as a key impediment for implementation.[16] A lack of policy coherence can arise from conflicting funding schemes. Conflicting funding schemes such as agricultural subsidies that promote unsustainable practices can perpetuate environmentally damaging activities and distort the market. And the scale of conflicting funding schemes is substantial. Governments

16 See Felix Kanungwe Kalaba, 'Barriers to Policy Implementation and Implications for Zambia's Forest Ecosystems' (2016) 69 *Forest Policy and Economics* 40–44.

currently spend US$500 billion each year on economic support that harms biodiversity—five times more than spending on biodiversity conservation measures.[17] OECD and G20 economies spend US$340 billion per year on fossil fuel support[18] and US$228 billion on support for farmers, of which US$116 billion can be considered as harmful to biodiversity and forests.[19] This is a complex relationship and is highly dependent on the stakeholders and relationships between people and institutions. On the one hand, fertilizer subsidies can reduce deforestation by increasing the yield on existing crop land and reducing the pressure to expand agricultural production into forested areas.[20] However, the same type of subsidies can accelerate deforestation if they prop up inefficient uses of land, encourage overuse of inputs and trigger an excessive depletion of natural resources.[21]

Policy coherence and coordination not only requires an investigation into whether policy objectives align, but also an alignment of the institutions that are tasked with implementation. An analysis of Ecuadorian forest policy demonstrates that whilst policy coherence is largely aligned, institutional responsibilities are fragmented, resulting in excessive duplication and a lack of coordination.[22] This is made further complicated by the fact that a robust forestry policy must also consider the cross-sectoral interests that influence deforestation, including energy and agriculture policy, especially given that these sectors have significant risk on forest cover in places such as South America, Asia and partially in the Congo Basin and West Africa.[23] In certain instances, it may be appropriate for forest governance to devolve to the local level and enable highly localized stakeholders to develop their own

17 OECD, *A Comprehensive Overview of Global Biodiversity Finance* (OECD Publishing 2020); World Bank, *Mobilizing Private Finance for Nature* (2020) 59.

18 OECD and International Energy Agency, 'Update on Recent Progress in Reform of Inefficient Fossil-Fuel Subsidies That Encourage Wasteful Consumption' (2019), available at https://oecd.org/fossil-fuels/publication/OECD-IEA-G20-Fossil-Fuel-Subsidies-Reform-Update-2019.pdf, accessed 30 May 2023.

19 OECD, *Towards Sustainable Land Use: Aligning Biodiversity, Climate and Food Policies* (OECD Publishing 2020), available at https://doi.org/10.1787/3809b6a1-en, accessed 30 May 2023.

20 Ryan Abman and Conor Carney, 'Agricultural Productivity and Deforestation: Evidence from Input Subsidies and Ethnic Favouritism in Malawi' (2020) 103 *Journal of Environmental Economics and Management* 102342.

21 Erwin Bulte, Richard Damania and Ramon Lopez, 'On the Gains of Committing to Inefficiency: Corruption, Deforestation and Low Land Productivity in Latin America' (2007) 54(3) *Journal of Environmental Economics and Management* 277–295.

22 Pradip Kumar Sarker, Richard Fischer, Fabian Tamayo, Bolier Torres Navarrete and Sven Gunter, 'Analyzing Forest Policy Mixes Based on the Coherence of Policies and the Consistency of Legislative Policy Instruments: A Case Study from Ecuador' (2022) 144 *Forest Policy and Economics* 102838.

23 Werna Raza, Bernhard Troster, Bernhard Wolfshehner and Markus Krajewski, *How Can International Trade Contribute to Sustainable Forestry and the Preservation of the World's Forests Through the Green Deal?* (European Union 2020) 11.

organization structures which can address the various intersecting issues relating to a community-owned forest in a holistic way. The devolution of forestry governance requires specialized support systems, such as access to micro-credit arrangements and arrangements to ensure equitable benefit sharing arrangements with local stakeholders. A meta-analysis of devolved forest governance structures demonstrates several advantages when compared to state-managed forests, such as improved forest cover.[24] However, there is no one-size-fits-all approach to designing forest governance. Community forest arrangements, including arrangements which confer property rights for conservation land use, can be undermined if the local network of actors continue to display an economic preference to continue deforestation.[25] The institutional settings must therefore be highly attuned to the policy environment that they operate, whether they have sufficient capability to coordinate, execute and address the underlying motivations of key actors.

Using Market-Based Instruments to Promote SFM

Timber Certification

Certification is one way in which investors can evaluate the performance of forest managers in meeting predefined ESG benchmarks, including fair wage entitlements for forestry workers and respect for local indigenous rights. Certification is an industry-led voluntary scheme which provides information and transparency to consumers that forest products are sustainably harvested and employ minimum ESG standards. The Forest Stewardship Council (FSC) and the Programme for the Endorsement of Forest Certification (PEFC) schemes are the two largest certification players in global forestry. Certification schemes can also extend to hybrid initiatives which employ a combination of government regulation and labelling. The FLEGT scheme requires timber-producing countries to enact minimum harvesting standards through legislation so that timber exporters can access the European market. For instance, in Indonesia, the FLEGT partnership with the European Union is enabled under their *Standar Verifikasi Legalitas Kayu* legislation, which allow private and

24 USAID, *Devolution of Forest Rights and Sustainable Forest Management Volume 1: A Review of Policies and Programs in 16 Developing Countries* (US Government 2012) ix, available at https://www.land-links.org/wp-content/uploads/2016/09/USAID_Land_Tenure_Devolution_of_Forest_Rights_and_Sustainable_Forest_Management_Volume_1.pdf, accessed 30 May 2023.

25 Yanto Rochmayanto, Dodik Ridho Nurrochmat, Bramasto Nugroho, Dudung Darusman, Arif Satria, Thorkil Casse, James Thomas Erbaugh and Donny Wicaksono, 'Devolution of Forest Management to Local Communities and Its Impacts on Livelihoods and Deforestation in Berau, Indonesia' (2023) 9(5) *Heliyon* e16115, available at https://doi.org/10.1016/j.heliyon.2023.e16115, accessed 30 May 2023.

community forest owners to export timber products to the European Union.[26] These voluntary schemes, and importantly the market access they provide, create powerful incentives for private actors to perform SFM; voluntary standards have shown to introduce higher levels of environmental conservation than those set by a country's legislation alone.[27]

However, noting the issues associated with certification schemes and WTO obligations discussed above, the saturation of voluntary schemes such as the FSC and PEFC within developing countries remains low. Currently, only 23% of FSC-certified and 9% of PEFC-certified forests are located within developing countries.[28] One of the key impediments for its low adoption is the lack of national certification procedures that enable forest managers to obtain FSC or PEFC certification and the lack of resources held by developing countries to monitor compliance.[29] Voluntary schemes require institutional resources and systems, such as trained officers and ability to monitor and report on compliance. At the project level, forest managers also face high direct and indirect costs to obtain FSC or PEFC certification, making it cost prohibitive.[30] As a result of these cost barriers, larger forest timber producers are able to access more markets and thus consolidate competition, whilst small-scale timber producers—which provides a major source of employment for rural communities in developing countries—remain locked out.[31] For many of these small-scale producers, they are required to perform collective action and combine their market power in order to compete on the global marketplace,[32] such as joining co-ops. These producers also face risk that FSC or PEFC certified timber may not attract a premium, and therefore do not see a return from the costs

26 See generally, Shawkat Alam, Tuti Herawati, Herman Hidayat and Stephen Wyatt, 'Forest Certification, State Regulation and Community Empowerment: Complementarity in Seeking a Viable Solution to Forest Degradation in Indonesia?' (2019) 22(1) *Asia Pacific Journal of Environmental Law* 27–47.

27 Ewald Rametsteiner and Markky Simula, 'Forest Certification—An Instrument to Promote Sustainable Forest Management' (2003) 67(1) *Journal of Environmental Management* 87–98.

28 Pratiwi Kartika and Cerdikwan Hariyadi (2020) 'The Programme for the Endorsement of Forest Certification (PEFC) and Its Contribution to Sustainable Forest Management in Indonesia' in A. Negi, J. Perez-Pineda and J. Blakenbach (eds), *Sustainability Standards and Global Governance*, available at https://doi.org/10.1007/978-981-15-3473-7_9.

29 P.B. Durst, P.J. McKenzie, C.L. Brown and S. Appanah, 'Challenges Facing Certification and Eco-Labelling of Forest Products in Developing Countries' (2006) 8(2) *International Forestry Review* 193–200, available at https://doi.org/10.1505/ifor.8.2.193.

30 Ibid.

31 Shawkat Alam, Tuti Herawati, Herman Hidayat and Stephen Watt, 'Forest Certification, State Regulation and Community Empowerment: Complementarity in Seeking a Viable Solution to Forest Degradation in Indonesia?' (2019) 22(1) *Asia Pacific Journal of Environmental Law* 27–47, 37.

32 See Luigi Orso, Ivan De Noni and Laura Viviana Marchisio, 'The Role of Collective Action in Leveraging Farmers' Performances: Lessons from Sesame Seed Farmers' (2017) 51 *Journal of Rural Studies* 93.

associated with undertaking the certification process. As a result, whilst certification aims to implement ESG outcomes, it may serve to intensify existing asymmetric power relationships within the sector in developing countries.

Land Tenure and Property Rights—A Necessary Precondition for SFM Trade and Investment

For most developing countries, fundamental rights and conditions such as political stability and highly regulated systems of land tenure and ownership remain elusive.[33] Land tenure—referring to the conditions under which land is held and occupied, and determines who can access and use land resources—remains an important prerequisite to practice SFM.[34] The rights of a landholder affect their ability to manage forests sustainably, and in most cases, forest resources are shared amongst a variety of different actors. In most joint and community forest schemes, local communities can access forests; however, harvesting may not be permitted without the formation of a forest management plan and is subject to government regulations.[35] According to the FAO, 73% of the world's forests are publicly owned, and in some regions public ownership is more dominant: 93% in Western and Central Africa, 99% in Western and Central Asia and 88% in South and Southeast Asia,[36] although such figures fail to account for the percentage of land subject to customary land rights.[37] Changes in government regulations, as well as unscrupulous actors who fail to recognize land tenure and property rights, undermine SFM. Illegal logging activities steal timber resources from tenured land to the detriment of landholders. This creates a chilling effect for any potential investment, public or private, as investors may lose the return on investment to illegal activity. Developing countries remain at particular risk as an immature legal system may be unable to enforce the rights of legitimate landholders, including customary rights possessed by indigenous communities.

In most developed countries, land tenure is assisted through titling. Whilst property rights do not have to be formalized to exist, titling can assist by creating a formal register of land interests that can be asserted against other actors, as well as creating indirect benefits such as growing a country's potential tax base.[38] However, titling can only work if there is a sufficient governance structure in place to make asserting such rights a reality. In addition, titling

33 Alam, Herawati, Hidayat and Watt (n 31).

34 Pia Katila, Constance McDermott, Anne Larson, Safia Aggarwal and Lukas Giessen, 'Forest Tenure and the Sustainable Development Goals—A Critical View' (2020) 120 *Forest Policy and Economics* 102294.

35 Ibid.

36 FAO, *Global Forest Resources Assessment: Main Report* (FAO 2020), available at https://doi.org/10.4060/ca9825en, accessed 1 June 2023.

37 Katila, McDermott, Larson, Aggarwal and Giessen (n 34).

38 Margaret Holland and Moustapha Diop, 'Strategies for Securing Tenure: The Promise and Pitfalls of Formalization' in Margaret Holland, Yuta Masuda and Brian Robinson (eds), *Land Tenure Security and Sustainable Development* (Cham Springer Nature 2022) 225, 229.

can create a negative effect for customary and other de facto rights holders by creating a form of de jure rights and institutionalize land-grabbing.[39] As a result, there is a need to ensure that local communities and customary rights holders are equitably engaged in the process to ensure that their rights are adequately protected. This is becoming increasingly important as 'land investments are more directed to countries with a high share of rural land under traditional systems and high diversity of land tenure systems',[40] and therefore there is a pressing need to ensure that private investment does not perpetuate land-grabbing or legitimization of nefarious actors to the detriment of customary rights holders and local forest communities.

In addition to titling and formalizing property rights, market mechanisms can also play a role in securing land tenure. One side effect from the use of certification schemes, such as FSC or PEFC as discussed earlier, is that practically it may act as a catalyst to resolve land tenure disputes.[41] Prior to certification and each year post-certification, forest management units are audited by independent third-party auditors under the FSC scheme and can issue corrective action requests (CARs) where there are issues in forest management. If there is an unresolved land tenure dispute prior to certification, auditors can issue CARs to require stakeholders to resolve their land dispute. Post-certification, auditors can issue CARs but can be given a time frame to resolve the issue. Critically, CARs are initiating conversations over land tenure and property rights which may lead to 'more community building relations and the development of a better system for monitoring illegal logging'.[42] However, despite this benefit associated with certification, Miteva et al notes that increased land tenure security can only extend to forests covered under a certification scheme, namely, forests that are only used for timber production, and will have limited effectiveness in isolated rural areas where costs for FSC compliance are too costly and the chances of being issued with a CAR becomes remote.[43]

Corruption Continues to Erode Confidence in Market-Based Instruments

Despite the critical role that private finance plays in securing a sustainable future, the decision to invest capital into SFM projects is primarily driven by the same considerations that drive other investment decisions: the need to

39 Ibid. 238.

40 C. Conigliani, N. Cuffaro and G. D'Agostino, 'Large-Scale Land Investments and Forests in Africa' (2018) 75 *Land Use Policy* 651, 652, available at https://doi.org/10.1016/j.landusepol.2018. 02.005, accessed 1 June 2023.

41 Daniela A. Miteva, Lea Fortmann and Roan McNab, 'Beyond the Traditional: Voluntary Market-Based Initiatives to Promote Land Tenure Security' in Margaret Holland, Yuta Masuda and Brian Robinson (eds), *Land Tenure Security and Sustainable Development* (Cham Springer Nature 2022) 269, 273–274.

42 Ibid. *Smartwood Forest Management 2006 CAR Verification Audit Report for PT Sumalindo Lestari Jaya in Samarinda, Kalimantan Timur* (Rainforest Alliance 2007).

43 Ibid. 275–276.

obtain a return on investment. Regardless of whether the return is realized through economic or non-economic gains, including ESG improvements, failing to realize a return is a key risk that must be managed. According to Lofqvist et al, asset managers and corporations continue to display a preference to utilize their capital towards low-risk investments or in areas that have an existing business presence.[44] There are several key motivators which attract private investment into sustainable forestry projects. The need to obtain net emissions reductions, promoting sustainability across a supply chain, or impact and sustainability positioning, are key motivators for private actors and can weigh into the decision to invest capital into a particular project.[45]

Conversely, the lack of knowledge around different types of interventions that can lead to emissions reduction, the lack of capacity to quantify impact, the failure to obtain a private benefit and the lack of storytelling potential are also lead determinants which prevent corporations from investing.[46] For the forestry sector in particular, the fact that investment into SFM is over long-term horizons, usually over ten or more years, make it an unattractive asset class.[47] Asset managers face additional risks given their fiduciary duties to obtain a financial return on investment, and a lack of standardization or knowledge over what works in terms of restoration investment.[48] Developing countries face additional hurdles when attempting to attract investment into SFM projects. Developing countries often do not possess the established good governance practices which are necessary for investors, including a stable policy and regulatory environment, transparency and accountability of forest actors. This section will consider these additional hurdles that developing countries face which prevent SFM finance from being deployed at scale.

The introduction of large sums of capital can only be effective where there are robust mechanisms in place to ensure transparency, accountability and good governance between institutions, investors, decision makers and forest communities. Institutional corruption is one of the leading contributing factors to the loss of effectiveness of both public and private forms of investment into SFM. Corruption costs the forest sector upwards of US$29 billion annually, with an average of 250 cases of forestry corruption identified in timber producing countries each year.[49] Corrupt actors can be organized into simple or complex networks, with INTERPOL finding that the most persons likely to be

44 Sara Lofqvist, Rachael Garrett and Jaboury Ghazoul, 'Incentives and Barriers to Private Finance for Forest and Landscape Restoration' (2023) 7 *Nature Ecology and Evolution* 707–715.

45 Ibid. 708–709.

46 Ibid.

47 Laurent Capolaghi and Francis Goddard, 'Forestry Funds: The Emerging Star of Alternative Investments' (EY 2023), available at https://www.ey.com/en_lu/private-equity/forestry-funds--the-emerging-star-of-alternative-investments, accessed 1 June 2023.

48 Lofqvist, Garrett and Ghazoul (n 44).

49 INTERPOL, *Uncovering the Risks of Corruption in the Forestry Sector* (INTERPOL 2016) 1.

involved in corruption include government officials from forestry agencies to facilitate the movement of illegal timber onto the market.[50] Corruption comes in many forms, and how it manifests itself is highly dependent on local governance arrangements.[51] Whilst bribery is the most utilized form of corruption,[52] other examples include failing to enforce legal rights or perform enforcement activities. Generally, corruption may manifest itself through two key ways: 'against the rule' corruption and 'according to the rule' corruption.[53] Against the rule corruption obtains public services that are not due to the briber or the implementation of public procedures, such as bribing a Minister to offer a logging concession without following due process.[54] According to the rule corruption facilitates the delivery of public services or the implementation of public procedures that are legal, for example, offering a bribe to speed up an approval process.[55] In many instances, corruption can include a hybrid combination of both forms of typologies. For instance, in Papua New Guinea, the forestry lease back scheme has enabled loggers to appear as agricultural developers in order to gain access to forest resources; however, systemic misuse of this scheme is not being prosecuted by state officials.[56]

Corruption can also manifest itself at various stages of policy formulation process and implementation. This includes weakening forest and carbon rights through policy lobbying to ensure that it benefits industry actors, manipulating data and falsely setting carbon reference levels so that there is no real net benefit for targeted action, officials sharing revenue and other rent-seeking behaviour rather than leaving benefits to local communities and failing to enforce land and forest rights.[57] Transparency International have recorded several instances of corruption directly relating to climate and forest finance, including a diversion of US$38 million of REDD+ funding, a reallocation of US$600 million of Reforestation Funds to finance politically favoured projects that did not contribute to the Fund's objectives and documented examples of over US$5 billion in losses, citing systematic financial mismanagement fraudulent practices by recipients and routine diversion of funds.[58] These examples underscore the importance of ensuring that there is sufficient oversight and

50 Ibid.

51 Hannah Harris, 'Corruption and the Forestry Industry in Papua New Guinea: Transnational Actors, Local Dynamics and Environmental Impact' (2019) 22(1) *Asia Pacific Journal of Environmental Law* 48–65.

52 Aksel Sunstrom, 'Understanding Illegality and Corruption in Forest Governance' (2016) 181 *Journal of Environmental Management* 779–790.

53 Fiona Meehan and Luca Tacconi, 'A Framework to Assess the Impacts of Corruption on Forests and Prioritise Responses' (2017) 60 *Land Use Policy* 113–122.

54 Ibid.

55 Ibid.

56 Harris (n 51).

57 Transparency International, *Corruption-free Climate Finance: Protecting Forests and People* (2021) 6.

58 Ibid.

transparency in place that can identify instances of corruption. Not only does corruption fail forest communities, but it also creates a disincentive for private actors to invest in forest communities if they perceive that their investment will have diminished ROI or lost altogether.

Quantifying the Impact of SFM Investments and Greenwashing

Developing countries face additional risks in being unable to adequately measure the outcomes associated with SFM finance for investors. This presents a serious issue as investors are unable to quantify the impact of their ESG investments, and due to the fiduciary obligations of asset managers and corporate directors, may be required to allocate their capital to other forms of investment and asset classes. New technology and scientific research can fill in these gaps.[59] In addition, developing countries face further difficulty due to the complexity of reporting and accounting frameworks. The benefits associated with SFM can be measured through the carbon that it can sequester (e.g., stock accounting, emissions accounting, and project emission reductions accounting),[60] or through the ecosystem services that they provide (e.g., through accounting standards such as the United Nations System of Environmental Economic Accounting: Ecosystem Accounting standard).[61] These different methodologies to measure the effectiveness of SFM result in information barriers and difficulties for investors to determine whether their investment achieves value for money or their ESG objectives.

In addition, benefits such as improved biodiversity outcomes are more difficult to quantify. The financial and economic implications of biodiversity risk remain poorly understood, in part, due to the limited requirement to reflect biodiversity as a material risk for financial disclosures.[62] There are some reporting frameworks that exist which address biodiversity impacts, such as the Exploring Natural Capital Opportunities, Risks and Exposure tool, developed by the Natural Capital Finance Alliance.[63] Yet according to Bonner et al, 'in general, the focus on financial measurement for determining materiality acts as a barrier to the identification of biodiversity and ecosystem services

59 World Bank, *Mobilizing Private Finance for Nature* (World Bank 2020) 60, available at https://pubdocs.worldbank.org/en/916781601304630850/Finance-for-Nature-28-Sep-web-version.pdf, accessed 8 June 2023.

60 See generally, Charlene Watson, *Forest Carbon Accounting: Overview & Principles* (UNDP 2015), available at: https://www.undp.org/publications/forest-carbon-accounting-overview-principles, accessed 8 June 2023.

61 See generally, Adrien Comte, C. Sylvie Campagne, Sabine Lange, Adrian Garcia Bruzon, Lars Hein, Fernando Santos-Martin and Harold Levrel, 'Ecosystem Accounting: Past Scientific Developments and Future Challenges' (2022) 58 *Ecosystem Services* 101486.

62 World Bank (n 59).

63 See Natural Capital Finance Alliance, 'Exploring Natural Capital Opportunities, Risks and Exposure' (NCFA 2023), available at https://encore.naturalcapital.finance/en, accessed 1 June 2023.

issues as material'[64] and there is no standardized taxonomy or methodology on which reporting can apply, and the necessary agreed baselines to measure biodiversity conservation impact.[65] On a practical level, the lack of standardized accounting to report and measure on biodiversity impact of a SFM investment makes it difficult for investors to assess risk and, resultingly, difficult to insure or hedge against this risk.[66] This will continue to be a growing concern as investors and the public become increasingly aware of the biodiversity impact associated with monocropping in order to obtain carbon credits, which can undermine the ESG credentials and social licence of an investment.

Being able to accurately quantify the benefits associated with SFM is vital in combating the growing issue the growing issue of corporate greenwashing. Whilst SFM has demonstrated a capability create a return on investment for the private sector, including both economic and non-economic returns, this is contingent on private investors possessing the social licence to conduct SFM activities within forest communities and deliver on ESG objectives. There is a relationship of trust between private companies, forest communities and governments, and there is an assumption that corporates conduct their activities that are conducive to sustainable development. Greenwashing—or when private actors make environmental claims or boost their green credentials without delivering any positive environmental or social impact—undermines this social licence. According to Netto et al, greenwashing can be levelled at both the firm or its products, and can range from 'executional' greenwashing (e.g. using natural landscape images to invoke green credentials) or a claim that selectively discloses a company's environmental performance.[67] Unclear environmental claims, failing to provide sufficient evidence that they are delivering ESG outcomes, setting environmental goals without a clear plan or roadmap to achieve implementation or using third-party certifications to obfuscate other environmental harms are examples of greenwashing in action. Certification is susceptible to corporate greenwashing as labelling may provide a product with the veneer of superior ESG performance to consumers.

64 J. Bonner, A. Grigg, S. Hime, G. Hewitt, R. Jackson, and M. Kelly, 'Is Natural Capital a Material Issue? An Evaluation of the Relevance of Biodiversity and Ecosystem Services to Accountancy Professionals and the Private Sector' (KPMG, Flora and Fauna International, and ACCA 2012); World Bank, *Mobilizing Private Finance for Nature* (World Bank 2020) 61, available at https://pubdocs.worldbank.org/en/916781601304630850/Finance-for-Nature-28-Sep-web-version.pdf, accessed 8 June 2023.

65 World Bank (n 59).

66 Ibid.

67 Sebastião Vieira de Freitas Netto, Marcos Felipe Falcão Sobral, Ana Regina Bezerra Ribeiro and Gleibson Robert da Luz Soares, 'Concepts and Forms of Greenwashing: A Systemic Review' (2020) 32(19) *Environmental Sciences Europe*, available at https://doi.org/10.1186/s12302-020-0300-3, accessed 1 June 2023.

Reform Options to Enhance SFM Through Trade and Investment

To address the key motivations for corporations and asset managers, including to obtain net-zero benefits, promote sustainability across the supply chain and the need to provide a return on investment due to fiduciary duties, policymakers must implement a range of tools to attract investment and provide the correct signals to the market. As indicated above, risk of failing to realize a return on investment remains a significant barrier which prevents private actors from utilizing their capital into SFM, as well as the illiquid nature of SFM as an asset class. However, there are ways to address risk and improve liquidity. In terms of the latter, capital flows into forestland investment enabling liquidity to rise.[68] Placing forest assets as a listed vehicle or packaging SFM investments in better investment products that meets the needs of institutional investors can also address the illiquidity of SFM.

Expanding markets and systems that can quantify benefits, implementing innovative green market–based instruments that can provide additional security for investors (e.g., green bonds), and subsidies which can provide long-term price securities and cost guarantees all assist in attracting private investment into sustainable forestry projects and practices.[69] However, it must be noted that developing countries often lack the capacity to implement such policy responses, especially subsidies that can provide security and insure against risk. Furthermore, developing countries must take an additional step in building their capacity and infrastructure that can enable greater quantification of benefits associated with sustainable forestry management.

Collective Initiatives to Combat Corruption: Greater Integration of Subnational Issues and Capacity Building

As previously discussed, corruption greatly reduces the effectiveness and amount of funding available for SFM. Whilst the state plays an important role to ensure its officials are not engaging in corrupt activities within the forestry sector, the private sector is an important partner in combatting corruption. Not only can the private sector ensure that its own actors do not engage in corrupt activities, but the private sector also plays a crucial role in ensuring that it does not facilitate or enable institutional corruption, especially 'according to the rule' corruption. There are several compliance programs relevant to private actors to combat corruption in the forestry sector. The International

68 Petdro Moura-Costa, Lionel Fretz and Gerald Kohn, 'Feasibility Analysis for an International Investment Promotion Entity for Sustainable Forest Management' in Mafa Chipera and Mahendra Joshi (eds), *The Private Sector Speaks: Investing in Sustainable Forest Management* (Centre for International Forestry Research 2001) 190.

69 Lofqvist, Garrett and Ghazoul (n 44) 711–712.

Organization for Standardization (ISO) 37001[70] standard provides a procedure for private actors to identify instances of bribery within their organization and supply chain. However, whilst ISO 31007 creates standards to assist auditors to identify corrupt activity, obtaining certification is not reliant that the organization has sufficient testing and assurance mechanisms in place to ensure that the standards are being deployed effectively.[71]

Collective initiatives to address forestry corruption are becoming increasingly used to protect SFM investments. Collective initiatives also drive compliance by creating reputational risks for companies that decide to voluntarily pledge to collective initiative commitments[72] and creating norms of behaviour and culture within the organization. Initiatives such as the World Economic Forum's Partnership Against Corruption Initiative[73] provide a good example of a collective initiative that obliges participants to report and act on instances of corruption. The EITI also creates a standard which requires countries to publish information relating to contracts, production, operating costs and revenues for forest resource companies, enabling the civil sector to scrutinize the relationship between private and government officials. However, these initiatives are voluntary with no 'hard' penalty imposed for non-compliance. In practice, effective use of initiatives such as EITI is also reliant upon a robust civil sector that can scrutinize this information and identify instances of corruption.[74]

Experiences on the ground suggest that these initiatives often lack integration with subnational issues and more localized governance structures. According to Le Billon et al, interviewees expressed that EITI was not relevant in Colombia as EITI was applied at the national level, despite most forest sector bribery occurring at the sub-national and local government levels.[75] Greater sensitivity to more localized decision-making bodies is needed to address corruption where it occurs. Second, one of the lead determinants for corruption is a serious failure to meet the material needs of regulators, including sufficient salary, equipment, funds and staffing

70 International Organization for Standardization, 'ISO 31007—Anti-Bribery Management Systems' (ISO undated), available at https://www.iso.org/iso-37001-anti-bribery-management.html, accessed 1 June 2023.

71 Amy Smith and Jason Grant, 'Keeping Better Company: Engaging the Private Sector to Reduce Forest Sector-Related Corruption Risk' (WWF 2021), available at https://www.worldwildlife.org/pages/tnrc-topic-brief-keeping-better-company-engaging-the-private-sector-to-reduce-forest-sector-related-corruption-risk#2, accessed 1 June 2023.

72 Ibid.

73 See generally, World Economic Forum, *Partnering Against Corruption Initiative* (WEF 2023), available at https://www.weforum.org/communities/partnering-against-corruption-initiative, accessed 1 June 2023.

74 Phillippe Le Billon, Paivi Lujala and Siri Aas Rustad, 'A Theory of Change for the Extractive Industries Transparency Initiative' (U4 Anti-corruption Resource Centre 2020) 35.

75 Ibid. 36.

arrangements.[76] The private sector, in partnership with development organizations, can play a lead role in addressing these capacity constraints being experienced by developing countries. Private investment can address the lack of equipment through public-private partnerships, but importantly, development organizations can work with industry to package forestry investment and create cost sharing arrangements.

Policy Coordination: Network Effects, Knowledge and Regulatory Gaps

Policy silos lead to duplication and diminish the opportunity for different areas of government to consider complex problems holistically, such as SFM investment. Creating policy networks, which amalgamate actors from different but related policy fields, is one method to break down silos. According to Baulenas et al., creating policy networks enables policymakers to share problem identification and fact-finding activities, build trust, and foster greater homogeneity in policy ideas and solutions. This approach can also enhance their readiness to engage in innovative policy changes needed to address cross-sectoral issues.[77] Increased use of inter-ministerial organizations is essential for ensuring that cross-cutting issues in forestry policy, such as those related to agriculture and energy, are effectively addressed. For example, the Mexican State of Chiapas has established an Inter-institutional Co-ordination Commission on Climate Change which coordinates the efforts of various climate change policy actors.[78] This is a live issue given that in many countries, the responsibility to perform SFM is distributed between several government agencies.

In Indonesia, the Ministry of Environment and Forestry, the Ministry of Agriculture, the Ministry of Energy and Mineral Resources, and the Ministry of Agrarian and Spatial Planning, each have responsibilities for developing and implementing policies related to biodiversity and ecosystems, climate, agriculture, bioenergy, and spatial planning, respectively. Each ministry has its own strategies in place to enhance private investment in these areas.[79]

Framework legislation or guiding policy documents also play an important role in mainstreaming issues and ensuring coherence amongst several

76 Michael Miller, 'Persistent Illegal Logging in Costa Rica: The Role of Corruption Among Forestry Regulators' (2011) 20(1) *Journal of Environment & Development* 50–68.

77 Eulalia Baulenas, Sylvia Kruse and Metodi Sotirov, 'Forest and Water Policy Integration: A Process and Output-Orientated Policy Network Analysis' (2021) 31(5) *Environmental Policy and Governance* 432–450; D. Nooteboom, *Adaptive Networks: The Governance for Sustainable Development* (Eburon 2006); C. Pahl-Wostl, 'A Conceptual Framework for Analysing Adaptive Capacity and Multi-Level Learning Process in Resource Governance Regimes' (2009) 19(3) *Global Environmental Change* 354–365.

78 See World Bank, CIAT and CATIE, *Climate-Smart Agriculture in Chiapas, Mexico* (The World Bank Group 2014).

79 OECD, *Towards Sustainable Land Use: Aligning Biodiversity, Climate and Food Policies* (OECD 2020), available at https://www.oecd-ilibrary.org/environment/towards-sustainable-land-use_3809b6a1-en, accessed 1 June 2023, chapter 4.

government agencies. Establishing clear objectives and requiring several government agencies and policy actors to adhere to these goals create better integration, shared understanding of the policy problem and agreed measures to determine success. However, examining how this was achieved in the Vietnamese National REDD+ Action Plan (NRAP) demonstrates that this is no easy task. In Vietnam, whilst the NRAP recognizes the role of private investment to reduce deforestation and improve SFM, how companies are implementing these objectives into their corporate plans remains a key knowledge gap.[80] In addition, the NRAP promotes coordination by giving a mandate to multiple government ministries to evaluate how their policies affect deforestation, thus mainstreaming this issue; however, in practice this mandate is subordinate to key legislation in each respective ministry and department, therefore relegating deforestation concerns.[81] This highlights that any guiding policy mandate or framework legislation requires extensive work on supporting policy work, legislation or regulations, which considers the views of key policy actors and specifies how each sector can achieve coherence with an overriding SFM objective.

For greater vertical integration, this depends largely on the level of centralization of SFM policymaking in developing countries. In terms of REDD+, some countries have instituted working groups that enable local and provincial governments to be represented in federal agencies. In Indonesia, province-level working groups on REDD+ meet monthly,[82] which allows 'ministries, agencies or committees to provide information and promote coordination between agricultural producers and subnational governments'.[83] This approach allows for a bi-directional flow of information and decision-making and allows local communities to voice their specific issues in obtaining SFM finance into the policymaking apparatus of federal and national governments. However, to enable meaningful vertical integration, developing countries require additional capacity building to ensure that sub-national governments and local organizations have sufficient access to information, expertise and resources to enable meaningful consultation, and for SFM finance in particular, have the expertise to identify barriers for greater SFM funding by the private sector, including barriers which prevent scaling up existing investments. This requires extensive knowledge sharing of financial and investment concepts, as well as monitoring and evaluation to identify the effectiveness of existing SFM funding in meeting ESG objectives.

80 Gabrielle Kissinger, Maria Brockhaus and Simon Bush, 'Policy Integration as a Means to Address Policy Fragmentation: Assessing the Role of Vietnam's National REDD+ Action Plan in the Central Highlands' (2021) 119 *Environmental Science & Policy* 85–92.

81 Ibid.

82 FCPF, *REDD+ Annual Country Progress Reporting (with semi-annual update)* (2015), available at https://www.forestcarbonpartnership.org/sites/fcp/files/2016/Oct/230916_Final%20NS_FCPF%20%20Country%20Progress%20Report.pdf, accessed 1 June 2023.

83 OECD, *Towards Sustainable Land Use: Aligning Biodiversity, Climate and Food Policies* (OECD 2020), available at https://www.oecd-ilibrary.org/environment/towards-sustainable-land-use_3809b6a1-en, accessed 1 June 2023, chapter 4.

There are also instances of greater coordination between governments and multilateral organizations to develop greater cohesion between the domestic sphere and global actors. Indonesia, the Democratic Republic of Congo, the Republic of Congo and Peru have established the International Tropical Peatlands Centre (ITPC), in collaboration with the United Nations Environment Programme and the FAO. The ITPC aims to foster greater south-south cooperation for SFM in peatland areas, including linking different stakeholders to enable greater investment in technical services and capacity building with the private sector.[84] Formalizing institutional arrangements, such as creating the ITPC, enables developing countries to share expertise on specific matters relating to SFM and multiply the impact of private investment into SFM by disseminating technical knowledge amongst developing country partners. The scope of the ITPC to consider SFM practices in a specific geological area also creates greater focus on key issues which are unique to this geology, such as the continued use of fire in peatland management and the intersecting socio-economic factors which drive continued peatland degradation. However, despite the creation of such centres of excellence to foster greater SFM investment, these bodies cannot replace investment that is still required within existing government departments and the regulatory powers that they possess. Bodies created through bilateral, regional or multilateral instruments must still have a strong domestic institution that is able to support its workstreams and implement regulations. Taking the ITPC as an example, the work performed by this centre is undermined as the Indonesian Peatland Restoration Agency still lacks direct authority over peatland areas and must overcome a lack of state funding.[85]

A Greater Role for NGOs: Quantifying Benefits, Greenwashing and Keeping SFM Investors Accountable

Whilst some measures for SFM can be accounted for, such as carbon stock or return on investment through timber production, other benefits, including social benefits or positive biodiversity outcomes, are difficult to quantify. This is due, in part, that these outcomes are highly context specific and would vary from project to project. For instance, a metric which highlights the amount of deadwood available on the forest floor may have implications for carbon accounting, however, depending on the ecosystem, may have substantially higher biodiversity impact as it increases the viability of saproxylic forest

84 See Priority Activity 4.7 under Ministry of Environment and Forestry, Indonesia and CIFOR, *International Tropical Peatlands Centre* (Republic of Indonesia 2019), available at https://www.tropicalpeatlands.org/resources/ITPC-Concept-Note-en-web.pdf, accessed 1 June 2023.

85 OECD (n 83).

species.[86] As a result, this leaves investors without the information that they need to make informed investment decisions and embrace SFM as a legitimate asset class for long-term investing. There are tools which consider the context specific nature of these goals to create criteria to enable companies to see if their SFM investment are meeting ESG objectives. The Future-Fit Framework requires companies to report their progress against 23 science-based 'break-even goals'; these goals are minimum requirements that companies must pass to ensure that they are not holding up implementation of the SDGs.[87] One such goal is that 'natural resources are managed with respect to the welfare of ecosystem, people and animals'.[88]

It is incumbent on investors to critically evaluate the claims made by companies towards their ESG credentials and the data that they use to evidence greater SFM implementation. Here NGOs are the missing link in providing independent, external scrutiny. Not only do NGOs play a critical role in facilitating FSC or PEFC obligations providing the training that can allow landholders to implement SFM.[89] NGOs can fill the technical capacity gap by providing the expertise that is required to accurately scrutinize data and demand better ESG performance from companies. Greater steps can be done to combat greenwashing in SFM. There are linkages in improving the monitoring and enforcement capacity of SFM actors who participate in labelling schemes such as FSC or PEFC to ensure that they are meeting stated ESG outcomes. But shareholders play an equally important role in ensuring that companies are accountable to the environmental performance claims that they are making to the market. With many developed countries having rules concerning director liabilities and disclosure requirements, an issue that has a material impact on a publicly listed company[90] can ensure that shareholders hold companies accountable for delivering on their ESG objectives. Shareholders can also initiate suits under common law claims, such as through fraudulent misrepresentation.

86 O.-P. Tikkanen, T. Heinonen, J. Kouki and J. Matero, 'Habitat Suitability Models of Saproxylic Red-Listed Boreal Forest Species in Long-Term Matrix Management: Cost Effective Measures for Multi-Species Conservation' (2007) 140 *Biological Conservation* 359–372; A. Zubizarreta-Gerendiaiin, T. Pukkala and H. Peltola, 'Effect of Wind Damage on the Habitat Suitability of Saproxylic Species in a Boreal Forest Landscape' (2019) 30(3) *Journal of Forestry Research* 879–889; Timo Pukkala, 'Measuring the Social Performance of Forest Management' (2021) 32 *Journal of Forestry Research* 1803–1818.

87 See Future-Fit Business, *Future-Fit Business Benchmark* (2023), available at https://futurefitbusiness.org/benchmark/, accessed 1 June 2023; OECD, *A Comprehensive Overview of Global Biodiversity Finance* (OECD Publishing 2020); World Bank, *Mobilizing Private Finance for Nature* (2020) 64.

88 Ibid.

89 Miteva, Fortmann and McNab (n 41) 277.

90 See US Securities and Exchange Commission, 17 CFR § 229.1011 (2017). See, for instance, class action suit against investors by the environmental claims of directors at *In re Danimer Scientific, Inc. Securities Litigation*, 1:21-cv-02708 (E.D.N.Y. May 14, 2021).

Certification: Addressing Supply and Demand Pressures

Alternatively, certification plays an important role in providing a system of ensuring ESG outcomes that is easily understood by investors and consumers. However, one of the main issues is the lack of saturation of FSC and PEFC within developing countries. As previously discussed, cost barriers prohibit its widespread adoption where it is not guaranteed that certification will enable a higher premium for timber products. This is both a demand-side and supply-side issue. On the demand side, greater efforts need to be made to require certification from timber consumers. Whilst initiatives such as the EU's FLEGT aim to address this demand-side issue by restricting market access for illegally harvested timber, such initiatives are not applied uniformly across the global marketplace. China remains one of the largest importers of illegal timber in the world, consuming between 39 and 69 million cubic metres of illegal timber[91] and accounts for 20% of China's total wood imports.[92] Most consumption of illegal timber comes from exotic species of rare timber, such as rosewood that is harvested for furniture production. Whilst China have recently revised their Forest Law to ban timber where 'he/she clearly knows was piratically felled or indiscriminately felled in forest regions',[93] this provision raises two key issues. First, the requirement to establish that the consumer 'clearly knows' is opaque, and consumers may circumvent this requirement by failing to perform due diligence to determine the origins of their timber. Consideration should be made to reform Article 65 of the Forest Law to shift the offence to a strict liability offence, however, provide enforcement bodies with flexibility to issue penalties based on whether there are aggravating or mitigating circumstances from the consumers conduct. Second, there is an issue of enforcement. Whilst having a de jure ban on illegally harvested timber are good first steps, most of the effort is tied up in having sufficient enforcement and investigative capacity. There is limited value in banning illegal timber and restricting market access if there is not enough enforcement across the supply chain, especially in large timber markets.

On the supply side, financial support is vital to timber producers to encourage uptake of certification schemes within developing countries. Whilst developing countries have limited financial capacity to provide direct subsidies to increase uptake, developed countries can assist by providing targeted assistance in this respect. Providing increased support for FSC or PEFC compliance is a direct way to assist the private sector to increase their investment into SFM. Governments may also consider imposing tariffs or other measures on non-certified timber to socialize the cost of capacity building in developing

91 Matthias Dieter, 'Analysis of Trade in Illegally Harvested Timber: Accounting for Trade via Third Party Countries' (2009) 11(8) *Forest Policy and Economics* 600–607.

92 Chatham House, *Illegal Logging & Related Trade: Lessons from the Global Response* (Chatham House 2010).

93 *Forest Law 2019* (China), Article 65.

countries from non-certified timber consumers. However, this comes with downstream issues as developing countries, who do not have the current capability to participate in FSC or PEFC, are effectively locked out from the global marketplace. Due care must be considered in ensuring that any tariffs collected on non-certified timber must be directly allocated for capacity building initiatives in full, with exemptions provided to enable LDCs to continue to participate in the global marketplace where they have demonstrated a roadmap to achieve certification. Moreover, funding to contrary schemes which promote environmentally damaging activities, rather than building the capacity of developing countries to undertake certification, is a significant potential source of finances that can promote SFM. Building the capacity for developing countries to effectively participate in certification is vital, as imposing additional requirements without providing support will only seek to perpetuate illegal logging, marginalize forest communities and fail to address the economic drivers that fuel illegal logging and land conversion. Finally, it is noted that trade issues associated with the use of certification schemes remain. Given the issues associated with the WTO remaining unable to hear trade appeals, it is doubtful that further clarification or guidance can be obtained in how the use of certification schemes may constitute a disallowable PPM in breach of GATT Article I obligations.

A Double-Edged Sword: Achieving Greater Certainty by Formalizing Property Rights

The experience of Mozambique provides a good example of both opportunities and barriers associated with formalizing property rights interests with a view of securing land tenure. Whilst land in Mozambique is owned by the state and cannot be sold, mortgaged or charged, a person can obtain access and benefit rights associated with a parcel of land by applying to the state for a Direito de Uso e Aproveitamento da Terra (DUAT). The 1997 Land Law recognized that the DUAT could be obtained through customary and good faith land occupation, thus formalizing customary land rights. Converting customary rights into de jure rights enables investors to negotiate lease agreements and other contractual arrangements with the community directly, as well as enabling the community to learn about the context of their rights within their newly formalized title.[94]

However, the introduction of the DUAT and enabling customary rights holders to apply for a DUAT comes with difficulties. According to Nhantumbo et al, lower levels of education and limited experience to effectively engage in the legal system result in communities often being disadvantaged and

94 Margaret Holland and Moustapha Diop, 'Strategies for Securing Tenure: The Promise and Pitfalls of Formalization' in Margaret Holland, Yuta Masuda and Brian Robinson (eds), *Land Tenure Security and Sustainable Development* (Springer Nature 2022) 225, 239.

less secure.[95] Customary rights holders and local communities often do not have the technical knowledge or legal experience to engage with the National Directorate of Land and Forests of the Ministry of Agriculture to claim such rights. Furthermore, the 1997 Land Law creates a double-edged sword for women, as most rural women obtain their rights to land through customary norms and practices as defined through their relationships with men.[96] As a result, the formalization of property rights may entrench gender inequality and lock women out from secure land tenure. Finally, the case of Mozambique also created practical issues in formalizing land rights. Many community actors lack sufficient identification documents, and it remains 'a practical difficulty in implementing any kind of conventional formalization of rights'.[97] Costs also remain a significant barrier, as the legal support, training to improve surveying capacity, and improvement in negotiation skills to reach agreement with the state and outside interests cost money.[98] NGOs can facilitate land tenure conflict resolution by providing support services that can resolve disputes.[99] Mapping services, alternative conflict dispute resolution mechanisms, providing advice on local operating parameters and conditions to private investors, and assisting in monitoring and enforcement are crucial activities which provide the foundation for greater land tenure and property rights for forest communities.

Conclusion

Global trade and investment play a critical role in perpetuating land use practices on forest ecosystems. Whilst historically this has resulted in overexploitation of forest landscapes to produce forest products or promote growth in related sectors such as agriculture, SFM has an opportunity to leverage market-based approaches to promote greater sustainable use and achieve better outcomes for social development and environmental conservation. Private actors are the key to implement SFM at scale. To date, whilst there is potential for greater SFM investment, private sector involvement has been minimal, suggesting that significant barriers exist for SFM to become an attractive asset class.

To address these risks, government policy and targeted action is required in several areas. First, corruption continues to erode investor confidence, and collective initiatives which partner with the private sector and consider sub-national and local governance arrangements can enable greater private

95 I. Nhantumbo and A. Salomão, *Biofuels, Land Access and Rural Livelihoods in Mozambique. International Institute for Environment and Development* (IIED 2010).

96 Simon Norfolk and Christopher Turner, *Improving Tenure Security for the Rural Poor: Mozambique—Country Case Study* (FAO 2007) 15.

97 Ibid. 27.

98 Ibid.

99 Miteva, Fortmann and McNab (n 41) 278.

sector SFM investment. Second, policy coherence and coordination remain fragmented. Most public funds continue to go into activities which undermine SFM, and existing governance arrangements require greater vertical and horizontal integration to create better, more coordinated policy. Vietnam's experiences in implementing more coordination demonstrate that regulatory gaps also need to be identified to allow coordinating agencies to have sufficient regulatory power and resources to implement SFM and make the sector more attractive to private investment.

Investors also require stringent data and remain informed that their investments are delivering their proposed ESG objectives. Greater capacity building to perform monitoring and enforcement is increasingly important, as unscrupulous entities are increasingly employing greenwashing to boost their environmental credentials without delivering any tangible impact on the ground. Related to this issue, certification plays an important role in boosting investor confidence. However, as this chapter has discussed, certification in schemes such as FSC or PEFC remains low in developing countries, as SFM landholders and managers face cost barriers to obtain certification. Furthermore, certification schemes are at risk of non-compliance with GATT obligations against the use of PPMs, which are often replicated in trade obligations found in regional trade agreements.

The Global North plays a key role in unlocking investment into SFM and promoting the use of trade measures, including tariffs, on non-certified timber or diverting resourcing to environmentally destructive activities being a potential avenue to raise certification in the Global South. Finally, land tenure remains a live issue. Formalization can address some land tenure issues; however, legal systems in developing countries need maturity and greater enforcement capabilities for formalization to result in any tangible benefit. In addition, this creates a potential issue for forest communities and indigenous rights holders, who may have their legitimate claims undermined by de jure rights holders. As this chapter has demonstrated, polycentric governance is required for a robust, fully functioning SFM. There is substantial work that needs to be performed to make SFM a more attractive proposition for private investment and provide developing countries and forest communities the capital that they need to break away from unsustainable practices.

9 GATS and the Liberalization of Water Services

Implications for Human Rights and the Environment

Introduction

It is universally recognized that ensuring access to safe drinking water and sanitation services for the world's impoverished populations is a significant developmental challenge of the 21st century. Addressing these challenges requires substantial investments in water delivery and management infrastructure, including supply systems, sewerage, and irrigation. One of the UN Millennium Development Goals (MDGs) was to halve, by the year 2015, the proportion of people unable to access or afford safe drinking water and those without basic sanitation. The SDGs, which succeeded the MDGs, aim further to ensure universal access to safe and affordable drinking water and sanitation by 2030. Despite progress, challenges remain significant. As of the latest reports, 2 billion people still lack access to safely managed drinking water, and 3.6 billion lack safely managed sanitation services. The investment needed to meet these SDG targets is now estimated to be substantially higher, reflecting both inflation and the increased scope of the goals.

Public services are often regarded as essential by people across most nations, and governments typically provide these services universally, acknowledging their significance in everyday life. The provision of clean water remains a significant essential service. Markus Krajewski highlights that the core reason for state involvement in these services is to fulfil public interest objectives,[1] which can vary based on societal values within different historical, social and economic contexts. Due to their critical role in addressing social, public health and environmental policy concerns, these services are sometimes also categorized as social or essential services, with these terms frequently used interchangeably. The definition of public services, however, is not uniform. In some cases, services enshrined in national constitutions and international human rights documents are considered public services.[2]

1 Markus Krajewski, 'Public Services and Trade Liberalisation: Mapping the Legal Framework' (2003) 6(2) *Journal of International Economic Law* 341, 344.
2 Jane Kelsey, *Serving Whose Interests? The Political Economy of Trade in Services Agreement* (Routledge 2008) 120.

DOI: 10.4324/9781003164951-10

Economists refer to these services, which are non-rivalrous and non-excludable and often cannot be efficiently provided by the market alone, as public goods. The WTO recognizes these as public services because they are predominantly supplied by public authorities, with private entities typically participating under government delegation. The introduction of international competition through these mechanisms invites a variety of new players into the market, enhancing efficiency and fostering innovation in water management and delivery. This opens up substantial commercial opportunities for large corporations equipped with the necessary capital, technology and expertise to operate on a global scale.

Indeed, from the mid-20th century, services that were typically categorized as public and government managed have evolved into intricate commercial frameworks involving a variety of participants and operating on an international scale. The division of public utilities such as electricity, water and telecommunications into separate phases—production, transmission, distribution and sales—illustrates this transformation. Moreover, sectors like education now utilize sophisticated, international service supply chains that function within competitive global markets. The late 1970s marked a pivotal shift in Western democracies with the rise of neo-liberal economic policies, which emphasized the privatization of public services, including water. This ideological shift not only led to the creation of water markets as we know them today but also dramatically changed the role of the state from being a direct provider of water services to acting primarily as a regulator.[3] This transition allowed private entities to assume control over water resources, fundamentally altering access to and the management of this vital resource. The state's new role focuses on overseeing these private operators, ensuring compliance with standards and fair practices in an effort to balance public needs with market dynamics. As such, over the past 50 years, water privatization has emerged as a significant trend in the water sector.[4]

For some, one of the key solutions to the global water crisis is the privatization of water services, which have traditionally been the domain of government-controlled monopolies. The World Bank, along with many others, believes that the privatization of the water industry is the most efficient way to provide clean water to the most people. The common argument is that private entrepreneurs are more efficient in increasing access of clean drinking water by assisting governments, providing infrastructure and providing critically needed funding. The World Bank's push for privatization was driven by

3 Jessica Budds and Gordon McGranahan, 'Are the Debates on Water Privatisation Missing the Point? Experience from Africa, Asia and Latin America' (2003) 7 *Environment & Urbanisation* 90–92.

4 Jason Morrision and Peter Gleick, 'Freshwater Resources: Managing the Risks Facing the Private Sector' (Research paper, Pacific Institute 2004); Maude Barlow and Barry Clarke, *Blue Gold: The Battle Against the Corporate Theft of the World's Water* (Earthscan 2002).

the promise that through privatization, the World Bank, together with TNCs, would be able to solve the world's water inequalities by providing clean and safe drinking water to places that previously did not afford this luxury. They pushed a social agenda and an ethical mission of poverty alleviation. Quite simply, says sociologist Michael Goldman of the University of Minnesota, 'in the name of poverty reduction, water privatisation become a key green neo-liberal project for the World Bank, which has cultivated elite transnational water policy networks to create the appearance of a worldwide consensus on a private future for water. Water should not be regarded merely as a traditional commercial commodity'.[5] In that regard, Fried notes:

> The debate between the economic dimensions of the costs of water services and the social dimensions of water begins with the issue of the universal right to water access. Market conditions must be clearly established, and the respective roles of the private sector and public authority must be discussed and defined.[6]

However, the global trend of water privatization has led to the consolidation of water services under the control of a few powerful multinational companies.[7] During the last decade, privatization of the water industry has affected millions of people. It has been implemented in both the developed and developing world. Its effects are seen specifically in the developing world, where a significant number of people have been placed under increased pressure due to their inability to afford the basic right. The wave of privatization in the developing world started in Latin America in the early 1990s, and it has spread to many countries in Africa and Asia as well. One of the reasons for the rapid rise of water privatization in developing countries was due to the World Bank's significant push for the privatization of the water industry. In country after country for many years, the World Bank has been quietly imposing a for-profit system of water delivery, leaving millions of people without access to water. The World Bank has been promoting the privatization of water by advocating the interests of a handful of transnational water corporations.

In 1997, the World Bank pressured Bolivia to privatize Cochabamba's water system, its third-largest city, by tying additional water development aid to privatization. By September 1999, Bolivia had non-transparently awarded Aguas

5 Budds (n 3) 87; J.J. Hukka and T.S. Katko, 'Refuting the Paradigm of Water Services Privatisation' (2003) 27 *Natural Resources Forum* 142. For a discussion of the debate as to whether water should be classified as a right or a commodity, see also K. Bakker, 'The "Commons" Versus the "Commodity": Alter-Globalization, Anti-privatization and the Human Right to Water in the Global South' (2007) 39 *Antipode* 430.

6 J. Fried, 'Water Governance, Management and Ethics: New Dimensions for an Old Problem' (2008) 6 *Santa Clara JIL* 1 at p. 2.

7 Marty Logan, 'Finance Corporations Said to Eye Water Privatization in U.S' *Inter Press Service*, 4 February 2003.

del Tunari, a subsidiary of the American engineering giant Bechtel, a 40-year exclusive concession to the city's water sources after a bidding process that featured only one bidder. Shortly after the privatization in November 1999, water prices soared by 35%,[8] triggering massive protests in Cochabamba. The Bolivian government responded with violent suppression, culminating in a declaration of martial law in April 2000. This led to the death of a teenager and injuries to over a hundred people during the ensuing unrest. Despite the protests, the residents continued to resist, forcing Bechtel to abandon the project. Bolivia then terminated the contract.[9] Bechtel subsequently filed for US$50 million in damages and lost profit in an ICSID arbitration case but withdrew the claim under international pressure. This series of events highlights the risks of privatizing public utility services, which often act as natural monopolies. In developing countries, weak regulations can leave communities vulnerable to exploitation by MNCs through high prices, poor service and service cutbacks, often leading to severe socio-economic and environmental consequences.

The commodification and privatization of water services can prioritize profit over public welfare, potentially leading to higher water prices and uneven distribution of water resources. The entry of international corporations into local markets might disrupt established practices and stir conflicts over water rights and access. In addition, privatization is often linked with significant reductions in employment as private companies seek to maximize profits through workforce downsizing. The ILO has observed that the privatization and restructuring of water, electricity and gas utilities generally lead to decreased employment levels, with reductions sometimes affecting up to 50% of the workforce.[10] This trend is particularly pronounced in certain forms of privatization, such as contracting out specific industry segments and complete privatization, especially when combined with restructuring efforts. Additionally, any increase in employment following privatization is uncommon and typically occurs only after extensive initial layoffs.

To address these issues, rigorous regulation and oversight are essential to balance the benefits of globalization with the needs of local communities. The integration of national policies, influenced by debt and aid conditionalities, contributes to a high level of international coherence affecting both

8 Jennifer Naegele, 'What Is Wrong with Full-Fledged Water Privatization?' (2004) 6 *Journal of Law and Social Challenges* 99, 105, 125.

9 Pierre Thielborger, 'The Human Right to Water Versus Investor Rights: Double-Dilemma or Pseudo Conflict?' in F. Francioni, E.U. Petersmann and P.M. Dupuy (eds), *Human Rights in International Investment Law and Arbitration* (Oxford University Press 2009) 499.

10 International Labour Office, 'Managing the Privatisation and Restructuring of Public Utilities (Water, Gas, Electricity)' (Report for the Discussion at the Tripartite Meeting on Managing the Privatization of Public Utilities, Geneva, 12–16 April 1999) Part 2, available at http://www.ilo.org/public/english/dialogue/sector/techmeet/tmpu99/tmpure2.htm#2.1.

the global North and South. The GATS,[11] negotiated during the Uruguay Round of WTO talks, plays a critical role in this context. Replacing the standalone GATT, GATS establishes binding rules on the international trade of services, including those related to water, thereby shaping how these services are globally managed and traded. The GATS profoundly influences the water and sanitation sector, potentially more than any other framework, by allowing WTO member states to open their water markets to global trade rules and market access. Nevertheless, there is considerable ambiguity regarding how GATS provisions are applied to water services and the consequent impacts on markets, consumers and the environment. This uncertainty, amplified by the Agreement's global reach, poses significant challenges for water markets and their management. The social consequences of privatization are most prominently observed in the water sector. Water is the most crucial substance for human survival, necessitating careful management and context-specific regulation. The factors influencing water management practices are diverse and interconnected, encompassing climate, demographics, technological capabilities, economic development and trade, consumption patterns and social and cultural processes.[12]

In addition, whilst water is often categorized as a good, complex issues frequently stem from the classification of various types of 'water services' crucial for providing drinking and domestic water. These services fall into four main categories: water collection and purification, which involves making water safe for consumption; water distribution, the process of delivering water to consumers; sewage treatment and wastewater management, which handle the sanitation and disposal of waste; and incidental water services, which cover the construction and maintenance of necessary infrastructure.[13] These services are yet to be classified formally within the WTO framework under the Services Sectoral Classification List, where only sewage services have been specified, under the general heading of environmental services.[14] This has international trade impacts, as paragraph 31(iii) of the Doha Ministerial Declaration calls for the 'reduction or, as appropriate, elimination of tariff and non-tariff barriers to environmental goods and services'. The proposal to include water services as 'environmental services' under the GATS is a matter that is vehemently opposed by many human rights and environmental NGOs, primarily

11 Marrakesh Agreement Establishing the World Trade Organization, opened for signature 15 April 1994, 1867 UNTS 3 ('*Marrakesh Agreement*'), annex 1B (*General Agreement on Trade in Services*) 1869 UNTS 183 (entered into force 1 January 1995).

12 O. Ünver, 'Global Governance of Water: A Practitioner's Perspective' (2008) 14(4) *Global Governance* 409–417.

13 Elisabeth Türk and Markus Krajewski, 'The Right to Water and Trade in Services: Assessing the Impact of GATS Negotiations on Water Regulation' *Paper Presented at the CAT+E Conference 'Moving forward from Cancún'*, Berlin, 30–31 October 2003, available at www.ciel.org/Publications/GATS_WaterHR_28Oct03.pdf, at p. 6.

14 Ibid.

because the WTO is perceived as an organization that has proven itself to be insufficiently concerned with genuinely promoting sustainable development, particularly when this involves giving primacy to the preservation of natural resources.[15] Finally, it is possible to interpret a 'right to water' from the 'right to life' under the ICCPR or from the rights to life, health and an adequate standard of living under the International Covenant on Economic, Social and Cultural Rights. Analysing water privatization through the lens of human rights helps to define clear objectives and responsibilities and provides a robust legal framework for addressing this issue.[16]

This chapter explores the potential implications of the GATS on water services. Water services require particular consideration in the liberalization debate given their vital role in promoting human development and their status as a human right. The GATS has the potential to benefit the sector by creating increased efficiencies and encouraging foreign investment. However, there is concern that treating services in much the same manner as goods ignores the social aspects of many services and risks undermining human rights. This chapter explores the impact of the GATS on the liberalization of water services. It examines how the GATS, as a framework within the WTO, influences global water service markets and the associated challenges and opportunities. This analysis is particularly focused on how the GATS treats water services not only as economic commodities but also as essential public goods, thereby intertwining trade liberalization with fundamental human rights and environmental sustainability. The chapter concludes by arguing that given the vital role of water services, greater certainty is required to ensure the effective operation of the GATS, the validity of domestic legislation and the facilitation of water services.

GATS: An Overview

The GATS is an international agreement within the framework of the WTO which seeks to progressively liberalize trade in services. The GATS was created to extend the multilateral trading system to the service sector in the same way that the GATT provides such a system for goods. The GATS applies to trade in all services, except 'services supplied in the exercise of governmental authority',[17] that is, services which are not supplied on a commercial basis or in competition with other service providers.[18] The term 'services supplied in the exercise of governmental authority' refers to any service that is neither provided

15 R. Nardone, 'Like Oil and Water: The WTO and the World's Water Resources' (2003) 19 *Connecticut Journal of International Law* 183, 197.

16 Melina Williams, ' Privatization and the Human Right to Water: Challenges to the New Century' (2007) 28 *Michigan Journal of International Law* 472.

17 *Marrakesh Agreement*, opened for signature 15 April 1994, 1867 UNTS 3, annex 1B ('GATS')1869 UNTS 183, art I:3(b) (entered into force 1 January 1995).

18 Ibid. art. 1:3(c).

on a commercial basis nor in competition with other service providers. Traditional examples of such services include healthcare, police protection, penitentiary services and basic education.

However, there has been a trend towards privatization in many member countries, and as a result, services that were once considered purely governmental are now increasingly subject to the rules of the GATS. This shift means that these services may now fall within the scope of GATS regulations. However, the ambiguity and narrowness of the public service exception may only save a limited number of governmental services. Thus the range of trade in services under GATS is all-encompassing.[19]

The GATS does not specifically define 'services', but Article I:2 defines 'trade in services' as 'the supply of a service' through one of four designated 'modes of supply':

1 From the territory of one Member into the territory of any other Member.
2 In the territory of one Member to the service consumer of any other Member.
3 By a service supplier of one Member, through commercial presence in the territory of any other Member.
4 By a service supplier of one Member, through presence of natural persons of a Member in the territory of any other Member.[20]

The GATS seeks to liberalize trade in services by imposing particular limits on measures affecting trade in services.[21] These measures refer to regulatory measures taken by federal, state and local administration, and those undertaken by non-governmental bodies through delegated governmental authority.[22] All domestic measures adopted by States must be consistent with obligations under the GATS. These obligations can be divided into general and specific rules. In essence, the GATS mandate potentially applies to activities conducted by all tiers of government—national, regional and local—as well as non-government bodies that exercise governmental authority. This makes GATS pertinent to numerous government entities and organizations that typically do not engage in or may not even be aware of international trade negotiations. The broad inclusion of such a wide range of entities under GATS is particularly significant given the nature of how water services are provided and how policies aimed at preserving water resources are developed and implemented.

Under the GATS, a measure does not need to directly regulate the trade or supply of services to affect trade in services. According to GATS, a measure is covered if it impacts the conditions of competition for the supply of a service,

19 Türk and Krajewski (n 13) 27.
20 GATS art 1.
21 *Marrakesh Agreement*, opened for signature 15 April 1994, 1867 UNTS 3, annex 1B ('GATS') 1869 UNTS 183, art I:1 (entered into force 1 January 1995).
22 Ibid. art I:3(a).

regardless of whether it governs other aspects. Article XXVIII of GATS provides examples of what constitutes 'measures by Members affecting trade in services'. This non-exhaustive list includes measures related to the purchase, payment or use of a service; the access to and use of services required to be offered to the public generally; and the presence, including commercial presence, of persons from a member country providing a service in another member's territory. Also, the definition of 'measures by Members affecting trade in services' is intentionally broad, reflecting the wide range of governmental actions that can influence service trade. This broad scope ensures that the MFN[23] treatment obligation under GATS applies to a wide array of regulatory measures, underscoring the expansive reach of the agreement in governing international trade in services.

The GATS general obligations apply to all member states and include all their services sectors and sub-sectors in the four modes of supply. The general obligations under GATS include the MFN principle[24] and transparency.[25] The MFN obligation applies even if a member has not made a specific commitment in a given service and requires non-discrimination among members in relation to services or services suppliers of a like nature.[26] The inherent risk of the MFN obligation is its potential to open the floodgates so that a limited trial of market liberalization of a particular service may bind that member to a far more expansive market opening than it ever intended.[27] Such a risk is particularly concerning for the water services sector because, as noted above, maximizing flexibility and leaving scope for dynamic regulatory adjustment is an important component of holistic and sustainable water services policy.

GATS also regulate market access[28] and impose a NT obligation.[29] The market access provision restricts States from imposing quantitative restrictions or domestic ownership requirements on services in order to ensure market access for foreign service suppliers. The NT obligation restricts Members from treating foreign suppliers in a manner less favourably than their domestic counterparts. These specific commitments apply only to individual service sectors nominated by a Member for liberalization. Article XVII of the GATS, the NT provision, mandates that members must treat 'like services' from other members no less favourably than their own domestically produced like services. This provision has the potential to broadly influence all GATS-related measures. However, its practical application is confined to areas that influence trade in services, excluding those covered by Articles XVI (Market Access) and VI (Domestic Regulation).

23 GATS Art II.
24 *Marrakesh Agreement*, art II.
25 *Marrakesh Agreement*, art. III.
26 A. Pereira, 'The Liberalization of Education under the WTO Services Agreement (GATS): A Threat to Public Educational Policy?' (2005) 2(3) *Manchester Journal of International Economic Law* (2005) 5.
27 Ibid. 18–19.
28 *Marrakesh Agreement*, art XVI.
29 *Marrakesh Agreement*, art XVII.

In the EC–Bananas III case,[30] the dispute resolution panel introduced a four-pronged test to assess whether a measure conflicts with the GATT NT provision. The test involves (1) verifying that the complainant has established that the member had a 'specific commitment' in the relevant service sector and mode of supply, (2) determining that the member has implemented a measure impacting the service supply in the concerned sector and mode, (3) confirming that the measure applies to both foreign and domestic like services or service suppliers, and (4) proving that the measure provides less favourable treatment to foreign suppliers compared to domestic counterparts.

While this test was developed in the context of the GATT, it remains uncertain whether a similar approach will be adopted by dispute resolution panels for GATS. The determination and application of this test in future GATS disputes could significantly affect the interpretation and enforcement of the NT provision within the framework of international trade in services. In theory, this approach provides flexibility, as each Member defines its own trade in services regime through specific commitments in its schedule of commitments.[31] In the context of water services, Members would accordingly have to nominate their water services for liberalization before Articles XVII and XVI apply.

The issue of domestic regulation in relation to the affordability and availability of services following privatization is addressed in Section III of this Article. It highlights that even with privatization, states retain the responsibility to ensure the provision of basic services through effective regulation. However, a paradox exists because the GATS does not afford members sufficient policy autonomy in crafting such regulations. Article VI of GATS contains several provisions aimed at ensuring that domestic regulations do not act as barriers to trade. Specifically, Article VI:1 mandates that members administer all general measures affecting trade in services in sectors with specific commitments in a reasonable, objective and impartial manner. Yet, GATS does not clearly define what constitutes reasonable, objective and impartial regulation, nor does it provide criteria to assess whether a member's domestic regulations meet these standards. This lack of clarity leaves significant questions about the application and enforcement of these principles, posing challenges for member states in navigating their regulatory responsibilities under GATS.

The stated purpose of Article VI.4 is to ensure that measures such as technical standards and licensing requirements are not 'unnecessary barriers to trade in services'. The procedures that the Article sets out for achieving its aim are for the Council for Trade in Services to establish bodies for the purpose of

30 World Trade Organization, 'European Communities—Regime for the Importation, Sale and Distribution of Bananas, WT/DS27/AB/R' (adopted 25 September 1997), available at https://www.wto.org/english/tratop_e/dispu_e/27abrw_e.pdf, accessed 19 August 2024.

31 Aaron Ostrovsky, Robert Speed and Elisabeth Türk, 'GATS, Water and the Environment: Implications of the General Agreement on Trade in Services for Water Resources' (Research Discussion Paper, Centre for International Environmental Law 2003) 16.

developing 'any necessary disciplines'. The permissible scope of these conditions is that they must be 'based on objective and transparent criteria, such as competence and the ability to supply the service', 'not [be] more burdensome than necessary to ensure the quality of the service', and 'in the case of licensing procedures, not in themselves [be] a restriction on the supply of the service'.[32] Particularly in relation to the requirement that particular measures are not 'more burdensome than necessary to ensure the quality of the service', the question of the extent to which the GATS will affect domestic water services policies remains largely unexplored. There is considerable ambiguity about whether and how concession contracts for water services—including policies that set out the negotiation of the financial arrangements contained therein—would be covered by the GATS.[33] If these policies were to fall under GATS Article VI.4, they would have to comply with the respective criteria and obligations for specific disciplines that will be negotiated under this mandate. Pricing arrangements for units of economic activity (e.g., of water extracted) have not yet been discussed under GATS Article VI.4.[34]

There is a wide range of domestic instruments concerning water services that could potentially be argued to fall within the ambit of Article VI.4. For example, land use restrictions that control the distribution of industry potentially affect local water quality and demand for water services, and therefore can serve as an important regulatory tool to preserve market access to water services.[35] In turn, the preservation and responsible management of groundwater is crucial for a country's ability to provide safe and clean water to its citizens. As regards technical regulations, they may include setting certain quality standards for water to be provided to human beings. Again, they constitute a policy tool central to the realization of the right to water. Thus, while these policies are crucial for domestic water management, they may—in the future—be covered by trade disciplines established under Article VI.4. However, from a human rights and sustainable development perspective, water policymakers should be free to design and implement policies that pursue objectives relating to access maximization, conservation, and quality standards without being primarily concerned with any corresponding reduction in trade or other economic impacts of these policies.[36] If disciplines under Article VI.4 threaten this approach, the ability of individual member states, which have the primary obligation to ensure human rights for their citizens, may be significantly compromised.

32 'WTO, GATS: Fact and Fiction—Misunderstandings and Scare Stories: The WTO Is Not After Your Water' (n.d.), available at www.wto.org/english/tratop_e/serv_e/gats_factfiction8_e.htm.

33 WWF and CIEL, GATS, Water and the Environment—Implications of the General Agreement on Trade in Services for Water Resources (Gland, World Wide Fund for Nature 2003) p. 39.

34 Ibid.

35 Türk and Krajewski (n 13) 11.

36 Ibid.

The Application of GATS to Water Services

In order to create a more certain picture of how GATS will apply to water services, it is useful to consider the text of the agreement to determine how and in what circumstances a Member would liberalize its water services under GATS. Water services have not been explicitly included in the classification system, and up to this point, there has been no commitment from member states in this field.[37] Nevertheless, the growing number of commitments within the environmental services sector, particularly concerning sewage and sanitation, prompts speculation about the duration for which water services will remain excluded from the Agreement. Given that both sewage and sanitation depend extensively on water, their operations significantly influence water utilization and resource distribution. Consequently, while the broader scope of water services might eventually fall under GATS commitments, the specific segment of drinking water could remain exempt. This separation within the water supply framework under the Agreement could pose internal challenges for water management, especially considering the industry's inclination towards a natural monopoly and the necessary collaboration between public and private entities.[38] The ongoing uncertainty and complexity in defining water services under the WTO and the GATS agreement present substantial challenges.

The Public Service Exception[39]

Proponents of the GATS reject concerns about public services and insist they are carved out through Article 1.3. In this respect, governments are allowed to pursue their policy objectives where services are 'supplied in the exercise of governmental authority' and on a non-commercial and non-competitive basis. While the terms 'commercial and 'competitive' are not defined, it is clear that there are very few services provided in the exercise of governmental authority that do not have either a commercial element or a competitor, and this is even in the case of water services which tend towards a monopoly structure.[40] Importantly, the nature and purpose of the service and its social characteristics are not relevant considerations. Therefore, while no WTO Members have made GATS commitments in regard to water, there is a strong likelihood that a State's GATS obligations can severely curtail its regulatory autonomy in the water services market.[41]

37 World Bank and WTO, I-TIP Services, available at http://i-tip.wto.org/services/(S(r2sl0omoomrwnqs4bwb02o4i))/default.aspx, accessed 4 August 2015.

38 Budds (n 3) 93.

39 *Marrakesh Agreement*, art I:3.

40 Türk and Krajewski (n 13) 8.

41 Shawkat Alam, Pundarik Mukhopadhaya and David Randle, 'The General Agreement on Trade in Services (GATS), Water, and Human Rights from the Perspective of Developing Countries' (2011) 58(1) *Netherlands International Law Review* 43, 121.

Market Access[42]

The GATS market access provision aims to eliminate a number of qualitative and quantitative barriers to trade in services, including quotas and monopolies. Although GATS does not specifically require the privatization of public services, privatization is often linked with the elimination of public monopolies.[43] This has particular significance for the provision of water services which tend towards a natural monopoly—a structure which is also fundamental to a government's ability to ensure the right to water.[44] The fact that the GATS commitments are almost impossible to rescind (the 'lock-in effect') means that regulators have to ensure that water allocation is properly done from the beginning.[45] This is particularly concerning for developing countries which tend to not have the capacity or infrastructure to undertake assessments of the potential and actual impact of services policies.[46]

National Treatment[47]

The NT provision seeks to prevent countries from adopting protectionist measures that discriminate against foreign companies in favour of domestic suppliers. However, this provision may frustrate the very policies necessary to facilitate the supply of water to the poor. There are essentially two main regulatory mechanisms to achieve this: universal services obligations (USOs) imposed on private providers, and directly subsidizing service providers.[48]

Given that the private sector is likely to be most interested in segments of markets that are more profitable, imposing USOs is a useful way for States to ensure that water is provided to the poorest of society whilst still allowing privatization in more profitable sectors.[49] However, the USOs have to be carefully formulated before States sign up to specific commitments, as they may not be later revoked (the lock-in effect).[50] Subsidies, on the other hand, may constitute anti-competitive behaviour or violate the NT provision.[51] Such a

42 *Marrakesh Agreement*, opened for signature 15 April 1994, 1867 UNTS 3, annex 1B ('GATS') 1869 UNTS 183, art XVI (entered into force 1 January 1995).
43 Türk and Krajewski (n 13) 7.
44 Rupa Chanda, 'Social Services and the GATS: Key Issues and Concerns' (2003) 31(12) *World Development* 1997, 2004–2006.
45 Malgosia Fitzmaurice, 'The Human Right to Water' (2006) 18 *Fordham Environmental Law Review* 537, 571.
46 United Nations Economic and Social Council, Report of the High Commissioner, *Economic, Social and Cultural Rights, Liberalization of Trade in Services and Human Rights*, UN Doc E/CN.4/Sub.2/2002/9, 25 June 2002, 15.
47 *Marrakesh Agreement* art XVII.
48 Türk and Krajewski (n 13) 10–13.
49 Ibid. 12.
50 Fitzmaurice (n 44) 572.
51 Ibid.

strict approach may have an adverse effect on the provision of water services and may impact on a State's ability to promote the right to development.

Domestic Regulation[52]

Under GATS Article VI, countries have a specific obligation to regulate those services where they have filed a commitment in a reasonable, objective and impartial manner.[53] Further, it seeks to ensure that measures such as technical standards and licensing requirements do not constitute unnecessary barriers to trade, and it includes a mandate for the development of new disciplines in this area. It is not clear what constitutes 'unnecessary trade barriers'; however, a necessity test has been proposed, which requires that a domestic regulation relating to qualifications, licensing and technical standards be no more trade restrictive than necessary to fulfil the policy objective of that regulation. That is, even where a domestic regulation is applied in a non-discriminatory manner, it may still be inconsistent with GATS if it is 'more trade restrictive than necessary'.[54]

The ultimate concern that arises in this context is the extent to which governments will retain their autonomy to select regulatory objectives.[55] A measure designed to facilitate a human right, such as water services, may have to consider its trade restrictiveness as one of its key elements.[56] The question arises whether this has the effect of subordinating human rights obligations to trade rules. From a sustainable development perspective, a human rights approach to trade holds the enjoyment of human rights (the social pillar) among the objectives of trade liberalization, not as an issue secondary to trade. Thus any judgement of the trade restrictiveness of a measure should also consider a State's human rights obligations.[57]

Liberalization of Water Services: Weighing Costs and Benefits

The debate surrounding the GATS features sharply contrasting views. On one hand, critics argue that GATS facilitates the transfer of public services from state control to profit-driven MNCs, thereby undermining the government's

52 *Marrakesh Agreement*, art VI.4.

53 World Trade Organization ('WTO'), *GATS—Fact and Fiction* (2001), available at http://www.wto.org/english/tratop_e/serv_e/gatsfacts1004_e.pdf.

54 Colin Kirkpatrick and David Parker, 'Domestic Regulation and the WTO: The Case of Water Services in Developing Countries' (2005) 28(10) *The World Economy* 1491, 1499.

55 Chanda (n 44) 2006.

56 Türk and Krajewski (n 13) 7–9.

57 United Nations Economic and Social Council, Report of the High Commissioner, *Economic, Social and Cultural Rights, Liberalization of Trade in Services and Human Rights*, UN Doc E/CN.4/Sub.2/2002/9, 25 June 2002, 16.

ability to regulate for social objectives.[58] They fear that this shift prioritizes profit over public welfare. On the other hand, proponents of GATS argue that it offers a flexible framework for its member states, imposing no obligations to privatize or deregulate any service sector. Instead, it allows countries the discretion to maintain public or private monopolies as they see fit. Proponents emphasize that it is up to individual states to decide the extent of liberalization in any sector.[59] However, as GATS does provide a platform for the negotiation and liberalization of public services, it could be argued that it inherently promotes liberalization by encouraging discussions on opening up service sectors to international competition. The concerns surrounding the GATS focus on the trade-off between commercial and efficiency interests on the one hand, and equity and developmental goals on the other hand.[60] In order to facilitate an objective assessment of GATS, the following sections will evaluate the opportunities and challenges posed by the liberalization of trade in services, and its potential application to water services.

GATS and Liberalization Benefits

In a general sense, the more efficient supply of services in a sector can facilitate economic growth and development. Specifically, the WTO asserts that services liberalization can promote economic performance, assist countries to capitalize on their competitive strengths, offer consumer savings, promote faster innovations and facilitate technology transfer.[61]

The ability to increase economic growth and the capacity of an economy is increasingly being viewed as a mechanism to assist governments to alleviate poverty and meet developmental goals.[62] This approach is supported by the WTO, which views trade liberalization and economic growth as tools to assist governments in promoting human welfare.[63] In addition, opening up to foreign commercial presence in trade in services can benefit recipient countries by increasing foreign investment. The availability of private capital

58 Scott Sinclair, 'How the World Trade Organisation's New "Services" Negotiations Threaten Democracy' (Canadian Centre for Policy Alternatives, 2000); David Hartridge, 'WTO Secretariat Hits False Attacks against GATS' (Speech Delivered at the European Services Forum, Brussels, 27 November 2000), available at http://www.esf.be/docs/hartridg.doc.

59 Rupa Chanda, 'General Agreement on Trade in Services: Implications for Social Policy-Making' (2003) 38(16) *Economic and Political Weekly* 1567, 1569, 1571–1572.

60 Lyla Mehta and Birgit la Cour Madsen, 'Is the WTO After Your Water? The General Agreement on Trade in Services (GATS) and Poor People's Right to Water' (2005) 29(2) *Natural Resources Forum* 154, 157.

61 World Trade Organization ('WTO'), *GATS—Fact and Fiction* (2001), available at http://www.wto.org/english/tratop_e/serv_e/gatsfacts1004_e.pdf.

62 Rebecca Bates, 'The Trade in Water Services: How Does GATS Apply to the Water and Sanitation Services Sector?' (2009) 31 *Sydney Law Review* 121, 132.

63 World Trade Organization ('WTO'), *GATS—Fact and Fiction* (2001), available at http://www.wto.org/english/tratop_e/serv_e/gatsfacts1004_e.pdf.

can reduce the total burden on government resources which could then be directed to improving the public sector or help facilitate the provision of an essential service which the government is unable to supply.[64] Liberalization can also lead to the transfer and provision of technical and managerial capacities to relevant sectors, which may assist states to better utilize their resources and develop in a more efficient manner.[65]

These positive implications sound appealing and suggest that global trade in services is advantageous for all Members, developing and developed countries alike. Specifically with respect to water, if such benefits are realized it would clearly benefit local communities as water quality, access and affordability would be improved and it would assist in meeting the needs of those lacking adequate water services.[66]

GATS and Liberalization Concerns

The liberalization of trade in services without sufficient government regulation and proper assessment can also have adverse implications. First, MNCs prioritize profit-making over social goals. It is common for them to engage only in profitable ventures and to pull out of investment projects if their potential for revenue is threatened. A case in point is the UK-based company Biwater, which withdrew from a private water project in Zimbabwe in 1999 because the targeted consumers were too impoverished to afford the tariffs necessary for the company to achieve its desired profit margins. Richard Whiting, Biwater's country manager for Zimbabwe, highlighted the divergence between private and social objectives, stating:

> Investors need to be convinced that they will get reasonable returns . . . We have to consider factors like the end users' ability to afford water tariffs . . . While these projects are socially viable, they unfortunately do not meet private sector profitability criteria.

The most common criticism is that the GATS would force companies to open up their services to foreign entities and result in a 'corporate takeover' of their service.[67] This concern is greatest in the case of social services, such as water, where states have an obligation to ensure the availability and accessibility of essential services, particularly to the poor. There is apprehension about the opening up of such services in terms of the impact on the costs, availability and quality of such services and on the realization of national

64 Chanda (n 44) 2000.

65 United Nations Economic and Social Council, Report of the High Commissioner, *Economic, Social and Cultural Rights, Liberalization of Trade in Services and Human Rights*, UN Doc E/CN.4/Sub.2/2002/9, 25 June 2002, 12–15.

66 Bates (n 62) 133.

67 Türk and Krajewski (n 13) 7.

policy objectives.[68] Indeed, such concerns are warranted. Given that foreign investment is primarily driven by commercial objectives, private capital will not necessarily be the most effective means of ensuring universal access to essential services that at times can be unprofitable.[69] Further, privatization that is leading to an increasingly large and powerful private sector can undermine domestic regulations through political pressures and 'regulatory capture'.[70] In the highly controversial plan to privatize water services in Bolivia, prices were to increase by 35%.[71] This serves as a stark example that water privatization is not necessarily efficient and cost-effective when considering questions relating to access and affordability of water services. Thus, while States often fail to universalize water services due to lack of finance, corruption and institutional inefficiencies, private bodies fail because profits are placed ahead of social development.[72]

A further concern raised is that GATS curtails the use of regulatory mechanisms, such as public subsidies to address various non-economic objectives. In liberalized water sectors, governments will still be required to establish and protect minimum water service standards for the advantage of the community.[73] However, Lang notes that such regulatory measures have the potential to be viewed as a barrier to trade and pose a threat of breaching the NT and MFN treatment provisions of GATS.[74] However, Chanda argues that these concerns are unwarranted given the voluntarily nature of the commitment process and the discretion of imposing limitations in the commitment schedules.[75] Noting this, Chanda's approach remains silent that the specification of such limitations requires a significant degree of administrative capacity and insight by a Member at the point of making a commitment. Often this is lacking for many developing countries.[76] This is further exacerbated by the power asymmetries between developing and developed countries, where the request-offer process under GATS allows powerful countries to exert significant pressure on poorer countries to respond quickly and positively to requests.[77] In this regard, it is appropriate for developed countries to fulfil the promises of technical assistance and capacity building under GATS.

68 Chanda (n 44) 2002.

69 United Nations Economic and Social Council, Report of the High Commissioner, *Economic, Social and Cultural Rights, Liberalization of Trade in Services and Human Rights*, UN Doc E/CN.4/Sub.2/2002/9, 25 June 2002, 13.

70 Ibid.

71 Fitzmaurice (n 45) 540.

72 Mehta (n 60) 157.

73 Bates (n 62) 134.

74 Andrew Lang, 'The GATS and Regulatory Autonomy: A Case Study of Social Regulation of the Water Industry' (2004) 7(4) *Journal of international Economic Law* 801, 806.

75 Chanda (n 44) 2002.

76 Mehta (n 60) 161.

77 Ibid. 162–163.

Evaluating Water Services Liberalization From a Human Rights Dimension

The GATS has stimulated considerable public debate and concern from developing countries, major international NGOs and civil society. There is concern that treating services in much the same manner as goods ignores the social aspects of many services. It is useful to recall at this point the principle of sustainable development encompasses three pillars: social, economic and environmental. The services sector is linked to the social aspect of sustainable development in the discussion of human rights. The liberalization (and privatization) of water services therefore requires particular consideration given the vital relationship between water and human rights and the possible impact on the market responsible for supplying this essential service.[78]

Water Privatization, States and Markets

Water privatization involves non-government entities, either local or foreign, owning and managing water supply infrastructure. International investment treaties like the GATS create frameworks that enable foreign companies to enter local markets and establish the conditions under which states must facilitate access. Although the involvement of the private sector in water and sanitation has a long history, these treaties are reshaping how these companies function within local environments. Traditionally, the management of water and sanitation has been considered a public good and thus the responsibility of the public sector. The liberalization of water services involves the entrance of private firms to the domestic water market. Historically, the water services sector has been in the domain of states and it is estimated that over 90% of the world's piped water is delivered by public bodies, at both national and local levels.[79] This is because of the essential nature of water services and the fact that they are often natural monopolies.[80]

However, despite public control, governments, particularly in developing countries, in reality fail to universalize water services.[81] State failure in this area can be attributed to a lack of finance, political interference, mismanagement and poor regulatory structures.[82] In this context, privatization has been promoted as the correct remedy based on the presumption that 'competition promotes efficiency and provides users with options that in turn, make infrastructure providers more accountable'.[83] Several OECD studies[84] highlight the potential

78 Bates (n 62) 128.

79 Chanda (n 44) 1998.

80 Caroline Dommen, 'Trade and Human Rights: Towards Coherence' (2005) 3 *International Journal on Human Rights* 7, 10.

81 Lang (n 74) 810.

82 Mehta (n 60) 155.

83 World Bank, 'World Development Report 1994: Infrastructure for Development' (Report, World Bank 1994) 33.

84 Rachel Thompson and Carole Pellegrino, 'Environmental Services: The "Win-Win" Role of Trade Liberalization in Promoting Environmental Protection and Economic Development'

for win-win outcomes for developing countries through the liberalization of trade and investment in water and waste management services. These studies point out how such reforms can lead to significant environmental and social benefits. For instance, expanding access to clean water and efficient waste collection services enhances the health and well-being of more citizens by creating cleaner human environments. Moreover, improvements to water infrastructure can reduce wastage and unequal access to this precious resource, often due to outdated systems prone to leaks and unauthorized access. The introduction of recycled effluent water for industrial use can further boost the availability of drinking water.

Additionally, the transformation of waste into alternative energy sources presents innovative energy solutions. The presence of foreign companies promotes environmental education and skills transfer, enriching local expertise in environmental management. These companies often introduce a broader range of environmental technologies that tackle problems more effectively and sometimes shift focus from remedial to preventive measures. They also tend to reinvest a portion of their profits into local environmental technology development, infrastructure upgrades and new investments, fostering a cycle of continuous improvement and sustainability. The liberalization of trade and investment in water and waste management services presents numerous economic and development advantages for developing countries. Key among these benefits is the alleviation of financial pressures on government budgets at both state and municipal levels. The savings garnered from these efficiencies can be redirected towards enhancing environmental policies, inspections and enforcement or can be used to bolster other social services and improve overall budget stability.

Furthermore, the development and operation of water and waste management facilities generate both skilled and unskilled employment opportunities for local populations in the design, construction and ongoing maintenance of these infrastructures. This influx of jobs contributes to stable economic growth and boosts the local tax base as both foreign and domestic investments are attracted to the community. Additionally, local private sector entities gain valuable experience in managing large or highly specialized projects. This expertise is not only crucial for local development but is also exportable, providing solutions to other nations with similar needs and conditions, thereby expanding the economic impact beyond local borders.

However, there is also the danger that private sector involvement may shift the focus of water service provision away from the public interest and in favour

(OECD Working Papers, 2000); OECD Joint Working Party on Trade and Environment, 'Environmental Goods and Services: An Assessment of the Environmental, Economic and Development Benefits of Further Global Trade Liberalisation' (OECD Working Papers 2000) 55–56 (this study is based on the review of over 60 examples of foreign private sector participation in the provision of water management services in developing countries); OECD, 'Assessing the Environmental Effects of Services Trade Liberalisation: A Methodology' (OECD Working Papers 2002).

of profit, excluding those unable to pay for the service. Given the essential role of water in promoting human health, caution is required in the application of privatization and liberalization policies to ensure the maintenance of basic service levels.

Water as a Human Right

While a human right to water is not explicitly recognized in the International Bill of Human Rights, more recent international human rights treaties include explicit references to the right to water.[85] Specifically, in 2002 the United Nations Committee on Economic, Social and Cultural Rights explicitly recognized the right to water as a human right in its General Comment No. 15 by emphasizing its importance in relation to other human rights.[86] The Committee also emphasized the responsibility of states in realizing the right to water which includes the provision of sufficient, safe, affordable water for personal and household use. Consequently, States are under an obligation to ensure universal access to basic water services for the promotion and protection of individual health and the well-being of their population.

Given that human rights obligations are enforceable on states, the privatization of an industry impacting human rights does not absolve the state of its responsibilities. Indeed, it is fundamentally the government's duty to ensure that the right to water is protected and upheld.[87] The General Comment clarifies that when water services are privatized, the duty to regulate and monitor the provision of water remains with the government. This includes ensuring that the right to water is fulfilled through measures such as subsidizing water for the poorest and most vulnerable, or establishing a tariff system that makes essential water use affordable, if not free.[88]

A State's ability to facilitate services may be compromised by international trade rules, including GATS, which may reduce a government's flexibility to implement water management policies.[89] Consequently, there appears to be an inescapable tension between the goals of the right to water and the goals of liberalization. Special consideration must be given to the liberalization (and privatization) of water services, given their nature as a public good

85 See *International Covenant on Economic, Social and Cultural Rights*, opened for signature 16 December 1966, 999 UNTS 3 (entered into force 3 January 1976) ('ICESCR'); *Declaration on the Right to Development*, GA Res 41/128, UN GAOR, 41st sess, 97th plen mtg, UN Doc A/Res/41/128 (1986); *Convention on the Elimination of All Forms of Discrimination Against Women*, opened for signature 18 December 1979, 1249 UNTS 13 (entered into force 3 September 1981).

86 Substantive Issues arising in the Implementation of the International Covenant on Economic, *Social and Cultural Rights: General Comment No 15*, UN ESCOR, 29th sess, UN Doc E/C.12/2002/11 (2002) ('*General Comment No 15*').

87 Williams (n 16) 501.

88 Ibid. 502.

89 Türk and Krajewski (n 13) 3.

and position as a human right. From a human rights perspective, the varying outcomes of privatization and private sector involvement in water services indicate that such approaches should be treated with caution. The promise of privatization as a solution to water access issues is not always realized.[90] In some LDCs, privatization has led to sharp increases in prices and social unrest, making essential water services even less accessible for the poorest populations. The risks associated with privatization are particularly severe in many LDCs due to heightened susceptibility to exploitation and unfair practices. This is exacerbated by limited resources, insufficient monitoring of MNCs, and a lack of robust legal frameworks.[91]

Commentators like Shiva argue that privatizing water services could pave the way for the privatization of water in all its forms.[92] Given these concerns, it is crucial to maintain some level of flexibility in the management and regulation of water services. Ensuring that privatization policies remain reversible and are not mandated by international trade law is essential for protecting water rights and addressing the unique challenges faced by vulnerable populations.

Conclusion

Trade liberalization presents both opportunities and challenges within the water services sector. Any decision regarding the operation of the GATS must acknowledge the human right to water and its vital nature as a human need and service. However, past experiences with water privatization schemes, together with the lack of clarity regarding the operation of the GATS, leave little reason to be optimistic. This coupled with the power asymmetries in the WTO negotiation processes can significantly disadvantage developing countries. The primary goal of water management is sustainability, which encompasses environmental, economic and infrastructural aspects into a cohesive operational framework. However, achieving this equilibrium is often difficult, as it requires providing sufficient services while maintaining the ecosystem's resilience. The water sector's monopolistic characteristics and emphasis on long-term investments play vital roles in planning for sustainability. Furthermore, the introduction of investment treaties such as the GATS, which allows new market

90 This point is further illustrated in General Comment No. 15 which emphasizes that third party, private intervention in the provision of water must be handled with caution: 'Where water services . . . are operated or controlled by third parties, States parties must prevent them from compromising equal, affordable, and physical access to sufficient, safe and acceptable water. To prevent such abuses an effective regulatory system must be established, in conformity with the [International Covenant on Economic, Social & Cultural Rights] and this General Comment, which includes independent monitoring, genuine public participation, and imposition of penalties for non-compliance.' General Comment, para. 24.

91 J. Dellapenna and J. Gupta, 'Toward Global Law on Water' (2008) 14 *Global Governance* 443.

92 V. Shiva, *Water Wars—Privatization, Pollution, and Profit* (South End Press 2002) 98.

entrants, introduces additional complexity. Considering these challenges, it is crucial for the WTO to reassess the implementation of GATS to ensure the sustainable and long-term delivery of water services.

In order for the GATS to be more aligned with developmental goals, there is a need for adequate economic, technical and social assessments of the potential and actual impact of services policies. It is also necessary to allow for flexibility in provisions, whereby commitments can be withdrawn if the changes that the country encounters warrant this.[93] This issue demands a thoughtful and cautious approach, as we have illustrated the negative socio-economic effects of privatizing and liberalizing public services. These practices can render services both inaccessible and unaffordable while also leading to unemployment. Kelsey precisely notes that 'the quality, affordability, and accessibility of services are crucial to social well-being, cohesion, and stability—and often to the sustainability of life itself'.[94] Potential tensions between WTO law and other spheres of international law governing water services need to be addressed in a manner that recognizes the primacy of the human right to water. Within the GATS framework, the social dimension of water services cannot be given mere lip service, especially when it comes to LDCs.[95] On this point, Bouguerra forcefully argues that

> It is unrealistic and scarcely imaginable that water should be wholly subject to the laws of the market, with no compensation and, above all, no help for deprived sections of the population.[96]

93 Mehta (n 60) 160.

94 Jane Kelsey, 'Confronting Trade-Related Human Rights in a GATS-Compatible World' (2007) 1 *Law, Social Justice & Global Development* 1, available at http://go.warwick.ac.uk/elj/lgd/2007_1/kelsey.

95 L. Bouguerra, *Water Under Threat* (Zed Books 2006) 118.

96 Ibid.

Bibliography

Books

Anghie A, *Imperialism, Sovereignty and the Making of International Law* (Cambridge University Press 2005)
Barlow M and Clarke B, *Blue Gold: The Battle Against the Corporate Theft of the World's Water* (Earthscan 2002)
Bercusson B and Estlund C, *Regulating Labour in the Wake of Globalization: New Challenges, New Institution* (Hart Publishing 2008)
Biersteker TJ, *Distortion or Development? Contending Perspectives on the Multinational Corporation* (Massachusetts Institute of Technology Press 1978)
Billon P, Lujala P and Rustad SA, *A Theory of Change for the Extractive Industries Transparency Initiative* (U4 Anti-corruption Resource Centre 2020)
Bouguerra L, *Water Under Threat* (Zed Books 2006)
Chatham House, *Illegal Logging & Related Trade: Lessons from the Global Response* (Chatham House 2010)
Chi Chi M, *Integrating Sustainable Development in International Investment Law, Normative Incompatibility, System Integration and Governance Implications* (Routledge 2018)
Cotula L, *Foreign Investment, Law and Sustainable Development* (IIED 2014)
Dolzer R and Schreuer C, *Principles of International Investment Law* (2nd edn, Oxford University Press 2014)
Dolzer R and Stevens M, *Bilateral Investment Treaties* (Martinus Nijhoff Publishers 1995)
ESCAP, *Handbook on Policies, Promotion, and the Facilitation of Foreign Direct Investment for Sustainable Development in Asia and the Pacific* (United Nations 2022)
Escobar A, *Encountering Development: The Making and Unmaking of the Third World* (Princeton University Press 1995)
Frank TM, *Fairness in International Law and Institutions* (Oxford University Press 1995)
Frank TM, *The Power of Legitimacy among Nations* (Oxford University Press 1990)
Gallagher K and Zarsky L, *Generalized System of Preferences Handbook on the Scheme of the United States of America* (The Enclave Economy MIT Press 2007) <https://unctad.org/system/files/official-document/itcdtsbmisc58rev3_en.pdf> accessed 10 February 2023
Gleeson D and Labonte R, *Trade Agreements and Public Health* (Palgrave Macmillan 2020)
'Guide to the Global Compact: A Practical Understanding of the Vision and Nine Principles 51' *UN Global Compact* (2002) <http://www.unglobalcompact.org/content/public_Documents/gcguide.pdf> accessed 12 July 2023

Harten GV, *Investment Treaty Arbitration and Public Law* (Oxford University Press 2007)
Henkin L, *The Age of Rights* (Columbia University Press 1990)
Hyde JN, *Economic Development Agreements* (Recueil des Cours 1962)
International Labour Organization, *Handbook on Assessment of Labour Provisions in Trade and Investment Agreements* (ILO 2017)
Jagers N, *Corporate Human Rights Obligations: In Search of Accountability* (Intersentia 2002)
Kelsey J, *Serving Whose Interests? The Political Economy of Trade in Services Agreement* (Routledge-Cavendish 2008)
Lowenfeld AF, *International Economic Law* (2nd edn, Oxford University Press 2008)
McLachlan C, Shore L and Weiniger M, *International Investment Arbitration: Substantive Principles* (Oxford University Press 2007)
Monash University Castan Centre for Human Rights Law, *Human Rights Translated: A Business Reference Guide* (United Nations Human Rights, Office of the High Commissioner for Human Rights 2008)
Moran T, *Does Foreign Investment Promote Development?* (Peterson Institute Press 2005)
Moran TH, Graham EM and Blomström M (eds.), *Does Foreign Investment Promote Development?* (Peterson Institute for International Economics 2005)
Nhantumbo I and Salomão A, *Biofuels, Land Access and Rural Livelihoods in Mozambique.* (International Institute for Environment and Development (IIED) 2010)
Nooteboom D, *Adaptive Networks: The Governance for Sustainable Development* (Eburon 2006)
OECD, *A Comprehensive Overview of Global Biodiversity Finance* (OECD Publishing 2020)
OECD, *Towards Sustainable Land Use: Aligning Biodiversity, Climate and Food Policies* (OECD 2020) <https://www.oecd-ilibrary.org/environment/towards-sustainable-land-use_3809b6a1-en> accessed 1 June 2023
OECD, 'Trade, Employment and Labour Standards: A Study of Core Workers' in *Rights and International Trade* (OECD Publishing 1996)
Pauwelyn J, *Conflict of Norms in Public International Law: How WTO Law Relates to Other Rules of International Law* (Cambridge University Press 2003)
Puvimanasinghe SF, *Foreign Investment, Human Rights and the Environment: A Perspective from South Asia on the Role of Public International Law for Development* (Martinus Nijhoff Publishers 2007)
Rodrik D, *Has Globalisation Gone Too Far?* (Institute for International Economics 1997)
Schacherer S, *Sustainable Development in EU Foreign Investment Law* (Brill Nijhoff 1988)
Schwarzenberger G, *Foreign Investments* (Stevens 1969)
Scierbeck J, 'Operational Measures for Identifying and Implementing Human Rights Issues in Corporate Operations', in Asbjorn Eide, Helge Ole Bergesen and Pia Rudolfson Goyer (eds), *Human Rights and the Oil Industry* (Intersentia 2000)
Seid SH, *Global Regulation of Foreign Direct Investment* (Ashgate 2002)
Seiderman I, *Hierarchy in International Law: The Human Rights Dimension* (Intersentia-Hart 2001)
Seidl-Hohenvelderm I, *International Economic Law* (3rd edn, Kluwer Law International 1999)
Shiva V, *Water Wars—Privatization, Pollution, and Profit* (South End Press 2002)
Sinclair S, *How the World Trade Organisation's New "Services" Negotiations Threaten Democracy* (Canadian Centre for Policy Alternatives 2000)
Sornarajah M, *The International Law on Foreign Investment* (2nd edn, Cambridge University Press 2004)
Sornarajah M, *The International Law on Foreign Investment* (3rd edn, Cambridge University Press 2010)
Steiner HJ and Alston P, *International Human Rights in Context* (Oxford University Press 2000)

Stiglitz J, *Globalization and Its Discontents* (W.W. Norton 2002)
Subedi SP, *International Investment Law: Reconciling Policy and Principle* (Oxford University Press 2008)
Tion in De Schutter O (ed), *Transnational Corporations and Human Rights* (Hart Publishing 2006)
Towards Sustainable Land Use: Aligning Biodiversity, Climate and Food Policies (OECD Publishing 2020) <https://doi.org/10.1787/3809b6a1-en> accessed 30 May 2023.
Turner S, *A Global Environmental Right* (Routledge 2013)
VanDuzer JA, Simons P and Mayeda G, *Integrating Sustainable Development into International Investment Agreements: A Guide for Developing Countries* (Commonwealth Secretariat 2012) <https://www.iisd.org/system/files/meterial/6th_annual_forum_commonwealth_guide.pdf> accessed 20 January 2024
Viñuales JE, *Foreign Investment and the Environment in International Law* (Cambridge University Press 2012)
Zarsky L, *International Investment for Sustainable Development: Balancing Rights and Rewards* (Earthscan 2004)

Contribution in Edited Books

Adams RJ and Turner L, 'The Social Dimension of Freer Trade' in ML Cook and HC Katz (eds), *Regional Integration and Industrial Relations in North America* (ILR Press 1994)
Ahmad Y and Carey E, 'Development Co-Operation During the COVID-19 Pandemic: An Analysis of 2020 Figures and 2021 Trends to Watch' in *Development Co-operation Profiles* (OECD Publishing 2021) <https://doi.org/10.1787/e4b3142a-en> accessed 3 June 2023
Akpan GS, 'Host Community Hostility to Mining Projects: A New Generation of Risk?' in Elizabeth Bastida, Thomas Walde and Janeth Warden-Fernandez (eds), *International and Comparative Mineral Law and Policy: Trends and Prospects* (Kluwer Law International 2005)
Alston P, 'The "Not-a-Cat" Syndrome: Can the International Human Rights Regime Accommodate Non-State Actors?' in Philip Alston (ed), *Non-State Actors and Human Rights* (Oxford University Press 2005)
Aspremont J, 'International Customary Investment Law: Story of a Paradox' in Tarcisio Gazzini and Eric De Brabandere (eds), *International Investment Law: The Sources of Rights and Obligations* (Martinus Nijhoff 2012)
Atik J, 'Legitimacy, Transparency and NGO Participation in the NAFTA Chapter 11 Process' in Todd Weiler (ed), *NAFTA Investment Law and Arbitration: Past Issues, Current Practices, Future Prospects* (Transnational Publishers 2004)
Bjorklund AK, 'National Treatment' in August Reinisch (ed), *Standards of Investment Protection* (Oxford University Press 2008)
Boer B, 'Introduction' in Ben Boer (ed), *Environmental Law Dimensions of Human Rights* (Oxford University Press 2015)
Cantegreil J, 'Implementing Human Rights in the NAFTA Regime—The Potential of a Pending Case: Glamis Corp v USA' in Pierre-Marie Dupuy, Francesco Francioni and Ernest-Ulrich Petersmann (eds), *Human Rights in International Investment Law and Arbitration* (Oxford University Press 2009)
Chandler G, 'The Responsibilities of Oil Companies' in Asbjorn Eide, Helge Ole Bergesen and Pia Rudolfson Goyer (eds), *Human Rights and the Oil Industry* (Intersentia 2000)
Deakin S, 'The Contribution of Labour Law to Economic and Human Development' in Guy Davidov and Brian Langille (eds), *The Idea of Labour Law* (Oxford University Press 2011)

De Schutter O, 'Transnational Corporations as Instrument of Human Development' in Philip Alston and Mary Robinson (eds), *Human Rights and Development: Towards Mutual Reinforcement* (Oxford University Press 2005)

Echeverra GME, 'Conflicts between Resource Development and Indigenous People' in *Mining and Oil & Gas Development in Latin America* (Mineral Law Series, Rocky Mountain Mineral Law Foundation 2001)

Fick BJ, 'Introduction' in Barbara J. Fick (ed), *International Labour Law* (Edward Elgar 2015)

Frankkental P, 'Why Socially Responsible Investment Requires More Risk for Companies Rather than More Engagement', in Rory Sullivan and Craig Mackenzie (eds), *Responsible Investment* (Greenleaf Publishing 2006)

Gao Z, Akpan G and Vanjik J, 'Public Participation in Mining and Petroleum in Asia and the Pacific: The Ok Tedi Case and Its Implications' in Donald N. Zillman, Alastair Lucas and George (Rock) Pring (ed), *Human Rights in Natural Resource Development: Public Participation in the Sustainable Development of Mining and Energy Resources* (Oxford University Press 2002)

Hirsch M, 'Interactions Between Investment and Non-Investment Obligations in International Investment Law' in P. Muchlinski, F. Ortino and Ch. Schreuer (eds), *The Oxford Handbook of International Investment Law* (Oxford University Press 2008)

Holland M and Diop M, 'Strategies for Securing Tenure: The Promise and Pitfalls of Formalization' in Margaret Holland, Yuta Masuda and Brian Robinson (eds), *Land Tenure Security and Sustainable Development* (Springer Nature 2022)

Joubin-Bret A, 'Admission and Establishment in the Context of Investment Protection' in August Reinisch (ed), *Standards of Investment Protection* (Oxford University Press 2008)

Jungk M, 'A Practical Guide to Addressing Human Rights Concerns for Companies Operating Abroad' in Michael K. Addo (ed), *Human Rights Standards and the Responsibility of Transnational Corporations* (Kluwer Law International 1999)

Kartika P and Hariyadi C 'The Programme for the Endorsement of Forest Certification (PEFC) and Its Contribution to Sustainable Forest Management in Indonesia' in A. Negi, J. Perez-Pineda and J. Blakenbach (eds), *Sustainability Standards and Global Governance* (Springer 2020) <https://doi.org/10.1007/978-981-15-3473-7_9>

Knoll-Tudor I, 'The Fair and Equitable Standard and Human Rights Norms' in Pierre-Marie Dupuy, Francesco Francioni and Ernest-Ulrich Petersmann (eds), *Human Rights in International Investment Law and Arbitration* (Oxford University Press 2009)

Kriebaum U, 'Privatising Human Rights: The Interface Between International Investment Protection and Human Rights' in A. Reinisch and U. Kriebum (eds), *The Law of International Relations: Liber Amicorum Huas Neuhold* (Eleven International Publishing 2007)

Kube V and Petersmann EU, 'Chapter 11: Human Rights Law in International Investment Arbitration' in Andrea Gattini, Attila Tanzi and Filippo Fontanelli (eds), *General Principles of Law and International Investment Arbitration* (Brill Publishing 2018).

MacDonald G and McLaughlin T, 'Extracting Conflict' in Rory Sullivan (ed), *Business and Human Rights: Dilemmas and Solutions* (Greenleaf Publishing 2003)

Miteva DA, Fortmann L and McNab R, 'Beyond the Traditional: Voluntary Market-Based Initiatives to Promote Land Tenure Security' in Margaret Holland, Yuta Masuda and Brian Robinson (eds), *Land Tenure Security and Sustainable Development* (Springer Nature 2022)

Moura-Costa P, Fretz L and Kohn G, 'Feasibility Analysis for an International Investment Promotion Entity for Sustainable Forest Management' in Mafa Chipera and Mahendra Joshi (eds), *The Private Sector Speaks: Investing in Sustainable Forest Management* (Centre for International Forestry Research 2001)

Muchlinski P, 'Corporate Social Responsibility and International Investment Law' in P. Muchlinski, F. Ortino and Ch. Schreuer (eds), *The Oxford Handbook of International Investment Law* (Oxford University Press 2008)

Novitz T, 'The European Union and International Labour Standards: The Dynamics of Dialogue Between the EU and the ILO' in Philip Alston (ed), *Labour Rights as Human Rights* (Oxford University Press 2005)

Orellana MA, 'Science, Risk and Uncertainty. Public Health Measures and Investment Disciplines' in Philippe Kahn and Thomas Walde (eds), *New Aspects of International Investment Law* (Martinus Nijhoff Publishers 2007)

Ortino F, 'Non-Discriminatory Treatment in Investment Disputes' in PM Dupuy, F Francioni and EU Petersmann (eds), *Human Rights in International Investment Law and Arbitration* (Oxford University Press 2009)

Park WW, 'NAFTA Chapter 11: Capital Exporters as Host States' in Gabrielle Kaufmann-Kohler and Blaise Stucki (eds), *Investment Treaties and Arbitration* (Basel 2002)

Petersmann E, 'Human Rights, Constitutionalism, and "Public Reason" in Investor-State Arbitration' in Christina Binder et al. (eds), *International Investment Law For the 21st Century: Essays in Honour of Christoph Schreuer* (Oxford University Press 2009)

Pring G and Noe SY, 'The Emerging International Law of Public Participation Affecting Global Mining, Energy and Resource Development' in Donald N Zillman, Alastair Lucas and George (Rock) Pring (eds), *Human Rights in Natural Resource Development: Public Participation in the Sustainable Development of Mining and Energy Resources* (Oxford University Press 2002)

Pritchard R, 'Privatisation and Private Provision of Infrastructure' in R Pritchard (ed), *Economic Development, Foreign Investment and the Law* (Kluwer Law International and International Bar Association 1996)

Reinisch A, '"Investment and . . .": The Broader Picture of Investment Law' in A. Reinisch and Ch. Knahr (eds), *International Investment Law in Context* (Eleven International Publishing 2008)

Rodrik D, 'Labor Rights in International Trade: Do They Matter and What Do We Do about Them?' in Robert Lawrence, Dani Rodrik and John Whalley (eds), *Emerging Agenda for Global Trade: High Stakes for Developing Countries* (Johns Hopkins Press for the Overseas Development Council 1996)

Salias MCG, 'Do Umbrella Clauses Apply to Unilateral Undertakings?' in Christina Binder et al. (eds), *International Investment Law For the 21st Century: Essays in Honour of Christoph Schreuer* (Oxford University Press 2009)

Schrijver NJ, 'A Multilateral Investment Agreement from a North-South Perspective', in EC Nieuwenhuys and MMTA Brus (eds), *Multilateral Regulation of Investment* (Kluwer Law International 2001)

Schutter OD, 'Transnational Corporations as Instrument of Human Development', in Philip Alston and Mary Robinson (eds), *Human Rights and Development: Towards Mutual Reinforcement* (Oxford University Press 2005)

Sengenberger W, 'Re-Structuring at the Global Level: The Role of International Labour Standards' in W Sengenberger and D Campbell (eds), *Creating Economic Opportunities: The Role of Labour Standards in Industrial Restructuring* (International Institute for Labour Studies 1994)

Simma B and Kill T, 'Harmonizing Investment Protection and International Human Rights: First Steps Towards a Methodology' in Christina Binder et al. (eds), *International Investment Law for the 21st Century: Essays in Honour of Christoph Schreuer* (Oxford University Press 2009)

Sinclair A, 'Bridging the Contract/Treaty Divide', in Christina Binder et al. (eds), *International Investment Law For the 21st Century: Essays in Honour of Christoph Schreuer* (Oxford University Press 2009)

Sornarajah M, 'A Coming Crisis: Expansionary Trend in Investment Treaty Arbitration' in Karl P. Sauvant (ed), *Appeals Mechanism in International Investment Disputes* (Oxford University Press 2008)

Ssenyonj M, 'Non-State Actors and Economic, Social and Cultural Rights' in Mashood A Baderin and Robert Mccorquodale (eds), *Economic, Social and Cultural Rights in Action* (Oxford University Press 2007)

Steinhardt RG, 'Corporate Responsibility and the International Law of Human Rights: The New Lex Mercatoria' in Philip Alston (ed), *Non-State Actors and Human Rights* (Oxford University Press 2005)

Tawil GS, 'Most Favoured Nation Clauses and Jurisdictional Clauses in Investment Treaty Arbitration' in Christina Binder et al. (eds), *International Investment Law for the 21st Century: Essays in Honour of Christoph Schreuer* (Oxford University Press 2009)

Thielborger P, 'The Human Right to Water Versus Investor Rights: Double-Dilemma or Pseudo-Conflict?' in F Francioni, EU Petersmann and PM Dupuy (eds), *Human Rights in International Investment Law and Arbitration* (Oxford University Press 2009)

Vadi VS, 'Reconciling Public Health and Investor Rights: The Case of Tobacco' in Pierre-Marie Dupuy, Francesco Francioni and Ernest-Ulrich Petersmann (eds), *Human Rights in International Investment Law and Arbitration* (Oxford University Press 2009)

Vandevelde KJ, 'A Brief History of International Investment Agreements' in Karl P Sauvant and Lisa Sachs (eds), *The Effect of Treaties on Foreign Direct Investment: Bilateral Investment Treaties, Double Taxation Treaties, and Investment Flows* (Oxford University Press 2009)

Weissbrodt D and Kruger M, 'Human Rights Responsibilities of Business as Non-State Actors' in Philip Alston (ed), *Non-State Actors and Human Rights* (Oxford University Press 2005)

Witte JM, 'A Trade Lever? The Potential and Limits of Promoting Core Labour Standards Through Social Clauses' in BJ Fick (ed), *International Labour Law* (IL 2015)

Woicke P, 'Putting Human Rights Principles into Development Practice through Finance: The Experience of the International Finance Corporation' in Philip Alston and Mary Robinson (eds), *Human Rights and Development: Towards Mutual Reinforcement* (Oxford University Press 2005)

Yannaca-Small K, 'Fair and Equitable Treatment Standard: Recent Developments' in August Reinisch (ed), *Standards of Investment Protection* (Oxford University Press 2008)

Zia-Zarifi S, 'Protection Without Protectionism: Linking a Multilateral Investment Treaty and Human Rights' in EC Nieuwenhuys and MMTA Brus (eds), *Multilateral Regulation of Investment* (Kluwer Law International 2001)

Ziegler AR, 'Most-Favoured-Nation (MFN) Treatment' in August Reinisch (ed), *Standards of Investment Protection* (Oxford University Press 2008)

Journal Articles

Abman R and Carney C, 'Agricultural Productivity and Deforestation: Evidence from Input Subsidies and Ethnic Favouritism in Malawi' (2020) 103 *Journal of Environmental Economics and Management* 102342

Afilalo A, 'Towards a Common Law of International Investment: How NAFTA Chapter 11 Panels Should Solve Their Legitimacy Crisis' (2004) 17 *Georgetown International Environmental Law Review* 51

Ahmad Y and Carey E, 'Development Co-Operation During the COVID-19 Pandemic: An Analysis of 2020 Figures and 2021 Trends to Watch' in *Development Co-operation Profiles* (OECD Publishing 2021) <https://doi.org/10.1787/e4b3142a-en> accessed 3 June 2023

Alam S, Herawati T, Hidayat H and Wyatt S, 'Forest Certification, State Regulation and Community Empowerment: Complementarity in Seeking a Viable Solution to Forest Degradation in Indonesia?' (2019) 22(1) *Asia Pacific Journal of Environmental Law* 27

Alam S, Mukhopadhaya P and Randle D, 'The General Agreement on Trade in Services (GATS), Water, and Human Rights from the Perspective of Developing Countries' (2011) 58(1) *Netherlands International Law Review* 13.

Baez C, Dearing M, Delatour M and Dixon C, 'Multinational Enterprises and Human Rights' (1999/2000) 8 *University of Miami International and Comparative Law Review* 183

Bakker K, 'The "Commons" Versus the "Commodity": Alter-globalization, Anti-privatization and the Human Right to Water in the Global South' (2007) 39 *Antipode* 430

Baltag C, 'The Role of *Amici Curiae* in Light of Recent Developments in Investment Treaty Arbitration: Legitimizing the System?' (2020) 35(1–2) *ICSID Review—Foreign Investment Law Journal* 279 <https://doi.org/10.1093/icsidreview/siaa021> accessed 20 January 2024

Bantekas I, 'Corporate Social Responsibility in International Law' (2004) 22 *Boston University International Law Journal* 309

Bates R, 'The Trade in Water Services: How Does GATS Apply to the Water and Sanitation Services Sector?' (2009) 31 *Sydney Law Review* 121

Baulenas E, Kruse S and Sotirov M, 'Forest and Water Policy Integration: A Process and Output-Orientated Policy Network Analysis' (2021) 31(5) *Environmental Policy and Governance* 432

Berik G and Rodgers YM, 'Options for Enforcing Labour Standards: Lessons from Bangladesh and Cambodia' (2010) 22 *Journal of International Development* 56

Blanton R and Blanton SL, 'Labor Rights and Foreign Direct Investment: Is There a Race to the Bottom?' (2012) 38(3) *Journal of International Interactions* 267

Brower CN, 'Whither International Commercial Arbitration: The Goff Lecture 2007' (2008) 24(2) *Arbitration International* 181

Brower CN and Schill SW, 'Is Arbitration a Threat or a Boon to the Legitimacy of International Investment Law' (2008–2009) 9 *Chicago Journal of Investment Law* 471

Brown RC, 'Promoting Labour Rights in the Global Economy: Could the United States' New Model Trade and Investment Frameworks Advance International Labour Standards in Bangladesh?' (2016) 155 *International Labour Review* 383–403

Budds J and McGranahan G, 'Are the Debates on Water Privatisation Missing the Point? Experience from Africa, Asia and Latin America' (2003) 7 *Environment & Urbanisation* 87

Bulte E, Damania R and Lopez R, 'On the Gains of Committing to Inefficiency: Corruption, Deforestation and Low Land Productivity in Latin America' (2007) 54(3) *Journal of Environmental Economics and Management* 277

Burke-White WW, 'The Argentine Financial Crisis: State Liability Under BITs and the Legitimacy of the ICSID System' (2008) 3 *Asian Journal of WTO & International Health Law and Policy* 199

Burke-White WW, Van Staden A, 'Investment Protection in Extraordinary Times: The Interpretation and Application of Non-Precluded Measures Provisions in Bilateral Investment Treaties' (2008) 48 *Virginia Journal of International Law* 309

Calvert J, 'Beyond "Once BITten, Twice Shy": Defending the Legitimacy of Investor-State Dispute Settlement in Peru and Australia' (2023) 30 *Review of International Political Economy* 1799 <https://doi.org/10.1080/09692290.2022.2134172> accessed 20 January 2024.

Cameron PD, 'Stability of Contract in the International Energy Industry' (2009) 27(3) *Journal of Energy and Natural Resources Law* 305

Carroll AB, 'Corporate Social Responsibility: The Centrepiece of Competing and Complementary Frameworks' (2015) 44 *Organizational Dynamics* 95

Chalamish E, 'The Future of Bilateral Investment Treaties: A De Facto Multilateral Agreement?' (2008–2009) 34 *Brookings Journal of International Law* 353

Chanda R, 'General Agreement on Trade in Services: Implications for Social Policy-Making' (2003) 38(16) *Economic and Political Weekly* 1567

Chanda R, 'Social Services and the GATS: Key Issues and Concerns' (2003) *World Development* 1997

Charney JI, 'Is International Law Threatened by Multiple International Tribunals?' (1998) 271 *Recueil des Course* 219

Comte A, Campagne CS, Lange S, Bruzon AG, Hein L, Santos-Martin F and Levrel H, 'Ecosystem Accounting: Past Scientific Developments and Future Challenges' (2022) 58 *Ecosystem Services*

Conigliani C, Cuffaro N and D'Agostino G, 'Large-Scale Land Investments and Forests in Africa' (2018) 75 *Land Use Policy* 651

Dellapenna J and Gupta J, 'Toward Global Law on Water' (2008) 14 *Global Governance* 437

Dieter M, 'Analysis of Trade in Illegally Harvested Timber: Accounting for Trade via Third Party Countries' (2009) 11(8) *Forest Policy and Economics* 600

Dommen C, 'Trade and Human Rights: Towards Coherence' (2005) 3 *International Journal on Human Rights* 7

Douglas Z, 'The Hybrid Foundations of Investment Treaty Arbitration' (2003) 74(1) *The British Yearbook of International Law* 151

Droiin RC, 'Promoting Fundamental Social Rights Through International Framework Agreements: Practical Outcomes and Present Challenges' (2010) 31 *Comparative Labour Law and Policy Journal* 591

Dunning JH, 'The Determinants of International Production' (1973) 25 *Oxford Economic Papers* 289

Dunning JH, 'The Eclectic Paradigm of International Production: A Restatement and Some Possible Extensions' (1988) 19(1) *Journal of International Business Studies* 1

Dunning JH, 'Toward an Eclectic Theory of International Production: Some Empirical Tests' (1980) 11 *Journal of International Business Studies* 9

Durst PB, McKenzie PJ, Brown CL and Appanah S, 'Challenges Facing Certification and Eco-Labelling of Forest Products in Developing Countries' (2006) 8(2) *International Forestry Review* 193 <https://doi.org/10.1505/ifor.8.2.193>

Echandi R and Newson M, 'Influence of International Investment Patterns in International Economic Law Rulemaking: A Preliminary Sketch' (2014) 17 *Journal of International Economic Law* 847

Faruque, Abdullah Al, 'Mapping the Relationship between Investment Protection and Human Rights' (2010) 11(4) *The Journal of World Investment and Trade* 539

Fitzmaurice M, 'The Human Right to Water' (2006) 18 *Fordham Environmental Law Review* 537

Francioni F, 'Access to Justice, Denial of Justice and International Investment Law' (2009) *European Journal of International Law* 729

Franck SD, 'The Legitimacy Crisis in Investment Treaty Arbitration: Privatizing Public International Law through Investment Decisions' (2005) 73 *Fordham Law Review* 1521

Fried J, 'Water Governance, Management and Ethics: New Dimensions for an Old Problem' (2008) 6 *Santa Clara JIL* 1

Fry JD, 'International Human Rights Law in Investment Arbitration: Evidence of International Law's Unity' (2007–2008) 18 *Duke Journal of Comparative and International Law* 77

Gallus N, 'An Umbrella Just for Two? BIT Obligations Observance Clause and the Parties to a Contract' (2008) 24(1) *Arbitration International* 157

Garcia F, Ciko L, Gaurav A and Hough K, 'Reforming the International Investment Regime: Lessons from International Trade Law' (2015) 18(4) *Journal of International Economic Law* 861

Ginsburg T, 'International Substitute for Domestic Institutions: Bilateral Investment Treaties and Governance' (2005) 25 *International Review of Law and Economics* 107

Gomez KF, 'Rethinking the Role of Amicus Curiae in International Investment Arbitration: How to Draw the Line Favorably for the Public Interest' (2012) 35(2) *Fordham International Law Journal* 517

Grossman C and Bradlow DD, 'Are We Being Propelled Towards a People-Centred Transnational Legal Order?' (1993) 9 *American University Journal of International Law and Policy* 1

Hang S, 'Investing in Human Rights: Using Bilateral Investment Treaties to Hold Multinational Corporations Liable for Labor Rights Violations' (2014) 37 *Fordham International Law Journal* 1215

Harris H, 'Corruption and the Forestry Industry in Papua New Guinea: Transnational Actors, Local Dynamics and Environmental Impact' (2019) 22(1) *Asian Pacific Journal of Environmental Law* 48

Harrison J, 'The Labour Rights Agenda in Free Trade Agreements' (2019) 20 *Journal of World Investment & Trade* 705

Hobe S, 'Global Challenges to Statehood: The Increasingly Important Role of Non-Governmental Organisations' (1997) 5 *Indiana Journal of Global Legal Studies* 191

Hodgson M, 'Costs in Investment-Treaty Arbitration: The Case for Reform' (2014) 1 *Transnational Dispute Management*

Hukka J and Katko T, 'Refuting the Paradigm of Water Services Privatisation' (2003) 27 *Natural Resources Forum* 142

ILO, 'Tripartite Declaration of Principles Concerning Multinational Enterprises and Social Policy' (1978) 17 *International Legal Materials* 422

Islam S, 'Something for Everyone' (1994) 157(16) *Far Eastern Economic Review* 82

Izadi J and Madirimov B, 'Effect of Foreign Direct Investment on Sustainable Development Goals? Evidence from Eurasian Countries' (2023) *Journal of Sustainable Finance and Investment.* <http://doi.org/10.1080/20430795.2022.2163846> accessed 20 January 2024

Johnson L and Sachs LE, 'The Outsized Costs of Investor-State Dispute Settlement' (2016) 16(1) *Academy of International Business Insights* 12

Johnson L, Sachs LE and Lobel N, 'Aligning International Investment Agreements with the Sustainable Development Goals' (2019) 58 *Columbia Journal of Transnational Law* 61

Kalaba FK, 'Barriers to Policy Implementation and Implications for Zambia's Forest Ecosystems' (2016) 69 *Forest Policy and Economics* 40

Kalicki J and Medeiros S, 'Fair, Equitable and Ambiguous: What Is Fair and Equitable Treatment in International Law?' (2007) 22(1) *ICSID Review: Foreign Investment Law Journal* 25

Kardos M, 'The Relevance of Foreign Direct Investment for Sustainable Development: Empirical Evidence from European Union' (2014) 15 *Procedia Economics and Finance* 1349 <http://doi.org/10.1016/S2212-5671(14)00598-X> accessed 20 January 2024.

Katila P, McDermott C, Larson A, Aggarwal S and Giessen L, 'Forest Tenure and the Sustainable Development Goals—A Critical View' (2020) 120 *Forest Policy and Economics* 102294

Kaushal A, 'Revisiting History: How the Past Matters for the Present Backlash against the Foreign Investment Regime' (2009) 50(2) *Harvard International Law Journal* 491

Kawharu A, 'The Admission of Foreign Investment Under the TPP and RCEP: Regulatory Implications for New Zealand' (2015) 16 *Journal of World Investment and Trade* 1050

Kelley G, 'Multilateral Investment Treaties: A Balanced Approach to Multinational Corporations' (2000–2001) 39 *Columbia Journal of Transnational Law* 483

Kelsey J, 'Confronting Trade-Related Human Rights in a GATS-Compatible World' (2007) 1 *Law, Social Justice & Global Development* 1 <http://go.warwick.ac.uk/elj/lgd/2007_1/Kelsey >

Kirkpatrick C and Parker D, 'Domestic Regulation and the WTO: The Case of Water Services in Developing Countries' (2005) 28(10) *The World Economy* 1491

Kissinger G, Brockhaus M and Bush SR, 'Policy Integration as a Means to Address Policy Fragmentation: Assessing the Role of Vietnam's National REDD+ Action Plan in the Central Highlands' (2021) 119 *Environmental Science & Policy* 85

Knahr C, 'Investments in Accordance with Host State Law' (2007) 4(5) *Transnational Dispute Management*

Koh H, 'Transnational Public Law Litigation' (1991) 100 *Yale Law Journal* 23

Krajewski M, 'Public Services and Trade Liberalisation: Mapping the Legal Framework' (2003) 6(2) *Journal of International Economic Law* 341

Kriebaum U, 'Human Rights of the Population of the Host State in International Investment Arbitration' (2009) *The Journal of World Investment and Trade* 653

Kucera D, 'Core Labour Standards and Foreign Direct Investment' (2002) 141 *International Labour Review* 31

Laitos J, 'The Public Use Paradox and the Taking Clause' (1993) 13 *Journal of Energy, Natural Resources, and Environment* 9

Lang A, 'The GATS and Regulatory Autonomy: A Case Study of Social Regulation of the Water Industry' (2004) 7(4) *Journal of international Economic Law* 801

Law D, 'Globalisation and the Future of Constitutional Rights' (2008) 102 *Northwest University Law Review* 1313

Lazdinis M, Angelstam P, Pulzl H, 'Towards Sustainable Forest Management in the European Union Through Polycentric Forest Governance and an Integrated Landscape Approach' (2019) 34(7) *Landscape Ecology* 1737

Legum B, 'Defining Investment and Investor: Who Is Entitled to Claim?' (2006) 22(4) *Arbitration International* 521

Liemt GV, 'Minimum Labour Standards and International Trade: Would a Social Clause Work?' (1989) 128 *International Labour Review* 434

Lofqvist S, Garrett R and Ghazoul J, 'Incentives and Barriers to Private Finance for Forest and Landscape Restoration' (2023) 7 *Nature Ecology and Evolution* 707

Mann FA, 'British Investment Treaties for the Promotion and Protection of Investments' (1981) 52 *British Year Book of International Law* 241

Mann FA, 'State Contracts and State Responsibility' (1960) 54 *American Journal of International Law* 572

Mann H, 'Reconceptualizing International Investment Law: Its Role in Sustainable Development' (2013) 17(2) *Lewis & Clark Law Review* 521

Mantilla G, 'Emerging International Human Rights Norms for Transnational Corporations' (2009) 15 *Global Governance* 279

McLachlan C, 'Investment Treaties and General International Law' (2008) 57 *International and Comparative Law Quarterly* 361

Meehan F and Tacconi L, 'A Framework to Assess the Impacts of Corruption on Forests and Prioritise Responses' (2017) 60 *Land Use Policy* 113

Mehta L and Madsen B, 'Is the WTO After Your Water? The General Agreement on Trade in Services (GATS) and Poor People's Right to Water' (2005) 29(2) *Natural Resources Forum* 154

Miller M, 'Persistent Illegal Logging in Costa Rica: The Role of Corruption Among Forestry Regulators' (2011) 20(1) *Journal of Environment & Development* 50

Muchlinski P, 'Caveat Investor? The Relevance of the Conduct of the Investor Under the Fair and Equitable Treatment Standard' (2006) 55 *International and Comparative Law Quarterly* 567

Naegele J, 'What Is Wrong with Full-Fledged Water Privatization?' (2004) 6 *Journal of Law and Social Challenges* 99

Nardone R, 'Like Oil and Water: The WTO and the World's Water Resources' (2003) 19 *Connecticut JIL* 183

Neugebauer GP, 'Indigenous Peoples as Stakeholders: Influencing Resource-Management Decisions Affecting Indigenous Community Interests in Latin America' (2003) 78 *New York University Law Review* 1227

Neumayer E and Soysa ID, 'Globalisation, "Women's Economic Rights and Forced Labour"' (2007) 30(10) *The Journal of World Economy* 1510

Newcombe A, 'Sustainable Development and Investment Treaty Law' (2007) 8(3) *Journal of World Investment and Trade* 405

Nowrot K, 'How to Include Environmental Protection, Human Rights and Sustainability in International Investment Law?' (2014) 15 *The Journal of World Investment & Trade* 612

Olney WW, 'A Race to the Bottom? Employment Protection and Foreign Direct Investment' (2013) 91(2) *Journal of International Economics* 191

Orbie J and Roozendaal GV, 'Labour Standards and Trade: In Search of Impact and Alternative Instruments' (2017) 5(4) *Politics and Governance* 1

Orso L, Noni ID and Marchisio LV, 'The Role of Collective Action in Leveraging Farmers' Performances: Lessons from Sesame Seed Farmers' (2017) 51 *Journal of Rural Studies* 93

Pahl-Wostl C, 'A Conceptual Framework for Analysing Adaptive Capacity and Multi-level Learning Process in Resource Governance Regimes' (2009) 19(3) *Global Environmental Change* 354

Pan Y, et al., 'A Large and Persistent Carbon Sink in the World's Forest' (2011) 333 *Science* 988

Pereira A, 'The Liberalization of Education under the WTO Services Agreement (GATS): A Threat to Public Educational Policy?' (2005) 2(3) *Manchester Journal of International Economic Law* 5

Petersmann E, 'Human Rights, International Economic Law and Constitutional Justice' (2008) 19(4) *European Journal of International Law* 769

Picherack JR, 'The Expanding Scope of the Fair and Equitable Treatment Standard: Have Recent Tribunals Gone Too Far?' (2008) 9(4) *Journal of World Trade and Investment* 255

Posner MH and Whittome C, 'The Status of Human Rights NGOs' (1994) 25 *Columbia Human Rights Law Review* 267

Pukkala T, 'Measuring the Social Performance of Forest Management' (2021) 32 *Journal of Forestry Research* 1803

Rametsteiner E and Simula M, 'Forest Certification—An Instrument to Promote Sustainable Forest Management' (2003) 67(1) *Journal of Environmental Management* 87

Ratner SR, 'Corporations and Human Rights: A Theory of Legal Responsibility' (2001) 111 *Yale Law Journal* 443

Renner M, 'Towards a Hierarchy of Norms in Transnational Law?' (2009) 26(4) *Journal of International Arbitration* 533

Richards DL, Gelleny RD and Sacko DH, 'Myth with a Mean Streak? Foreign Economic Penetration and Government Respect for Human Rights in Developing Countries' (2001) 45 *International Studies Quarterly* 219

Robbins J, 'The Emergence of Positive Obligations in Bilateral Investment Treaties' (2005–06) 13 *University of Miami International & Comparative Law Review* 403

Rochmayanto Y, Nurrochmat DR, Nugroho B, Darusman D, Satria A, Casse T, Erbaugh JT, Wicaksono D, 'Devolution of Forest Management to Local Communities and Its Impacts on Livelihoods and Deforestation in Berau, Indonesia' (2023) 9(5) *Heliyon* e16115 <https://doi.org/10.1016/j.heliyon.2023.e16115> accessed 30 May 2023

Ruggie JG, 'Business and Human Rights: The Evolving International Agenda' (2007) 101 *American Journal of International Law* 819

Ruggie JG, 'Just Business: Multinational Corporations and Human Rights' (2014) 123(2) *Journal of Business Ethics* 361

Ryan CM, 'Meeting Expectations: Assessing the Long-term Legitimacy and Stability of International Investment Law' (2007–2008) 29 *University Pennsylvania Journal of International Law* 725

Sands P, 'Treaty, Custom and the Cross-fertilization of International Law' (1998) 10 *Yale Human Rights and Development Law Journal* 3

Sarker PK, Fischer R, Tamayo F, Navarrete BT and Gunter S, 'Analyzing Forest Policy Mixes Based on the Coherence of Policies and the Consistency of Legislative Policy Instruments: A Case Study from Ecuador' (2022) 144 *Forest Policy and Economics* 102838

Schreuer C, 'Diversity and Harmonization of Treaty Interpretation in Investment Arbitration' (2006) 3(2) *Transnational Dispute Management*

Schreuer C, 'Fair and Equitable Treatment in Arbitral Practice' (2005) 6 *Journal of World Investment and Trade* 357

Sheffer MW, 'Bilateral Investment Treaties: A Friend or Foe to Human Rights?' (2011) 39 *Denver Journal of International Law and Policy* 483

Sikkink K, 'Nongovernmental Organisations and Transnational Issue Networks in International Politics' (1995) 89 *American Society of International Law Proceedings* 413

Simma B and Alston P, 'The Sources of Human Rights Law: Custom, Jus Cogens, and General Principles' (1988–89) 12 *Australian Yearbook of International Law* 82

Singer B, 'Financing Sustainable Forest Management in Developing Countries' (2016) 18(1) *International Forestry Review* 96

Singhania M and Saini N, 'Demystifying Pollution Haven Hypothesis: Role of FDI' (2021) 123 *Journal of Business Research* 516 <https://doi.org/10.1016/j.jbusres.2020.10.007> accessed 20 January 2024

Spar D, 'Foreign Investment and Human Rights' (1999) 42(1) *Challenge* 55

Stefans S, 'The Amorality of Profit: Transnational Corporations and Human Rights' (2002) 20 *Berkeley Journal of International Law* 45

Su K, Shen W, 'Environmental Protection Provisions in International Investment Agreements: Global Trends and Chinese Practices' (2023) 15(11) *Sustainability* 8525 <https://doi.org/10.3390/su15118525> accessed 19 January 2024

Sunstrom A, 'Understanding Illegality and Corruption in Forest Governance' (2016) 181 *Journal of Environmental Management* 779

Thielbörger P, 'The Human Right to Water Versus Investor Rights: Double-Dilemma or Pseudo-Conflict?' (2009) *Human Rights in International Investment Law and Arbitration* 499

Thomas DC, 'International NGOs, State Sovereignty, and Democratic Values' (2001) 2 *Chicago Journal of International Law* 389

Tienhaara K, 'Regulatory Chill in a Warming World: The Threat to Climate Policy Posed by Investor-State Dispute Settlement' (2018) 7(2) *Transnational Environmental Law* 229 <http://doi.org/10.1017/S2047102517000309> accessed 20 January 2024

Tikkanen OP, Heinonen T, Kouki J and Matero J, 'Habitat Suitability Models of Saproxylic Red-Listed Boreal Forest Species in Long-Term Matrix Management: Cost Effective Measures for Multi-Species Conservation' (2007) 140 *Biological Conservation* 359

Triantafilou EE, 'Amicus Submissions in Investor-State Arbitration after Suez v. Argentina' (2008) 24(4) *Arbitration International* 571

Tsogas G, 'Labour Standards in International Trade Agreements: An Assessment of the Arguments' (1999) 10(2) *International Journal of Human Resource Management* 351

Ünver O, 'Global Governance of Water: A Practitioner's Perspective' (2008) 14 *Global Governance* 409

Uriz GH, 'To Lend or Not to Lend: Oil, Human Rights, and the World Bank's Internal Contradictions' (2001) 14 *Harvard Human Rights Journal* 197

Vandevelde KJ, 'Investment Liberalisation and Economic Development: The Role of Bilateral Investment Treaties' (1998) 36 *Columbia Journal of Transnational Law* 522
Vasciannie S, 'The Fair and Equitable Treatment Standard in International Investment Law and Practice' (2000) 70 *British Yearbook of International Law* 99
Vieira de Freitas Netto S, Falcão Sobral MF, Bezerra Ribeiro AR and da Luz Soares GR, 'Concepts and Forms of Greenwashing: A Systemic Review' (2020) 32(19) *Environmental Sciences Europe* <https://doi.org/10.1186/s12302-020-0300-3> accessed 1 June 2023
Vogt JS, 'The Evolution of Labor Rights and Trade—A Transatlantic Comparison and Lessons for the Transatlantic Trade and Investment Partnership' (2015) 18 *Journal of International Economic Law* 827
Walde TW, 'The "Umbrella" Clause in Investment Arbitration: A Comment on Original Intentions and Recent Cases' (2005) 6 *The Journal of World Investment and Trade* 183
Wasserstrom R and Reider S, 'Oil Firms in Environmentally Sensitive Areas: Learning to Balance Stakeholder Interests' (1997) 95(33) *Oil and Gas Journal* 23
Weiler T, 'Balancing Human Rights and Investment Protection: A New Approach for a Different Legal Order' (2004) 27 *Boston College International and Comparative Law Review* 429
Weiler T, 'Comment on International Law on Investment: The Minimum Standard of Treatment (MST)' (2004) 2(1) *OGEL—Oil, Gas and Energy Law Intelligence* <http://www.gasandoil.com/ogel/>
Weissbrodt D and Kruger M, 'Norms on the Responsibilities of Transnational Corporations and Other Business Enterprises with Regard to Human Rights' (2003) 97 *American Journal of International Law* 901
Williams M, 'Privatization and the Human Right to Water: Challenges to the New Century' (2007) 28 *Michigan Journal of International Law* 472
Witkowska J, 'Foreign Direct Investment and Sustainable Development in the New EU Member States: Environmental Aspects' (2011) 14(3) *Comparative Economic Research* 5
Yang PK, 'A Critique of ICSID's Amicus Curiae Decisions in Philip Morris v. Uruguay: Review of Amicus Submissions in a Fragmented World' (2021) 14(2) *Contemporary Asia Arbitration Journal* 245 <https://ssrn.com/abstract=3976975> accessed 20 January 2024
Yanyan H, Fuzhong C, Huini W, Jian X, Zhexiao X and Rabia A, 'The Impacts of FDI Inflows on Carbon Emissions: Economic Development and Regulatory Quality as Moderators' (2021) 9 *Frontiers in Energy Research* <http://doi.org/10.3389/fenrg.2021.820596> accessed 20 January 2024
Zandvliet R, 'Trade, Investment and Labour: Interactions in International Law' (Meijers-reeks 2019) <https://scholarlypublications.universiteitleiden.nl/access/item%3A2977132/view> accessed 15 March 2024
Zubizarreta-Gerendiaiin A, Pukkala T, Peltola H, 'Effect of Wind Damage on the Habitat Suitability of Saproxylic Species in a Boreal Forest Landscape' (2019) 30(3) *Journal of Forestry Research* 879
Zugliani N, 'Human Rights in International Investment Law: The 2016 Morocco-Nigeria Bilateral Investment Treaty' (2019) 68 *International and Comparative Law Quarterly* 761

Articles

Aaken AV, 'Fragmentation of International Law: The Case of International Investment Protection' University of St. Gallen Law School, Working Paper No. 2008-1 <http://ssrn.com/abstract=1097529> accessed 23 June 2023.
Alvarez JE and Khamsi K, 'The Argentine Crisis and Foreign Investor: A Glimpse into the Heart of the Investment Regime' International Institute for Law and

Justice, IILJ Working Paper 2008/5, 2008 <http://www.iilj.org/publications/docuemtns/2008_5.AlvarezKhamsi.pdf> accessed 12 June 2022

Boie B, 'Labour Related Provisions in International Investment Agreements' Employment Sector Employment Working Paper No. 126, ILO, 2012

Bonner J, Grigg A, Hime S, Hewitt G, Jackson R and Kelly M, 'Is Natural Capital a Material Issue? An Evaluation of the Relevance of Biodiversity and Ecosystem Services to Accountancy Professionals and the Private Sector' (KPMG, Flora and Fauna International, and ACCA 2012)

Boyd D, 'Paying Polluters: The Catastrophic Consequences of Investor-State Dispute Settlement for Climate and Environment Action and Human Rights' (Special Rapporteur on the Issue of Human Rights Obligations relating to the Enjoyment of a Safe, Clean, Healthy and Sustainable Environment, UN General Assembly, Doc Number A/78/168, 13 July 2023) <https://documents-dds-ny.un.org/doc/UNDOC/GEN/N23/205/29/PDF/N2320529.pdf?OpenElement> accessed 20 January 2024

Cosbey A, 'International Investment Agreements and Sustainable Development: Achieving the Millennium Development Goals' (International Institute for Sustainable Development 2005) <http://www.iisd.org>

Directorate-General for External Policies Policy Department, 'Labour Rights in Export Processing Zones with a Focus on GSP+ Beneficiary Countries' (European Union 2017) <http://www.europarl.europa.eu/RegData/etudes/STUD/2017/603839/EXPO_STU(2017)603839_EN.pdf>

Donado A and Wälde K, 'Globalization, Trade Unions and Labour Standards in the North', Employment Working Paper No. 119 ILO (2012)

Ebert FC and Posthuma A, 'Labour Provisions in Trade Arrangements: Current Trends and Perspectives' (International Labour Organization, International Institute for Labour Studies 2011)

Expert Mechanism on the Right to Development, 'Right to Development Under International Investment Law' (Human Rights Council, 3–5 April 2023, A/HRC/EMRTD/7/CRP.2) 8 <https://www.ohchr.org/sites/default/files/documents/issues/development/emd/session7/A_HRC_EMRTD_7_CRP.2%20for%20the%20web.pdf> accessed 20 January 2024

Gordon K and Pohi J, 'Environmental Concerns in International Investment Agreements' (OECD, Working Papers on International Investment, 2011) <https://www.oecd-ilibrary.org/finance-and-investment/environmental-concerns-in-international-investment-agreements_5kg9mq7scrjh-en> accessed 20 January 2024.

Guide to the Global Compact: A Practical Understanding of the Vision and Nine Principles (UN Global Compact, 2002) 51 <http://www.unglobalcompact.org/content/public_Documents/gcguide.pdf>

Hallward-Driemeier M, 'Do Bilateral Investment Treaties Attract FDI?' (World Bank 2003) 22 <http://econ.worldbank.org/files/29143_wps3121.pdf>

Hallward-Driemeier M, 'Do Bilateral Investment Treaties Attract FDI? Only Bit . . . . They Could Bit' Policy Research Working Paper 3121 <http://econ.worldbank.org/files/29143_wps3121.pdf> accessed 12 January 2024

Harten GV, 'Key Flaws in the European Commission's Proposals for Foreign Investor Protection in TTIP' Osgoode Hall Law School Legal Studies Research Paper Series No. 16, Volume 12 issue 4, York University, Toronto (2016) <http://papers.ssrn.com/sol3/papers.cfm?abstract_id=2692122>

Hendy J, 'A Threat to the Sovereignty of Courts and Parliaments' (*Graya*, No. 128 2015)

Koplow D and Steenblik R, *Protecting Nature by Reforming Environmentally Harmful Subsidies: The Role of Business* (Earth Track 2022) <https://www.earthtrack.net/document/protecting-nature-reforming-environmentally-harmful-subsidies-role-business> accessed 3 June 2023

Lowe V, 'Changing Dimension of International Law' University of Oxford Faculty of Law Legal Studies Research Paper Series Working Paper No 4/2007, March 2007 <http://papers.ssrn.com/Abstract=970727> accessed 17 May 2023.

Mann H, 'International Investment Agreements, Business and Human Rights: Key Issues and Opportunities' (International Institute for Sustainable Development 2008)

Moon G, 'Protecting Human and Environmental Rights in International Investment Agreements' (East Asia Forum 2021) <https://www.eastasiaforum.org/2021/08/06/protecting-human-and-environmental-rights-in-international-investment-agreements/> accessed 20 January 2024

Morrison J and Gleick P, 'Freshwater Resources: Managing the Risks Facing the Private Sector' (Research paper, Pacific Institute 2004)

Newcombe A, 'Canada's New Model Foreign Investment Protection Agreement' (2004) <https://www.international-arbitration-attorney.com/wp-content/uploads/2014/08/205arbitrationlawCanadianFIPA_001.pdf> accessed 17 March 2024

OECD, 'Assessing the Environmental Effects of Services Trade Liberalisation: A Methodology' (OECD Working Papers, 2002)

OECD, 'Interpretation of the Umbrella Clause in Investment Agreements' (Working Papers on International Investment, no. 2006/3, October 2006) <www.oecd.org/investment>

OECD Joint Working Party on Trade and Environment, 'Environmental Goods and Services: An Assessment of the Environmental, Economic and Development Benefits of Further Global Trade Liberalisation' (OECD Working Papers, 2000)

Ostrovsky A, Speed R and Türk E, 'GATS, Water and the Environment: Implications of the General Agreement on Trade in Services for Water Resources' (Research Discussion Paper, Centre for International Environmental Law, 2003)

Penfold B, 'Labour and Employment Issues in Foreign Direct Investment: Public Support Conditionalities' Working Paper No. 95, ILO <https://www.ilo.org/wcmsp5/groups/public/@ed_emp/@emp_ent/@multi/documents/publication/wcms_101040.pdf> accessed 19 November 2022

Peterson LE, 'Human Rights and BITs: Mapping the Role of Human Rights in Investor-State Arbitration' (Rights and Democracy, International Centre for Human Rights and Democratic Development, 2009)

Peterson LE, 'International Human Rights in Bilateral Investment Treaties and Investment Treaty Arbitration' (International Institute for Sustainable Development 2003)

Potter B, 'Vertical and Horizontal Races: The Impact of Multinational Corporations on Host Country Human Rights Regimes' (International Studies Association, 2009)

Richardson B and Harrison J, 'Labour Rights in Export Processing Zones with a Focus on GSP+ Beneficiary Countries' (Directorate-General for External Policies Policy Department, European Parliament) <https://www.europarl.europa.eu/RegData/etudes/STUD/2017/603839/EXPO_STU(2017)603839_EN.pdf> accessed 5 August 2024

Suda R, 'The Effect of Bilateral Investment Treaties on Human Rights Enforcement and Realization' Hauser Global Law School Program, Global Law Working Paper 01/05, New York University School of Law

Thompson R and Pellegrino C, 'Environmental Services: The "Win-Win" Role of Trade Liberalization in Promoting Environmental Protection and Economic Development' (OECD Working Papers, 2000)

Türk E and Krajewski M, 'The Right to Water and Trade in Services: Assessing the Impact of GATS Negotiations on Water Regulation' Paper Presented at the CAT+E Conference 'Moving Forward from Cancún', Berlin, 2003, <www.ciel.org/Publications/GATS_WaterHR_28Oct03.pdf>

WTO, 'GATS: Fact and Fiction—Misunderstandings and Scare Stories: The WTO Is Not After Your Water' n.d. <http://www.wto.org/english/tratop_e/serv_e/gats_factfiction8_e.html>

Presented Papers

Davarnejad L, 'Strengthening the Social Dimension of International Investment Agreements by Integrating Codes of Conduct for Multinational Enterprises' Paper Presented at OECD Global Forum on International Investment, 27–28 March 2008

Kalderimis D, 'Investment Treaties and Public Good' Paper Presented to Asian International Economic Law Network Inaugural Conference, 29 June 2009

Mosely L and Uno S, 'Racing to the Bottom or Climbing to the Top? Foreign Direct Investment and Human Rights' Paper Presented at the Annual Meetings of the American Political Science Association, August 29–September 1, 2002, Boston

Peterson LE and Kevin RG, 'International Human Rights in Bilateral Investment Treaties and in Investment Treaty Arbitration' Paper Presented by the International Institute for Sustainable Development (IISD) for the Swiss Department of Foreign Affairs, 2003

Schutter OD, 'A Human Rights Approach to Trade and Investment Policies' A Paper Presented to the Conference on Confronting the Global Food Challenge: Finding New Approaches to Trade and Investment That Support the Right to Food', held on 24–26 November 2008, Geneva, Switzerland

Türk E, Krajewski M, 'The Right to Water and Trade in Services: Assessing the Impact of GATS Negotiations on Water Regulation' Paper Presented at the CAT+E Conference 'Moving forward from Cancún', Berlin, 30–31 October 2003 <www.ciel.org/Publications/GATS_WaterHR_28Oct03.pdf>

Official Reports and Publications

Alfred-Maurice de Zayas, 'Report of the Independent Expert on the Promotion of a Democratic and Equitable International Order' United Nations Human Rights Council, 14 July 2015, 13th session (UN Doc A/HRC/30/44, Human Rights Council 2015)

'Beyond Voluntarism: Human Rights and the Developing International Legal Obligations of Companies' (International Council on Human Rights Policy 2002)

'Bilateral Investment Treaty Policy Framework Review: Government Position Paper of Republic South Africa' (Pretoria, June 2009)

Capolaghi L and Goddard F, 'Forestry Funds: The Emerging Star of Alternative Investments' (EY, 2023) <https://www.ey.com/en_lu/private-equity/forestry-funds—the-emerging-star-of-alternative-investments> accessed 1 June 2023.

Committee on Economic, Social and Cultural Rights (CESCR), 'General Comment No. 15: The Right to Water' (UN Doc. E/C.12/2002/11 2003)

Cotula L, 'Briefing 2: Investment Treaties' (International Institute for Environment and Development 2007)

'Development and International Economic Cooperation: Transnational Corporations' (U.N. ESCOR, 2d See, Agenda Item 7(d), para. 13, U.N. Doc E/1990/94, 1990)

'Draft United Nations Code of Conduct on Transnational Corporations' (U.N. Center on Transnational Corporations, Special Sess. (Mar. 7–18, 1983 and May 9–20, 1983), U.N. Doc.E/C.10/1982/6 1986)

The Evolving Debate on Trade & Labour Standards, IOE Information Paper (International Organisation of Employers, Geneva 2006)

Expert Mechanism on the Right to Development, 'Right to Development Under International Investment Law' (Human Rights Council, 3–5 April 2023, A/HRC/EMRTD/7/CRP.2), p. 8 <https://www.ohchr.org/sites/default/files/documents/issues/development/emd/session7/A_HRC_EMRTD_7_CRP.2%20for%20the%20web.pdf> accessed 20 January 2024

FAO, 'Global Forest Resources Assessment: Main Report' (FAO 2020) <https://doi.org/10.4060/ca9825en> accessed 1 June 2023

FCPF and REDD+, 'Annual Country Progress Reporting' (with semi-annual update 2015), <https://www.forestcarbonpartnership.org/sites/fcp/files/2016/Oct/230916_Final%20NS_FCPF%20%20Country%20Progress%20Report.pdf> accessed 1 June 2023

Grasselli MCG and Postolachi I, 'Promoting and Enforcing Compliance with Labour Provisions in Trade Agreements: Comparative Analysis of Canada, European Union and United States Approaches and Practices' (ILO 2023)

Horta K, 'The Chad/Cameroon Oil and Pipeline Project-Reaching a Critical Milestone' (World Rainforest Movement) <http://www.wrm/org.uy/countries/cameroon/Horta.html> accessed 15 March 2024

Human Rights Committee, 'General Comment No. 31: The Nature of the General Legal Obligation Imposed on States Parties to the Covenant' (CCPR/C/21/Rev.1/Add.13 2004)

Human Rights Council, 'Protect, Respect and Remedy: A Framework for Business and Human Rights' (8th Session Agenda item 3, A/HRC/8/5 2008)

International Institute for Sustainable Development, 'Southern African Development Community, Model Bilateral Investment Treaty Template with Commentary' (IISD, 2012) <https://www.iisd.org/itn/wp-content/uploads/2012/10/sadc-model-bittemplate-final.pdf>

International Investment Agreements, 'Latest Developments in Investor-State Dispute Settlement' (IIA MONITOR No. 1 (2008), UNCTAD, Geneva, 2008)

International Investment Agreements: Trends and Emerging Issues, 'UNCTAD Series on International Investment Policies for Development' (UN New York and Geneva, 2006)

International Labour Office, 'Managing the Privatisation and Restructuring of Public Utilities (Water, Gas, Electricity)' (Report for the Discussion at the Tripartite Meeting on Managing the Privatization of Public Utilities, Geneva, 1999) <http://www.ilo.org/public/english/dialogue/sector/techmeet/tmpu99/tmpure2.htm#2.1>

International Law Commission, 'Fragmentation of International Law: Difficulties Arising from the Diversification and Expansion of International Law' (Report of the Study Group UN Doc A/CN.4/L682, ILC 2006)

International Organization for Standardization, 'ISO 31007 Anti-Bribery Management Systems' (ISO, undated) <https://www.iso.org/iso-37001-anti-bribery-management.html> accessed 1 June 2023

INTERPOL, 'Uncovering the Risks of Corruption in the Forestry Sector' (INTERPOL 2016)

Investment Policy Monitor, No. 1 (UNCTAD, Geneva 2009) <www.unctad.org/en/docs/webdiaeia200911_en.pdf> accessed 21 July 2022

Iran-US Claim Tribunal Report Vol 19 (1989-III) <https://www.state.gov/iran-u-s-claims-tribunal/>

'Is Natural Capital a Material Issue? An Evaluation of the Relevance of Biodiversity and Ecosystem Services to Accountancy Professionals and the Private Sector' (KPMG, Flora and Fauna International, and ACCA, 2012)

John Ruggie, '2008 Report of the SRSG to the UN Human Rights Council on the Issue of Human of Human Rights and Business' (2008)

'Labour Rights in Export Processing Zones with a Focus on GSP+ Beneficiary Countries' Directorate-General for External Policies Policy Department

Luke Eric Peterson, 'International Human Rights in Bilateral Investment Treaties and Investment Treaty Arbitration' (International Institute for Sustainable Development 2003)

Luke Eric Peterson, 'International Sustainable and Ethical Investment Rules Project, All the Roads Lead Out of Rome: Divergent Paths of Dispute Settlement in Bilateral Investment Treaties' (Nautilus Institute for Security and Sustainable Development 2002)

Morrison J and Gleick P, 'Freshwater Resources: Managing the Risks Facing the Private Sector' (Pacific Institute 2004)

NAFTA Free Trade Commission, 'Statement on Non-Disputing Party Participation' (7 October 2003)

Natural Capital Finance Alliance, 'Exploring Natural Capital Opportunities, Risks and Exposure' (NCFA, 2023) <https://encore.naturalcapital.finance/en> accessed 1 June 2023.

Norfolk S and Turner C, 'Improving Tenure Security for the Rural Poor: Mozambique—Country Case Study' (FAO, 2007)

OHCHR, 'Human Rights, Trade and Investment' (E/CN.4/Sub.2/2003/9, OHCHR 2003)

Peterson LE, 'Human Rights and BITs: Mapping the Role of Human Rights in Investor-State Arbitration' (Rights and Democracy, International Centre for Human Rights and Democratic Development, Canada 2009)

Priority Activity 4.7 under Ministry of Environment and Forestry, Indonesia and CIFOR, 'International Tropical Peatlands Centre' (Republic of Indonesia 2019) <https://www.tropicalpeatlands.org/resources/ITPC-Concept-Note-en-web.pdf> accessed 1 June 2023

'Recent Developments in International Investment Agreements (2007–June 2008)' (IIA MONITOR No. 2 (2008), United Nations, Geneva, 2008)

Report of the High Commissioner for Human Rights, U.N. Economic and Social Council, 'Human Rights, Trade and Investment' (E/CN.4/Sub.2/2003/9, ECOSOC 2003)

Report of the Special Rapporteur on the Issue of Human Rights Obligations Relating to the Enjoyment of a Safe, Clean, Healthy and Sustainable Environment (Human Rights Council Thirty-seventh session 26 February–23 March 2018 Agenda item 3, A/HRC/37/59, Human Rights Council 2018)

Ruggie J, 'Guiding Principles on Business and Human Rights: Implementing the United Nations "Protect, Respect and Remedy" Framework' (Report of the Special Representative of the Secretary-General on the Issue of Human Rights and Transnational Corporations and Other Business Enterprises, Human Rights Council 2011)

Ruggie J, 'Guiding Principles on Business and Human Rights: Implementing the United Nations "Protect, Respect and Remedy" Framework' Report of the Special Representative of the Secretary-General on the Issue of Human Rights and Transnational Corporations and Other Business Enterprises (A/HRC/17/31, Human Rights Council, Seventeenth session, Agenda item 3, Promotion and Protection of All Human Rights, Civil, Political, Economic, Social and Cultural Rights, Including the Right to Development, UN General Assembly, 2011)

Ruggie J, 'Presentation of Report to United Nations Human Rights Council' (Geneva, 2009)

Ruggie J, 'Protect, Respect and Remedy: A Framework for Business and Human Rights' (8th Session Agenda item 3, A/HRC/8/5 Human Rights Council 2008)

Ruggie J, 'Report of the Special Representative of the Secretary-General on the Issue of Human Rights and Transnational Corporations and Other Business Enterprises' (A/HRC/4/035, Human Rights Council 2007)

Ruggie J, 'Statement on the Issue of Human Rights and Transnational Corporations and Other Business Enterprises to the Department of Trade and Industry' (South Africa 2009)

Smartwood, 'Forest Management 2006 CAR Verification Audit Report for PT Sumalindo Lestari Jaya in Samarinda, Kalimantan Timur' (Rainforest Alliance 2007)

Smith A and Grant J, 'Keeping Better Company: Engaging the Private Sector to Reduce Forest Sector-Related Corruption Risk' (WWF, 2021) <https://www.worldwildlife.org/pages/tnrc-topic-brief-keeping-better-company-engaging-the-private-sector-to-reduce-forest-sector-related-corruption-risk#2> accessed 1 June 2023

Southern African Development Community, 'SADC Model Bilateral Investment Treaty Template with Commentary' (July 2012)

Special Representative of the Secretary-General Business and Human Rights, R (A/HRC/11/13, Human Rights Council 2009)

Transparency International, 'Corruption-free Climate Finance: Protecting Forests and People' (2021)

UN Committee on Economic, Social and Cultural Rights, 'Substantive Issues Arising in the Implementation of the International Covenant on Economic, Social and Cultural Rights: General Comment No. 15' UN ESCOR, 29th sess (UN Doc E/C.12/2002/11 2002)

UNCITRAL, 'Possible Reform of Investor-State Dispute Settlement (ISDS) Note by the Secretariat' (Vienna 2017) <https://documents-ddsny.un.org/doc/UNDOC/LTD/V17/067/48/PDF/V1706748.pdf?OpenElement> accessed 20 January 2024

UNCTAD Report, 'Development Implications of International Investment Agreements' (IIA Monitor No. 2, United Nations, Geneva 2007)

UNCTAD, 'Economic Development in Africa, Rethinking the Role of Foreign Direct Investment' (2006) <https://unctad.org/system/files/official-document/gdsafrica20051_en.pdf> accessed 15 March 2024

UNCTAD, 'International Investment Agreement Navigator' <https://investmentpolicy.unctad.org/international-investment-agreements> accessed 26 April 2022

UNCTAD, 'Investment Policy Framework for Sustainable Development' (New York and Geneva 2015)

UNCTAD, 'Investor-State Dispute Settlement Cases: Facts and Figures 2020' (IIA Issues Note, 2020) <https://unctad.org/system/files/official-document/diaepcbinf2021d7_en.pdf> accessed 20 January 2024

UNCTAD, 'Most Favoured-Nation Treatment' (United Nations Conference on Trade and Development, UNCTAD Series on Issues in International Investment Agreement 1999)

UNCTAD, 'National Treatment' (Vol. IV, UNCTAD/IIT/11 1995)

'UNCTAD's Reform Package for the International Investment Regime' (New York and Geneva, 2018)

UNCTAD, 'The Role of International Investment Agreements in Attracting Foreign Direct Investment to Developing Countries' (United Nations, Geneva and New York 2009)

UNCTAD, 'World Investment Report' (2003) <https://unctad.org/publication/world-investment-report-2003>

UNCTAD, 'World Investment Report 2021: Investing in Sustainable Recovery' (2021) <https://unctad.org/system/files/officialdocument/wir2021_en.pdf> accessed 23 April 2022

United Nations, 'World Investment Report 2003' (United Nations, New York and Geneva 2003)

United Nations Economic and Social Council, 'Report of the High Commissioner, Economic, Social and Cultural Rights, Liberalization of Trade in Services and Human Rights' (UN Doc E/CN.4/Sub.2/2002/9, ECOSOC 2002)

United Nations Environment Programme, 'State of Finance for Nature. Time to Act: Doubling Investment by 2025' (United Nations 2022) <https://wedocs.unep.org/20.500.11822/41333> accessed 29 May 2023

The United States' 2003 Trade Policy Agenda <www.ustr.gov/reports/2003.html>

USAID, 'Devolution of Forest Rights and Sustainable Forest Management Volume 1: A Review of Policies and Programs in 16 Developing Countries' (US Government, 2012) ix <https://www.land-links.org/wp content/uploads/2016/09/USAID_Land_Tenure_Devolution_of_Forest_Rights_and_Sustainable_Forest_Management_Volume_1.pdf> accessed 30 May 2023

Watson C, 'Forest Carbon Accounting: Overview & Principles' (UNDP 2015) <https://www.undp.org/publications/forest-carbon-accounting-overview-principles> accessed 8 June 2023

World Bank, 'Mobilizing Private Finance for Nature' (World Bank 2020) <https://pubdocs.worldbank.org/en/916781601304630850/Finance-for-Nature-28-Sep-web-version.pdf> accessed 8 June 2023.

World Bank, 'Nature and Development Brief: Scaling up Finance for Nature' (World Bank 2022) <https://thedocs.worldbank.org/en/doc/b08b82598c0bb418ee7f73a49ff3fdfd-0320012022/original/3-Nature-Finance.pdf>

World Bank, 'World Development Report 1994: Infrastructure for Development' (Report, World Bank 1994)

World Bank, CIAT, and CATIE, 'Climate-Smart Agriculture in Chiapas, Mexico' (The World Bank Group 2014)

'World Investment Report' (United Nations, New York and Geneva, 2003)

World Trade Organization ('WTO'), 'GATS—Fact and Fiction' (2001) <http://www.wto.org/english/tratop_e/serv_e/gatsfacts1004_e.pdf>

WWF and CIEL, GATS, 'Water and the Environment—Implications of the General Agreement on Trade in Services for Water Resources' (Gland, World Wide Fund for Nature 2003)

Websites and Blogs

Aaronson SA, Rioux M, 'Striking a Proper Match? Strategies to Link Trade Agreements and Real Labor Rights Improvements' <https://www.ids.trade/files/news/2008/GLG%20Report.pdf> accessed 15 March 2024.

Cosbey A, 'International Investment Agreements and Sustainable Development: Achieving the Millennium Development Goals' (IISD 2005) <http://www.iisd.org>

Department of Labor, 'Labour Principles' <https://www.dol.gov/agencies/ilab/naalc> accessed 23 December 2023.

Future-Fit Business, 'Future-Fit Business Benchmark' (2023) <https://futurefitbusiness.org/benchmark/> accessed 1 June 2023

Garcia LG, 'The Role of Human Rights in International Investment Law' <https://www.matrixlaw.co.uk/wp-content/uploads/2016/05/The-role-of-human-rights-in-international-investment-law.pdf> accessed 21 October 2023

'Harnessing Investment for Sustainable Development: OECD FDI Qualities Initiative' <https://www.oecd.org/investment/sustainable-investment/> accessed 15 March 2024

Hartridge D, 'WTO Secretariat Hits False Attacks against GATS' (2000) <http://www.esf.be/docs/hartridg.doc>

Neumayer E and Spess L, 'Do Bilateral Investment Treaties Increase Foreign Direct Investment to Developing Countries' (2005) LSE Research Online <https://eprints.lse.ac.uk/627/01/World_Dev_(BITs).pdf>

Newcombe A, 'Canada's New Model Foreign Investment Protection Agreement' August 2004 <https://www.international-arbitration-attorney.com/wp-content/uploads/2014/08/205arbitrationlawCanadianFIPA_001.pdf> accessed 17 March 2024

Tobin J and Rose-Ackerman S, 'Bilateral Investment Treaties: Do They Stimulate Foreign Direct Investment' <www.upf.es/dret/civil/clef/sra.pdf>

UNCTAD, 'Investment Dispute Settlement Navigator' (UNCTAD 2024) <https://investmentpolicy.unctad.org/investment-dispute-settlement> accessed 20 January 2024

'The UN Global Compact' <https://unglobalcompact.org/> accessed 14 March 2024

UN Global Compact, 'UN Compact for the New Century' <http://unglobalcompact.org/un/gc/unweb.nsf/content/thenine.htm>

Unilever, 'Human Policy Statement' (2023) <https://spcommreports.ohchr.org/TMResultsBase/DownLoadFile?gId=37573> accessed 12 March 2024

Working Group on Business and Human Rights, 'Corporate human rights due diligence—identifying and leveraging emerging practices' <https://www.ohchr.org/EN/Issues/Business/Pages/CorporateHRDueDiligence.aspx> accessed 23 October 2023
World Bank and WTO, 'I-TIP Services' <http://i-tip.wto.org/services/(S(r2sl0om oomrwnqs4bwb02o4i))/default.aspx> accessed 4 August 2015
World Economic Forum, 'Partnering Against Corruption Initiative' (WEF 2023) <https://www.weforum.org/communities/partnering-against-corruption-initiative> accessed 1 June 2023
WTO, GATS: 'Fact and Fiction—Misunderstandings and Scare Stories: The WTO Is Not After Your Water' (n.d.) <www.wto.org/english/tratop_e/serv_e/gats_factfiction8_e.htm>

Newspaper Articles and Press Releases

Logan M, 'Finance Corporations Said to Eye Water Privatization in U.S.' *Inter Press Service* (2003)
Rahman M, 'Proposed Revisions in the EU-GSP Scheme: Implications for Bangladesh' *The Daily Star* (24 October 2021)
World Bank, 'Defying Predictions, Remittance Flows Remain Strong During COVID-19 Crisis' *World Bank* (2021) <https://www.worldbank.org/en/news/press-release/2021/05/12/defying-predictions-remittance-flows-remain-strong-during-covid-19-crisis?cid=ECR_E_NewsletterWeekly_EN_EXT&deliveryName=DM104029> accessed 3 June 2023

Others

Crawford J, 'Treaty Contract in Investment Arbitration' (The 22nd Freshfields Lecture on International Arbitration, London 29 November 2007)

Index

Note: Page numbers followed by n indicate a note.

For Product Safety Concerns and Information please contact our EU representative GPSR@taylorandfrancis.com Taylor & Francis Verlag GmbH, Kaufingerstraße 24, 80331 München, Germany